Parachutist

Parachutist

PETER HEARN

Foreword by

Air Chief Marshal Sir Neil Cameron
K.C.B., C.B.E., D.S.O., D.F.C.

ROBERT HALE · LONDON

ISBN 0 7091 5413 5
Robert Hale & Company
Clerkenwell House
Clerkenwell Green
London EC1R 0HT

Filmset by Specialised Offset Services Limited, Liverpool
and printed in Great Britain by
Lowe & Brydone Limited
Thetford, Norfolk

To the memory of
Bill Roden

Contents

Foreword by Air Chief Marshal Sir Neil Cameron   11
Preface   13

1   "Bob's Your Uncle"   15

2   Knowledge Dispels Fear   41

3   "Le Lieutenant Anglais a Perdu Son Poignet!"   51

4   Trials and Errors   65

5   Moussatchevo   77

6   "Got the Cards, Snowy?"   87

7   North America   99

8   The Day We Nearly Saw the King of Siam   107

9   Jungle Rescue Team   119

10   Free Wine   127

11   A Means of Transport   139

12   Lady Be Good   145

13   Problem Parachuting – Desert and Jungle   157

14   Falcons and Other Birds   171

15   P.T.S.   185

Bibliography   183

Index   185

Illustrations

Between pages 64 and 65

The first jump, from the balloon cage
Anti-entanglement drill in the hangar, 1957
Forward landing practice from the slides, 1957
Sliding down the slipstream from the door of the Beverley
Jumping from the Beverley boom, over Weston
Pau, 1959
Filing into the Nord Atlas
The P.T.S. free-fall team in Australia, 1959
Leaving the Beverley in the 'full cross' position
More relaxed, a year later
Moussatchevo, 1960
The French canopy
The American 'Conquistador'
The 'six' in training
The first Royal Air Force parachute display team, 1961
" 'Way ... *hayyyyy*,' we shouted as we all stepped backwards"

Between pages 128 and 129

Author, Snowy and Rudi at Paya Lebar
Snowy coming in on reserve at Paya Lebar
R.A.F. Detachment Special Forces, 1966
S.A.S. free faller in flight
With the 1971 Falcons in Hong Kong
Tracking across Hong Kong harbour at 8,000 feet
Touch down, still smoking, in Hong Kong
Falcons at play
The 1973 Falcons bale out at 12,000 feet

Between pages 128 and 129

Prince Charles being fitted up to make a water jump, 1971
Fifty-nine men set off for a mass free fall
" ... fifty-nine of us, straight over the tailgate at a run"
Author congratulating Flight Sergeant Andy Sweeney on his
thousandth descent
A major NATO exercise in Turkey

Foreword

by Air Chief Marshal Sir Neil Cameron,
K.C.B., C.B.E., D.S.O., D.F.C., R.A.F.

It has been the proud task of the Royal Air Force since 1940 to train all military parachutists in this country. The beginnings were uncertain in the early wartime days, but parachuting has always attracted sterling characters and under the guidance of the late Group Captain Maurice Newnham, and others, parachuting soon became a highly professional business and the early work at the Central Landing Establishment at Ringway near Liverpool culminated in the large-scale airborne operations of the 1939-45 war such as Normandy, Arnhem and finally the Rhine Crossing.

Luckily military parachuting did not end with the war and as the years went by a new generation of R.A.F. parachute instructors appeared. One of them was Peter Hearn, a university graduate and a physical fitness specialist. He wrote this book whilst he was the Commanding Officer of No.1 Parachute Training School Royal Air Force Abingdon, but he had come through the school first as a trainee instructor before finishing in command fourteen years later.

One of his main tasks during this period was to develop the techniques of free-fall parachuting which had a military application. This country was well behind in this field with France and the Eastern European countries out in front. However it was not long before Peter Hearn and his colleagues in the business, such as John Thirtle and others, were well up with the state of the art. As often happened, their equipment was not of the highest class because of a shortage of money, but what they lacked in equipment they made up in skill, courage and enthusiasm and it was not long before the British parachutist could go to the world parachuting championships and take their place with the best.

It is not easy to put across the wonderful exhilaration and sheer excitement of a parachute drop, be it from balloon, from aircraft static line or free fall, to someone who has never done it. The author has achieved this admirably. As a very experienced parachutist himself Peter Hearn has also managed to get across the spirit, morale and panache of the parachutist by a delightful use of the understatement.

The professional parachutist will get a thrill from this book as well as those

who have never had the opportunity to jump. Altogether it is a fitting tribute
to those men who have been the Royal Air Force's parachute instructors
down the years. "Knowledge Dispels Fear" is the motto of No.1 Parachute
Training School, but without a little fear and a lot of challenge many of the
characters who parachute would never have been attracted.

Preface

The story of a parachutist. Not a particularly expert nor prolific parachutist. Many have jumped more often and with more skill than I. Parachuting is a varied feast, and in no one aspect of it have I specialized enough really to excel. As a sport jumper I competed in times when the actual possession of a parachute and a modicum of luck in using it were enough to gain a place in the national team; as a military parachutist I have never jumped in anger; as a member of a parachute rescue team I never actually rescued anyone; as a trials parachutist I have proved little; as a display jumper I have perhaps gained some experience; as an instructor of others ... well, there are better than I. What I have done, however, is to try most of the dishes in the feast, and I was around when some of them were being concocted. Thus it is breadth of experience rather than outstanding expertise that I offer as credentials for this story.

For those who are perhaps expecting melodrama, I should add that I have never 'stared death in the face'. I have never hurtled earthwards fighting with a tangle of rigging lines; never become inextricably entwined with another parachutist's canopy in mid-air; never missed death-dealing power cables by inches. But then not many of us do. Only those in newspapers. Most of us can log our thousand or so jumps with no great problems or publicity. So I offer my story not as an exceptional parachutist, but as a typical one.

Many people have helped me put it together, some through inspiration, others with more direct assistance. The former are too numerous to mention, for they include just about every parachutist that I have met or read about or heard about. To them, my fellow parachutists, I owe the greatest debt.

I am grateful to Air Chief Marshal Sir Neil Cameron not only for providing the Foreword to *Parachutist* and for valuable guidance in the writing of it, but also for the personal encouragement that he gave me as Station Commander of Royal Air Force Abingdon during my formative parachuting years.

My Station Commander at Abingdon whilst I was preparing the book was Group Captain Roy Jenkins, to whom I am also indebted for further advice and encouragement.

For practical assistance and contributions I am grateful to the late Group

Captain Maurice Newnham, to Danny Sutton, Errol Minter, Ron Smith, Jock Fox, Norman Hoffman, Dick Mullins, Doug Peacock, Snowy Robertson, Pete Williams, Geordie Charlton, Stan Phipps, Keith Teesdale, Tommy Maloney, Frank Gavin, Gwynne Morgan, the late Geoff Greenland, John Meacock, Ron Ellerbeck, and Bob Sinclair. I only regret that so many of the wonderful stories I collected from them remain – as yet – untold.

For professional advice I thank Mr H.H. Edmonds of the Publications Clearance Branch of the Ministry of Defence.

For the typing chores I thank Corinne Turner and Marjorie Husband.

Above all, for being the wife of a parachutist, I thank Ed.

March 1975

1 / "Bob's Your Uncle"

"What's up, sir? Fingers cold?"

"Yes, Flight."

They weren't really cold. They just found it unusually difficult to do simple things: like adjusting the buckles of a parachute harness.

"Make sure your leg straps are nice and tight now. Don't want to trap the family jewels, do we ... ?" The Flight Sergeant checked and rechecked — tightening here, loosening there — until the webbing harnesses hugged us tight. "Right — reserves on! Top D rings remember, and line up for inspection. That's it, sir — number one, over here ... "

Number one ... Christ!

"Helmets on." They were made of brown canvas and foam rubber, and fastened under the chin with a tie-string. They had been used by many before us. Inside they were black, and smelt of sweat and Brylcream. Outside, they were adorned with crayoned wit. "Dig here," said one. They kept your ears warm, and gave an appearance of great daring. We didn't feel very daring.

The Flight Sergeant checked us yet again, thoroughly. "Stick — right turn ... quick march!" With our parachutes heavy on our backs we marched awkwardly out of the hangar into thin November sunlight. We kept in step across the tarmac, then lost it on the quiet grass of the airfield.

"Nice day for it then. Nice little bit of breeze. Ground nice and soft. Just the job."

The Flight Sergeant strode beside us towards the silver barrage balloon that was waiting on the grass with its big ears drooping lazily. It stirred restlessly on the short length of cable that tethered it to the winch lorry, but otherwise ignored us completely.

" ... and don't forget to have a good look at your canopy as soon as it's open, then get on with the rest of your drills ..."

A canvas-roofed cage of wood and metal hung beneath the balloon's belly, supported by wires that looked very thin. The airman sitting at the winch controls was chewing a piece of grass.

" ... so keep your feet and knees together, and Bob's your uncle."

The Flight Sergeant halted us, and disappeared into the cage, where he rattled things for a moment, then poked his head out again.

"Right. Lead on, number five."

We stepped in, one after the other, myself last to take up the number one position, nearest the door. I edged into the corner, as far as I could get. The Flight Sergeant hooked the static lines of our parachutes to the strong point in the roof of the cage, then checked each one with a sharp tug.

"Number one okay?"

"Number one okay."

"Number two okay?"

"Number two okay."

"Number three okay?"

"Number three okay."

We were all okay, we said. A thin metal bar was hooked across the open door.

"Up eight hundred feet, five men jumpinggggggg," bellowed the Flight Sergeant.

"Up eight hundred feet, five men jumpinggggggg," echoed the winch operator, and before any of us could disagree, the cable was paying out with a whirr, and the cage tilted, and rose. I peered gingerly over the side and watched as the earth receded in utter silence. It was like a green tide going out.

"Now don't forget, come forward one at a time when I tell you – right into the door – and let me see some good exits."

The rigging wires began to whine as we rose into a stronger, cooler breeze. A chequerboard of fields was stretching away to a hazy horizon. Such a long way down ...

" ... and a good pull on the correct liftwebs when you've assessed your drift, then just watch the ground, and Bob's your uncle ... "

Oh Christ ... Why hadn't I stayed a physical fitness officer?

" ... and if you should do anything wrong, I expect Flight Lieutenant Wiltshire will tell you about it over the loud hailer ..."

All the moisture had drained from my throat, and seeped into my knees. The Flight Sergeant had stopped talking. The silence was terrifying. He was looking over the side of the cage, watching the signal flags below. Perhaps they had lost the blue one! Perhaps we'd have to go down! Perhaps ... He stepped back suddenly and the metal bar dropped with a clatter like the clap of doom.

"Come forward number one!"

No more chat. No more Bob's your uncle. Just a statement of fact that propelled me against all reason into the open, swaying door to stand trembling on the edge of eight hundred feet of nothing, looking down in horror at the little toy figures looking up at me, then there was a sharp thump on the shoulder and another statement of fact in my left ear –

"GAAAAOOOOOOOOOOooooooooo ... "

– that dwindled and disappeared above me as my stomach rose into my chest and my boots appeared before my disbelieving eyes and the cold air rushed past me ... then a swoosh and a whuump as the liftwebs grabbed me by the shoulders and put my stomach and my boots back, and everything was still and quiet except for me going "Huuuuuuhhhhhh".

I had done it! I had done it! I had ...

"Get on with your drills, number one," said the loud hailer.

I looked up at the canopy. It was beautiful! A big white mushroom ... a giant nylon jellyfish ... a ...

"Number one ... get on with it ... "

I looked down. The green tide was coming in again, as quietly as it had gone out, but now with a frightening inevitability. I tried to prepare myself to meet it. Back liftwebs down ... chin on chest ... elbows in ... legs tight together ... and the grass suddenly rushed up and rolled all over me. I laid there for a moment, with the loud hailer saying unkind things about me. It could say what it bloody well liked. I had jumped ... I had jumped ...

Ten days earlier, I had reported to Royal Air Force Abingdon. About sixty of us had gathered in the lecture room. Most wore denims and camouflaged smocks and red berets. A handful, like myself, were in blue. In common we all wore big boots and strained expressions as we sat on hard seats listening attentively to the Royal Air Force officer who addressed us from the stage.

"Welcome to Number One Parachute Training School," he said.

The stage, his thick-soled jumping boots, and his brevet made him ten feet tall. He told us that jumping out of aeroplanes was not a natural thing to do, that it was against all human instinct, and that we would be very frightened. We all nodded in agreement and wondered why we'd come. But the ten foot tall officer went on to assure us that we would all overcome that fear, and would derive great satisfaction from so doing. He then told us about the course: Number 456 basic parachute training course for regular soldiers of the airborne forces, plus a few Royal Air Force volunteers for training as parachute jumping instructors. The basic course would last four weeks, he explained. There would be a few days of ground training first, during which we would be taught the simple skills of parachuting before we actually had to apply them in the air. Then eight descents – two from the balloon, followed by six from aircraft. The aircraft would be Beverley and Hastings, and the dropping zone was at Weston on the Green, ten miles north of Oxford. The training was well supervised, and as long as we did what we were told, nobody need get hurt, and were there any questions? There weren't, and the ten foot tall officer smiled at us as though it was all a huge joke, and left.

"Everyone outside then!" bellowed an authoritative voice. We all formed up in threes to be marched to the training hangar. "Fall in with the troops, Sir. No class distinction 'ere. Officers 'it the ground as 'ard as 'umans. By the left ... at the double ... *March*! lef ri lef ri lef ri lef ri ..."

At the hangar, the course was divided into sections of eight, and an instructor allocated to each section. As trainee instructors, we merited a Flight Sergeant. He was crisp and ramrod straight in freshly laundered overalls. SUTTON said the name tag over the breast pocket. He took us into the hangar – a dusty circus of swings and mats and slides and ladders, with camouflaged figures hanging in harnesses, leaping from ramps, whirring down from somewhere in the roof on the end of thin cables, tramping in booted unison from the dummy fuselage of a Hastings, and the voices of the instructors rising above the dust and the movement and the effort.

"Starboard stick – actiooonnnnn *stations* ... "

"Side left landings this time ... "

"Getcherlegstogether!!"

"GAAOOOOOO ... "

We became part of the hangar. A self-conscious part at first, until we realized that everyone was too intent upon their own survival to take note of the clumsiness of others. Then we settled down to learn the basic skills of military parachuting.

We learnt how to jump from the door of an aircraft, with a hard drive and in a compact position so that the slipstream wouldn't find a wandering limb to grab. "Go out of that door like a leaf, and you'll spin like a leaf," we were promised.

We learnt the 'aircraft drills' – the essential checks and the preparation of equipment to be carried out in the aircraft prior to jumping.

We learnt the 'flight drills'. How to check the parachute canopy when it had opened; how to operate the reserve parachute if it hadn't; how to steer away from each other to avoid entanglements; what to do if they couldn't be avoided; how to reduce the drift and oscillation of the parachute in preparation for landing.

We learnt how to land. How to absorb an impact that was a combination of the inevitable downward velocity and a horizontal movement caused by wind-drift and parachute oscillation. The body position, we soon learnt, was all important. "Chin on chest, shoulders rounded, elbows in, legs right underneath you, knees slightly bent, feet tight together, and Bob's your uncle ... " Hit the ground in that position, and all you had to do was roll with the drift, spreading the fall over the side of the leg, across the buttocks, and over the broad of the back in a smooth flowing movement. "Flow, sir, floooowwww ... not thump thump thump like that ... "

We learnt about the parachute itself. The 'X' type – standard equipment for British airborne forces. We learnt how to fit it, how to check it, and how to care for it. How it was made, and how it worked. It would be attached to a strong point in the balloon or aircraft by a 'static line' which, when you jumped, would automatically pull open the pack to allow rigging lines and canopy to deploy in a carefully regulated sequence. Fully developed, it would have a flying diameter of 28 feet, and would lower us to earth at about 18 feet per second. There might be a little oscillation, the Flight Sergeant warned us. Oscillation presupposed that the thing was open, so we wouldn't mind a little bit of that, we thought.

We learnt from lectures, films, and demonstrations. But above all we learnt from constant practice and repetition. We jumped, we rolled, we hurled ourselves out of mock aircraft doors, we swung in suspended harnesses, until conscious effort was replaced by reflex action.

Whilst we learnt the physical skills of military parachuting, we were also – without being fully aware of it – being mentally prepared. The ground was taken progressively further away from us. The 'fan', up in the hangar roof, gave us our first sensation of leaping into space – only 30 feet of space, but that was enough with only a thin cable for support and two fan blades beating the air to retard the plunge towards the floor. Then the outdoor exit trainer, on which the jump from the door was arrested rather abruptly and the body was then whisked away on an inclined cable to simulate the sensation of launching oneself into an aircraft slipstream. Anyone who jumped with a loosely fitted harness discovered why it was called the "knacker cracker". Thence to the high tower, for controlled descents and landings from 90 feet.

We were totally immersed in a parachuting atmosphere, which also helped to dispel some of its mystery. There was almost an air of normalcy about it. There was a certain nonchalance in the way in which the instructors fitted their parachutes and prepared to go off for their own descents, although we couldn't really believe that they enjoyed it. We would watch troops in more advanced stages of training than ourselves march out to the aircraft for the first sortie of the morning, and their happy return in approximately the same numbers a couple of hours later would raise hopes of our own survival.

But neither the training progression, nor the example of others, nor the Flight Sergeant's assurances that Bob was our uncle, could banish fear as we closed on the day of our first jump. Reason now told us that all would be well, but those butterflies in the belly are creatures not of reason but of instinct, and instinct still advised us to have nothing to do with leaping into space. So the big question remained unanswered: could we do it? Well, on that November morning at Weston on the Green, we had found out, like thousands before us, that we could ...

There was a second jump from the balloon that morning, then we drove back through Oxford in a coach filled with the noise of everyone telling everyone else how easy it was. All talking, nobody listening.

Back in the hangar the Flight Sergeant told us what we had done wrong on our first two descents, then had us back on the mats and in the harness swings to get it right. More landings, more flight drills, more exit training. And as soon as they thought that we were ready for it, we were waiting on the tarmac at Abingdon to emplane for our first jump from an aircraft, and those butterflies were busy again.

There was a long time to wait. A long time to think about it. But at last the Beverley trundled round. A winged double-decker: twenty men upstairs, forty down. We climbed into its metal belly and sat down on the banks of seats that lined each side of the fuselage. Two rows of white faces looking at each other from beneath the low brims of airborne helmets. We fastened our seatbelts. The doors were closed, and the aircraft trundled off again. It seemed a long way to the end of the runway. "We're going by road," someone said, but nobody laughed. The engines rose to full voice, and the Beverley surged forwards to lift surprisingly and steeply into the air.

Huddled back into my seat, wedged between the men on either side, I closed my eyes and started to go through the drills in my mind again ... left foot forward for port exit. Close to the man in front. Good drive out through the door. Check the canopy. Kick out of twists, if there were any. There were sure to be ...

The Beverley was swaying and bumping a little.

Yes ... kick out of twists, then what? All-round observation, that's right. Then steer away from anyone who looks too close for comfort ... assess the drift ... prepare for landing ...

The despatcher was positioning the strops on the overhead cables, one strop in front of each man. Suddenly the engines were roaring twice as loudly at us as the doors at the rear of the fuselage were opened.

"First sticks – STAND UP!"

The despatcher's voice could barely be heard over the steady thunder of the aircraft. The first three men on each side clambered to their feet. They hooked their static lines to the strops, staggering a little as the aircraft banked into its run for the dropping zone. We craned forward in our seats to watch the sticks move towards the roaring doors. The slipstream was whipping the despatcher's overalls. The red light glowed, then the green, and the three pale-faced men of the port stick disappeared from sight one after the other, then the three on the starboard side, with the despatchers yelling their numbers and the strops clattering against the rear of the doors. We sat back, envying the first ones because they didn't have to wait any longer. Round again, the Beverley still lurching uncomfortably, then levelling up for another run, and six more were gone.

Someone started to retch into his sick-bag. I felt my own stomach rebelling. Oh no! Not that! I'd rather have twists, Lord ... please give me twists, Lord, but don't let me be sick ... Round again. The empty seats came creeping up the aircraft towards us. Then it was us, standing, fumbling through the checks.

"Tell off for equipment check!"

"Three okay."

"Two okay."

"One okay, port stick okay."

"Port stick ... Actionnnn *stations!*"

We lurched towards the door, bemused by noise and nausea and inspired by a distinct longing to get it all over with. Red on ... green on ... following the man in front of me straight through the rectangle of light with no great conscious effort, to be grabbed by a giant hand and flung through the air in a confusion of tilting horizons and blue sky, then the harness tightening as the canopy took a long, deep breath of fresh air. I looked up. It was all there. And He hadn't given me any twists after all. I turned in the harness and looked around me. Nobody to steer away from. And below, all that lovely green grass, and everything so quiet after the uproar of the aircraft. Just swaying there gently in the sky, so soothing, so peaceful ... just that damned loud hailer again. All right, all right!

Subsequent descents, like the initial ground training, were progressive in nature. Something new and more demanding was added to each jump. There were longer sticks; then simultaneous sticks, troops jumping from both doors at the same time, which made the need for good all-round observation and the avoidance of entanglements more acute; and descents with seventy-pound weapon containers, hooked to the parachute harness for exit then lowered on a suspension rope for flight and landing. And between jumps, it was back in the hangar. "Sir, you might make a parachutist one day, but not if you make many more landings like that one ... Now then, sir, in the block and tackle if you don't mind ... "

My mind swung between emotional extremes: fear before a jump, exhilaration during it, and a sort of cockiness afterwards. The cockiness was knocked out of me on the night descent.

"All you have to do is relax," said the Flight Sergeant. "Just hold a good position, relax, and Bob's your uncle."

After slithering down the slipstream to find myself swinging alone in the darkness, with the dim horizons rising threateningly all round, and impenetrable blackness below, the Flight Sergeant's sound advice fled into the night, and I stiffened in fear. When Weston rushed up at me out of the darkness, the blow zigzagged up my spine and exploded in little stars around my head.

The eight jumps and the basic course were over. The troops paraded smartly and proudly to receive their airborne wings from the ten foot tall officer, while we watched from the side of the parade ground. For us, as potential instructors, that was just the beginning of our training. We now had to learn to teach what we ourselves had just been taught.

As qualified physical training instructors, we had some knowledge of the principles of teaching. Now we had to apply those principles to the specific techniques of parachuting. We analysed each skill, every movement, and found how best to teach it in simple progressions, how and when to use the various pieces of apparatus, the faults to watch for and how to correct them. We practised teaching each other, under the critical eye of the Flight Sergeant.

It was also necessary for us to know how to organize and operate a parachuting programme, which involved the preparation of troops and the supervision of their para-fitting; despatching them from balloon and aircraft; and marking and manning the dropping zone. Despatching from the aircraft I did not like. Standing braced against the aft edge of the door with the slipstream tugging at my flying overalls as though urging me to join it, the smile of encouragement that was meant to inspire those about to jump invariably froze into a grimace of horror when the green light came on and the troops hurtled past with a clatter of boots and strops and with little regard for me. Fortunately my role as an officer would eventually be on the dropping zone – the DZ – rather than in the door. Flight Lieutenant Bob Wiltshire took us out into the Berkshire countryside and on to Salisbury Plain to teach us how to select DZs suitable for troops or supplies to be dropped on. We then learnt how to calculate the 'release point' in relation to wind conditions, dropping height, length of sticks, and the direction of the aircraft's flight track; how to place the marker panels to guide the aircraft on to that point; how to use the ground-to-air radio; and the points to watch for and if necessary to correct with the loud-hailer during an actual descent. There was more to this P.J.I. business than we had thought.

Throughout this training, we were logging more jumps. We learnt from each one, often the hard way. Fear was disappearing, dispelled by knowledge, as the school motto promised that it would be. Knowledge that our equipment was sound; knowledge of our own increasing ability; knowledge that for every potential hazard there was a prevention, and knowledge that if the prevention should fail, there was usually a cure. In fact, real fear at this stage was not of jumping, but of failing to jump well enough – of making a nonsense of it before others. We were developing a cautious enthusiasm for and a certain pride in our parachuting. I still wasn't very good. On one jump from the balloon, we were to fly our reserve parachutes after the main canopy had opened, and ride the two down, for experience. When I pulled the red handle on the top of the chest-mounted reserve pack, the white nylon flopped out with no show of interest, and despite my efforts to shake some life into it, wrapped itself slowly and malevolently round my legs. I landed heavily, to gusts of laughter, for there is nothing more amusing to a P.J.I. than another P.J.I. in trouble.

In all that we did, safety was the keynote. Safety, achieved through constant supervision, through meticulous checking, through careful progression, through thorough briefing. Men's lives, we were constantly reminded, would be in our hands. Safety had to become a way of life.

For the final phase of our training we were attached to a basic course again, not as pupils this time, but as supernumerary instructors. Under critical supervision, we put our new-found teaching abilities to the test. We were also, at this stage, allowed into the inner sanctum – the crewroom. We learnt more there of the P.J.I. and of the nature of P.T.S. than we did in the hangar and the lecture rooms.

Our worthiness to wear the P.J.I. brevet had been under constant review throughout the training, and our numbers had dwindled accordingly. Now we were finally examined in theory and in practice. I didn't do very well in either but nevertheless found myself at last in Wing Commander Jimmy Blythe's office.

Seated impressively behind his desk, he asked me a few routine questions, which I answered as best I could.

"What would you do, Hearn," he then asked, "if as a young syndicate officer you were running a balloon jumping programme out at Weston and your syndicate Flight Sergeant came up to you and respectfully suggested that it would be better to shift the balloon to another part of the DZ?"

I would have told the Flight Sergeant to get stuffed, but I caught Bob Wiltshire's eye as he stood a little behind the CO. "Shift it" he was mouthing silently.

"I would shift it, sir."

"Good," said the Wing Commander, and handed me my brevet.

2/ Knowledge Dispels Fear

"We ought to have a corps of at least five thousand parachute troops," wrote Winston Churchill on 6 June 1940. "Pray let me have a note from the War Office on the subject."

The War Office raised its eyebrows. Create a new offensive weapon at a time when we ourselves faced imminent invasion? Within weeks of the collapse of France and the withdrawal of our battered armies from Dunkirk? When all our remaining military resources would surely be needed to counter the onslaught of a powerful enemy? And anyway, who the devil knew anything about parachute troops?

The Germans did. They in turn had learnt from the Russians, who had been developing an airborne capability since 1927, shortly after General Billy Mitchell had been scoffed at in the United States for even suggesting such an idea. The British officers who saw twelve hundred men and eighteen field guns dropped in the Red Army manoeuvres of 1936 reported that military parachuting was spectacular but of little tactical value. The Germans said nothing, went home, raised an elite force within the Luftwaffe, and developed with characteristic thoroughness an impressive airborne delivery system of their own. Using static line operated parachutes with a single suspension point that dangled men spider-like beneath their canopies, they jumped from their Junkers 52s from as low as 300 feet above the ground. By mid-1940 this force had already been put to good use in the German invasions of the Low Countries and Norway, and now the Home Guards of our own southern counties were anxiously scanning the summer skies for the first signs of the dreaded paratroopers.

But we in England had no practical knowledge of military parachuting techniques, nor did we possess any equipment specifically designed for airborne delivery. However, despite the dearth of knowledge and equipment, and notwithstanding the abundance of scepticism and outright opposition, Winston Churchill had spoken, and within the month there arrived at Ringway Airport, Manchester, two rather puzzled officers — Major John Rock of the Royal Engineers, and Squadron Leader Louis Strange, a former Royal Flying Corps pilot. They were jointly to command the parachute training element of a new unit, to be known as the Central Leading Establishment. Neither of them knew anything about parachuting.

They were joined by a staff of six Army and nine R.A.F. volunteers, who, apart from a few parachute packers and fabric workers among the latter, also had no experience of this uncertain form of transport. It was obvious that ideas and equipment would have to be improvised. Fortunately, that handful of pioneers were men of great ingenuity, as well as courage.

The only parachutes immediately available were the manually operated type used for aircrew training. A thousand of these were despatched to Ringway. The R.A.F. was exceedingly reluctant to divert any aircraft from their 'proper' task of dropping bombs to the highly suspect one of dropping people, but six Whitley bombers were eventually and grudgingly provided. Local defence commanders were advised that friendly parachutists would soon be making practice parachute drops on to Tatton Park and were not to be shot, and on 13 July the first trial descents were made. They were 'pull off' jumps.

This was the system that had been used before the war to give aircrew some parachuting experience. Clinging to the strut of a large biplane, such as the Vimy, the parachutist would at the correct height and moment pull the ripcord and allow the billowing canopy to drag him off the wing into space. To afford a perch from which the parachutist could be plucked from the Whitley, the rear gun turret was removed, and replaced by a small platform. Captain Lindsay recorded one of those first descents:

I found myself on a small platform about a foot square, at the very back of the plane, hanging on like grim death to the bar. The two rudders were a few feet away on either side of me; behind me was nothing whatsoever. As soon as I raised myself to my full height, I found that I was to all purposes outside the plane, the slipstream of air in my face almost blowing me off. I quickly huddled up, my head bent down and pressed into the capacious bosom of Flight Sergeant Brereton. He held up his hand for me to watch. The little light at the side changed from yellow to red. I was undeniably frightened, though at the same time filled with a fearful joy. The light changed to green, and down fell his hand. I put my hand across to the D ring in front of my left side and pulled sharply. A pause of nearly a second and then a jerk on each shoulder. I was whisked off backwards and swung through nearly one hundred and eighty degrees, beneath the canopy and up the other side. But I was quite oblivious to this. I had something akin to a blackout. At any rate, the first thing I was conscious of after the jerk on my shoulders was to find myself, perhaps four seconds later, sitting up in my harness and floating down to earth. The only sensation I registered was one of utter astonishment at finding myself so suddenly in this remarkable and ridiculous position.*

* *By Air to Battle* – the approved H.M.S.O. account of the British Airborne Division .

This was neither psychologically nor practically the best method of going to war, and an alternative and preferred system of exit was provided by making a circular hole in the floor of the Whitley's fuselage. It was far from ideal:

The Whitley was about as awkward and uncomfortable for the job as could be imagined. The door was much too small to allow men to pass through it quickly when wearing parachutes and equipment, and the only practicable alternative was to make a circular hole in the floor of the fuselage. The cramped interior into which the men had to crawl on their hands and knees was dark, draughty and smelly. The exit hole was for all the world like an outsize in those manholes which give access to drains or coal cellars. No small degree of skill and determination was necessary to project oneself through this hole or funnel – for it was nearly three feet deep – and it was absolutely vital to maintain a perfectly upright and rigid position as otherwise one's face scraped the side with most disagreeable results.*

With the unit thus equipped, the training of a few hardy volunteers commenced. For those first descents 'through the hole' with the R.A.F. training 'chutes, the ripcord was operated by a line attached to the aircraft. With this system, the canopy was freed first from the pack, followed by the rigging lines, which caused a heavy shock-load on the parachutist and the risk of him becoming entangled in his canopy if he made a bad exit – which Driver Evans of the Royal Army Service Corps did on 25 July, to become Britain's first airborne fatality. Training ceased. Two weeks later it recommenced with a new design of statichute, manufactured by the 'GQ' Parachute Company, which became known universally as the 'X' type. The development sequence was reversed so that the rigging lines were withdrawn first from the pack and put under tension before the weight of the falling body pulled the canopy into the air, to give a smoother opening and to lessen the risk of entanglement.

A welcome measure of parachuting expertise was added to the staff when a professional jumper called Harry Ward arrived at Ringway. As an aircraft rigger in the Royal Air Force, Harry had made his first jump in 1926, and in 1932, out of the Service, he had joined Cobham's Air Circus as a stunt parachutist. He was not a good teacher, but he brought to the unit his personal skill, fearlessness, and practical example – qualities most valuable, for there was not much else. Ground training facilities were almost non-existent. Parachutes were repacked in the airmen's dining hall, between meals. And the parachute was still far from foolproof, for excessive twists, or a leg caught in the rigging lines, could prevent the canopy from inflating, with

* *Prelude To Glory* by Maurice Newnham.

fatal consequences. There was no reserve parachute. But the attitude of trainees towards malfunctions and accidents was one of fatalistic acceptance. In the trucks returning from Tatton Park, or over an evening pint or two, they would raise their voices and mock the inherent hazards of their chosen trade, to the tune of 'John Brown's Body'.

"Is everybody happy?" said the Sergeant, looking up,
Our hero feebly answered "Yes", and then they hooked him up.
He jumped into the slipstream, and he twisted twenty times,
And he ain't going to jump no more.
    The lines they wrapped around his neck, the D rings broke his dome,
The liftwebs tied themselves in knots around each skinny bone,
The canopy became his shroud as he hurtled to the ground
And he ain't going to jump no more.
    The ambulance was on the spot, the jeeps were running wild,
The medicos they clapped their hands and rolled their sleeves and smiled,
For it had been a week or two since the last 'chute had failed,
And he ain't going to jump no more.
    He hit the ground the sound was 'splat', the blood went spurting high
His pals were plainly heard to say "Oh what a way to die"
They rolled him up still in his 'chute, and poured him from his boots,
And he ain't going to jump no more.
    Glory, glory, what a hell of a way to die.
Glory, glory, what a hell of a way to die.
Glory, glory, what a hell of a way to die,
And he ain't going to jump no more.

Despite early training problems, by February 1941 the newly created force was ready to declare its presence, albeit in a small way. Thirty-seven men of No.11 Special Air Service Battalion jumped from six Whitleys into Italy to blow up the Traquino viaduct. Although the damage that they caused was light, and although the whole raiding party was subsequently captured, the psychological impact – particularly on the Italians – of this arrival from the sky was considerable.

But at home there was still much scepticism, and a marked disinclination to support this new concept. Those few who now firmly believed in airborne assault struggled on, seeking to advertise through demonstrations, and trying all the time to improve parachuting safety and instructional methods.

In April the balloon made its first appearance at Tatton Park, to become a most valuable but initially unpopular training aid. Although it reduced the risk of parachuting malfunctions by eliminating slipstream interference to man and canopy, the very cold-bloodedness of dropping through the silent hole that took up most of the floor of the open, rickety cage was off-putting. Ron Smith, another Ringway man who retired as a Squadron Leader in 1974, tells of Lofty Humphries — one of the original 1940 instructors — despatching on one occasion from the balloon:

> He got to the last man — a particularly nervous lad, obviously not too keen, who eventually succumbed to Lofty's persuasive tones and equally persuasive six feet four inches, and slid over the edge. Somehow he didn't quite make it, and finished up hanging by his hands from the sill, looking up at Lofty with his eyes sticking out like chapel pegs. Very casually Lofty leant over the edge and gently said to the hapless pupil, "You'll be quite safe lad. Just reach up with both your hands and I'll take hold of you and pull you back in." With a look of gratitude in his eyes the young soldier took his hands from the sill to reach up for Lofty's, and disappeared with a shriek, to make his first descent. He went on to complete the course.

Also in April 1941, Winston Churchill visited Ringway. Some 400 trained paratroopers paraded, and in near gale conditions forty men jumped from five well-worn Whitleys. It was perhaps the determination and enthusiasm of this force rather than the scale of its demonstration that impressed Churchill, for shortly after his visit it was confirmed that a Parachute Brigade of four battalions was to be formed. It was the breakthrough.

To meet this commitment, a vast expansion of the makeshift facilities and of the Ringway staff was needed. Wing Commander Maurice Newnham, who had taken over command of the school in May and was, like Louis Strange, a former R.F.C. pilot of renown, pressed for a single Service staff of professional instructors, to be drawn from the Physical Fitness Branch of the Royal Air Force. When this was agreed upon, the Army instructors who had given such fine service during the first and formative year of parachute training withdrew to run the pre-drop training of prospective paratroopers at the Army Depot at Hardwick, and volunteers for P.J.I. training from within the Physical Fitness Branch arrived at Ringway. Not all of them stayed. And not all those who did stay were accepted. But the thirty-five who passed the two-week course and survived Newnham's critical interview were outstanding men, of backgrounds ranging from ballet dancer to champion boxer, but with enthusiasm and a great spirit of adventure in common.

On 1 November 1941 the unit became known as the Parachuting Training School, and the Royal Air Force assumed full responsibility for the parachute training of airborne soldiers.

There was still on the staff a hard-core of the original R.A.F. instructors, including Harry Ward, now promoted to Squadron Leader to fill the post of Chief Parachuting Instructor. There was a complementary post of Chief

Ground Instructor now established, and into it was posted in October 1941 Squadron Leader John Callastus Kilkenny, known ever since as 'J.C.K.'. His immediate task was to devise methods and a syllabus of ground training that would adequately prepare trainees for the parachuting phase of their course. He brought to this job the professionalism of a trained teacher, the physical skills and knowledge of an outstanding sportsman, an analytical mind, and an insistence on perfection that was to drive many to distraction, but which all were to respect. Like Maurice Newnham, he had been 'asked' to do the job, and had no inclination to parachute at all, but also like Newnham he knew there was no substitute for practical experience, and that the example of the senior instructional staff was of utmost importance. Again like Newnham, he broke a leg in gaining that experience.

"J.C.K. worked all day and half the night", recalls Erroll Minter, one of the 1941 N.C.O.s, eventually to become one of the most experienced P.J.I. officers in the business. "A dedicated man. I remember one night, at about half past seven, he called half a dozen of us out of the Sergeants' Mess and took us to the hangar. We put a line of mats up against the wall, and all we did for about an hour was to run up the wall as far as we could until we fell over backwards, while J.C.K. stood there balancing on his broken leg and scribbling in his notebook. He thought he might learn something about backward landing techniques by watching our natural protective reactions as we fell over."

From analysis such as that and from the application of proven teaching principles, J.C.K. developed basic parachuting techniques and a system of ground training that have not left his successors much scope for initiative. The ten-man section (a Whitley load) under one instructor was the basis of his training philosophy, and his syllabus of ground training, although developed in detail with subsequent experience, set the pattern for all of us to follow. The landing technique of rolling the impact over the less vulnerable parts of the body was largely his, and much of the equipment on which the basic skills were taught in the hangar was devised by J.C.K.: indeed, the hangar soon became known as 'Kilkenny's Circus'. Not all new ideas were his, for he had a staff of inventive minds from which to pick the best suggestions, polish them, and put them into practice, but to J.C.K. must go most of the credit for turning parachuting from a flirtation with fortune to a matter of some skill.

One of those other inventive minds belonged to Julian Gebolys, a Pole, and a parachutist of some experience. Inspired by Maurice Newnham, who was concerned at the continuing high incidence of injuries and convinced that the answer lay in some better means of controlling the parachute during the descent, Gebolys was largely responsible for one of the major advances in parachuting techniques. The early 'X' type had two single liftwebs, leading up from the shoulders. The only flight technique that was taught was the old professional trick of twisting the liftwebs to turn the body to face in the direction of drift, thus avoiding backward landings. There was no recognized method of reducing drift, nor of damping out the violent oscillations which were a feature of the 'X' type and a major cause of injuries.

"Then someone got the idea of splitting the liftwebs, so that we had four of them — two forward and two back liftwebs", recalled Danny Sutton. "Then we were sent up and told that whatever was happening, we were all to pull down our forward liftwebs during flight. Well, we did, and some of us really piled in, and we didn't think much of it. And the next time we went up to jump we were told that we were all to pull down our back pair of liftwebs this time, and of course, some of us took a real old hammering, but it proved what they wanted to find out, and then we were told that next time, if we were drifting forwards to pull on back liftwebs, and if we were drifting backwards to pull on front liftwebs, and of course — that was it!"

It has echoed round the hangar to this day. "You are drifting FORWARDS ... pull down on your BACK liftwebs ... " Or vice versa. Drift and oscillation were reduced with one simple movement, and injury rates fell at P.T.S. by 28 per cent when the technique was fully introduced.

Danny Sutton was typical of many who joined the staff of P.T.S. at that time:

I joined the Service as a general duty airman and went to Swinderby where there was a Polish squadron flying Wellingtons and Fairey Battles, and all I did for six months was peel spuds and scrub tables in the Sergeants' Mess. Well I didn't think that was doing much to win the war, so I asked the S.W.O. if I could remuster to something else, and he said what could I do? Well, I'd been a good gymnast before the war, almost national class, and I told him that, and he said I should try for P.T.I. So I went to St Athan with No.18 War Course, and passed out as a corporal P.T.I. and went to Great Yarmouth. I remember them bombing the brewery there ... Anyway, then there was this paper calling for volunteers from the P.T. Branch for training as parachute jumping instructors. I'd already volunteered for air gunner, but nothing seemed to be happening, so I thought I'd have a go. I still felt a bit out of things as a P.T.I., you see. So I got to Ringway, and I was a bit apprehensive. It was a big course — about eighty of us. On our first aircraft descent, from the Whitley in front of the one I was on, we had a fatality. I landed, and there he was, all covered up. Corporal Nelson, it was. Well, that sorted them out a bit. A lot of chaps chucked it in after that. About half of them. But to me, I thought, well ... it can't happen to me. You think like that, don't you?

I thought I'd press on. It couldn't happen to me. But it did sort that course out ...

Using aircraft that were never designed for parachuting purposes, parachutes that did not always forgive a bad exit, and with no reserve, fatalities were inevitable. But Danny Sutton's philosophy was shared by all, instructors and pupils alike. It couldn't happen to them. It wasn't that they were unafraid. In the early stages of training in particular, fear was very real to them. But again they could sing about it, and exalt the overcoming of it in a particularly soldierly way:

> When first I came to P.T.S., my C.O. he advised,
> "Take lots and lots of underwear, you'll need them, I surmise."
> But I replied, "By Gad, Sir! No matter what befall,
> I'll always keep my trousers clean, when jumping through the hole."

> I went into the hangar, instructor by my side,
> And on Kilkenny's circus had many a glorious ride.
> "On these ingenious gadgets," said he, "soon you'll learn to fall,
> And keep your feet together, when jumping through the hole."

> I worked hard in the hangar, and soon felt quite a man,
> Until I jumped from thirty feet, supported by a fan.
> I thought my end had really come, the floor seemed far below,
> But it was just another step, to jumping through the hole.

> I saw the gorgeous parachute, with camouflage design.
> I heard the Warrant Officer shoot such a lovely line.
> "This lovely bit of stuff, lads," said he, "upon my soul,
> Is sweeter than your sweetheart, when jumping through the hole."

> One morning very early, damp and cold and dark,
> They took me in a so-called bus, to a place called Tatton Park.
> In keeping with the weather, said I to one and all,
> "I take a dim and misty view of jumping through the hole."

> They fitted me with parachute, and helmet for my head.
> The Sergeant looked with expert eye, "They fit you fine," he said.
> "I'll introduce you now to Bessie, that is what we call
> The balloon from which you soon will be jumping through the hole."

> "Okay, up six hundred, four to drop!" said he.
> "Four to drop! Good God!" I cried, "and one of them is me!"
> Then clinging very grimly to the handles in the floor
> I cursed the day I'd volunteered for jumping through the hole.

> I hit my pack, I rang the bell, I twisted twenty times,
> Got both my feet entangled in my rigging lines,
> But floating upside down to earth I didn't care at all,
> For I had kept my trousers clean when jumping through the hole.

It was not until late 1943 that the 'hole' was to be replaced by a more civilized method of leaving the aircraft – through the side door of the Dakota.

By May of 1942, 250 men per week were receiving their airborne wings at the school. Amongst the trainees was now a growing number of men of other nationalities – Poles, Czechs, Yugoslavs, Dutchmen, Frenchmen, Norwegians, Belgians and Canadians were amongst those who acquired the necessary confidence and skills at P.T.S. to parachute on to enemy-held soil. There were special sections who trained the 'Lambs', the exceptionally brave and often anonymous men and women of clandestine organizations such as Special Operations Executive. The instructors of these 'specials' also flew with their charges to despatch them into the night over occupied Europe.

In February of that year the viability of small-party airborne operations had been effectively shown by the successful raid on the Bruneval radio location unit, when 120 men of No.2 Parachute Battalion parachuted into France at night; surprised and overcame the Germans who were guarding the installation; examined and removed important items of equipment; and withdrew by sea at a cost of one man killed and seven missing. Later that year began the series of major airborne operations that were to justify the faith of the pioneers of the concept. The 1st Parachute Brigade jumped into North Africa to fight with such distinction that an impressed enemy bestowed upon them the title of 'The Red Devils'. The enemy was further impressed at Primasole Bridge in Sicily, 1943; on the left flank of the Normandy landings, 1944; and at Arnhem later in the same year.

Twenty-five P.J.I.s from Ringway flew with their erstwhile pupils in the American Dakotas that dropped the 1st Airborne Division at Arnhem. Danny Sutton had been one of them ...

I was with one hundred and fifty six Battalion. Great bunch of lads, they were. I had a stick of twenty. Major Pott was the stick commander. He was a religious man, and he was reading his Bible on the way over. I was chatting with the lads, and they were all concerned with me getting messages back to their families. There was a lot of flak as we came in over the coast, and we were rolling all over the place, but I got 'em ready okay. They had a tremendous amount of kit, a lot of it stuffed in their smocks. Fat as pigs, they looked. But they went out all right. No bother. A good stick ...

Danny only met two of them again. One was Major Pott.

Whereas the Germans never again employed their paratroopers in major airborne assaults after their eventually successful but very costly landings in Crete in 1940, our own airborne commanders – in particular Generals 'Boy' Browning and 'Windy' Gale – learnt the lessons that each major operation had to offer, and applied them in the next. The culmination was operation

'Varsity'. In March 1945, four years after that windy day at Ringway when five old Whitleys and a few gliders had demonstrated our airborne potential to Winston Churchill, the 6th Airborne Division crossed the Rhine in 240 Dakotas and 425 towed gliders to spearhead the final allied assault into the enemy heartland.

It was the last, as well as the most successful, of the great airborne assaults.

The Parachute Training School had every reason to be proud of its former pupils. There had been established at Ringway a mutual respect and an enduring bond between the P.J.I. and the airborne soldier, which those of us who have come later on the scene have inherited, admired, and endeavoured to perpetuate – but have never been able to re-create fully. It was a kinship born of a shared adventure into something unknown; of wartime pressures; and of eventual success in the face of physical dangers and vast administrative obstacles.

By the end of the war, P.T.S. had been given the prefix 'No.1' to distinguish it from its offspring that had been established at Chaklala in India, and at Kabrit in the Middle East. The No.1 P.T.S. crest was formally approved in July 1944, bearing its by then well-proven motto – "Knowledge Dispels Fear".

It was ironic that after their greatest work was done and when many instructors had left the service, the P.J.I. was eventually authorized to wear a brevet to signify his trade. Ringway was handed back to the Manchester City Corporation, and a stained glass window in the city's main airport building serves still as a reminder of those who taught and those who learnt the early skills of military parachuting.

No.1 P.T.S. moved to Upper Heyford, in Oxfordshire. The task was still heavy. Replacements for the Parachute Regiment still required training, and the first pupils of the newly formed Territorial Army airborne units made their appearance. Many other nations too had by now decided that a force of elite paratroopers was an essential part of their military line-up, and trainees of many tongues appeared at the school. Instructors from Australia, Rhodesia, South Africa, Iraq, Burma, Thailand, Egypt, Israel, Ghana, Kenya and the Sudan were to learn their trade at No.1 P.T.S. and subsequently adapt our training systems to their own requirements and environments, and training teams of British P.J.I.s were to help in the establishment of many foreign 'schools'.

In 1950 the school moved again – to R.A.F. Abingdon. The much-loved Dakota was replaced by the Valetta and the Hastings – the latter, with a door on each side of the fuselage, provided the first experience of simultaneous stick jumping. In 1955 the Beverley arrived, a workhorse of great capacity but limited range. Also in that year, the reserve parachute was introduced, not primarily for humane reasons, but for NATO standardization.

Those like myself who have never jumped without the comfort of a reserve parachute view with admiration those who did so as a matter of course. Yet it was an innovation that surprisingly enough was not met with the overwhelming eagerness that one might suppose. In fact, there were those who considered it to be a damn nuisance. For the soldier, it was extra weight: it was less ammunition. For the P.J.I., it grossly obstructed his view of the ground coming up to meet his boots for those immaculate stand-up landings. Perhaps an extreme opinion was that expressed by an Italian sport-parachutist in the 1954 world parachuting championships, who was loaned a reserve and jumped thus for the first time in his parachuting life. His main canopy failed to open fully, and the reserve was duly operated. When he had landed safely, the owner of the reserve parachute ran to him, expecting heartfelt thanks. Instead, he found the Italian kicking the reserve across the DZ and swearing loudly, "The first a-time I wear a second 'chute what happens? My bloody main doan' open!"

But despite a few murmurs from the old-timers, the reserve was a life-saver, and well worth the few inconveniences that it may have caused.

In 1956, British airborne soldiers again put their parachutes to serious use when No.3 Battalion of the Parachute Brigade dropped into El Gamil airfield as part of the Suez operation.

And in 1957, of no significance to anyone but myself, I had arrived at No.1 P.T.S.

The organization and methods of training were still much as J.C.K. had devised them. Courses were divided into syndicates of about forty men, each in the charge of a P.J.I. 'syndicate' officer. These groups were further broken down into sections of eight, each with its own Sergeant P.J.I. whose job it was to teach the basic practicalities of parachuting to his own small group of men. The role of the syndicate officer – which I became after receiving my brevet – was to organize the daily training programme for his course, supervise the instruction in the hangar and on the outdoor towers, lecture on parachuting theory, and to brief and debrief for each major event, including every jump. During dropping, the officer's place was on the DZ, behind the loud-hailer, giving advice that was usually general in nature, and widely ignored. We had an officer of renowned short-sightedness, who one day mislaid his spectacles.

"Don't worry – I'll tell you when they're out, and I'll cover any emergencies. You just give them the patter," said Flight Lieutenant Bob Wiltshire.

The Beverley lumbered overhead. Faces were raised expectantly. Nobody jumped. A dummy run. But "They're out!" cried Bob. "Kick out of twists ... steer away everyone ... steer away ... " bellowed our short-sighted officer, and we rolled on the grass as he gave a perfect talk-down to an empty sky. However, loud-hailer advice was useful in the occasional emergency – a blown periphery that required a reserve parachute to be operated; an impending entanglement that needed to be steered away from; a man hurtling across the sky on his wrong liftwebs in a strong breeze.

There was no other job like it, we thought. One was dealing with people of all ranks, units and backgrounds, unified by apprehension. They arrived at P.T.S. wondering if the bold decision they had taken several months earlier had been such a good idea after all. Having accepted a challenge, they were now face to face with it. It became a battle – as it is for every parachutist – between innate pride and inherent fear, and our job of helping pride to win was fascinating and rewarding.

As course followed course I threw my lecture notes away. It was implanted. I knew what I was talking about. I didn't have to look at the Flight Sergeant any more for the answers to the awkward questions. I was jumping with more authority too. I was developing that sense of awareness, the precise assessment of approach to the ground, the timing and the confidence that enabled one to control the 'X' type canopy and step casually out of the air for a stand-up landing – occasionally. I jumped whenever I had the chance, from balloon or aircraft. 'Fiddling', it was called. I didn't consciously decide that I would chase the jumps: I just found that I was doing it. I realized, almost with alarm, that I was enjoying it. Particularly pleasant was dropping through the 'aperture' in the boom of the Beverley. One just kept walking towards the rear of the 'upper deck' until you fell through the large rectangular hole in the floor, to slither down the slipstream as though on a giant slide, while the static line did its stuff above your head. I even volunteered to jump as 'drifter'* on night descents, and the wiser ones shook their heads.

* Before training descents, an instructor jumps as 'drifter' on the first run over the DZ to ensure that the drift has been correctly calculated.

It might have been easy to fall into the way of thinking that military parachuting was an enjoyable end in itself. That it was but a means to an end was a lesson that we fortunately had ample opportunity to learn when between courses and at weekends we were sent to help the teams of P.J.I.s who were detached from P.T.S. to work and live permanently with the major airborne formations. Their task was to provide continuation training and exercise support for their units.

With the Detachment to 16 Parachute Brigade I helped lay the markers on the DZs on Salisbury Plain, and lit the flares as the Beverleys came looming in at 1,000 feet to fill the sky with parachutists. I watched the heavy equipment platforms drift down under their awesome cluster of sixty-foot 'chutes, then, as the aircraft engines faded and we loaded the DZ kit on to our landrover, I watched silent men service their equipment, check their weapons, merge into groups, and file quietly into the dusk of the Plain – to start their work, as we finished ours.

In Studland Bay, outside Poole Harbour, I clung to the rail of a moored landing craft, saying "Roger zero six, clear to drop" and feeling ashamedly seasick as the Hastings ran in to deliver its sticks of Royal Marine commandos into the sea at the beginning of a beach-reconnaissance exercise.

In Denmark, with a powdering of snow on the ground and the night air sweetly crisp, we shone Aldis lamps at the dark silhouette of a Hastings and watched twelve black blobs drift silently into the stubble field: the Special Air Service on their way to plant dummy explosives on the Lillebaelts bridge – if the Danes didn't get them first.

On York racecourse, on Newcastle's Town Moor, at Wormwood Scrubs, on Hankley Common, on airfields between Hawkinge and Arbroath – on small DZs up and down the country – we dropped the Territorials of 44 Parachute Brigade from the 'mobile' balloons, for the furtherance of their parachuting skills and the delight of local children.

No, military parachuting was not an end in itself. It was a transport system, serving the same function as a three-ton truck: it took the soldier to where his real business began.

But that didn't stop me enjoying it. I had been on the staff of No.1 P.T.S. for a year when there occurred one of those magical moments that occasionally happen in parachuting. I had a course of some forty Territorial soldiers, who were well behind in their training, for fog had lain in the Thames Valley like a mouldy wet blanket for over a week. We sat drumming our fingers on our desks in the offices on the airfield side of the hangar, looking out at the prehistoric shapes of the grounded Beverleys barely visible fifty yards away on the pans. Every so often we would pick up the telephone and bother the met man, until at last – no doubt through exasperation – he suggested the possibility of a break that afternoon. The Squadron Commander said that I could give it a try, using the balloon on the airfield at Abingdon, so we roused the balloon crew, loaded men and parachutes on to the coaches, and drove slowly round the peri-track through mist that was as thick as ever.

We found the balloon, looking thoroughly miserable, with its ears drooping and wet. We waited for the promised clearance, and nothing happened. In a mood of rebellious frustration I loaded the cage with instructors, put myself in the Number One slot by the door, and told the Flight Sergeant to give us a shout on the loud-hailer when eight hundred feet of cable had payed out. The Flight Sergeant's doubtful eyes and the wet grass disappeared almost immediately and we rose through dank swirls of mist that muffled both sight and sound. Then, above us, the fog began to glow. We all looked up. It was like surfacing from a deep dive into sunlit waters, as we suddenly broke into brilliant sunshine that painted the balloon a dazzling silver and threw sharp shadows on the cage. We hadn't seen shadows for a fortnight. We looked around us in wondrous silence. Below, for as far as we could see and in every direction, stretched unbroken rolls of pure white cotton wool. The balloon jerked gently to a halt two hundred feet above it. We were motionless, the only feature in a vast blue dome with a white floor. The sole possessors of the sun. Absolute silence.

Was there really an airfield below that blanket? And people?

"Eight hundred feet ... " called a distant and muted voice. Yes, there were ...

We shouldn't have jumped. Not without being able to see the signal flags, and the angle of the cable ... and the ground. But there was something compulsive about that cotton wool. It looked so solid, as though you could leap down on to it and go floundering off ankle-deep to the horizons. I nodded to the despatcher. He looked surprised, but dropped the bar. I stood in the door.

"I can't see the flags," he said.

I looked down at the impenetrable cloud.

"You've got a blue," I promised him.

"Cheerio then ... "

I jumped. The cotton wool hurtled up, and swaddled me just as my canopy opened. I hauled on the front liftwebs to make sure I wasn't drifting into the cable, then peered down through the damp mist for a sign of the ground, and saw it coming up just in time to let up the left liftweb for a sideways landing. I heard the others dropping around me, and found the coaches and the anxious Flight Sergeant. We were back in the land of mortals.

It was not going to clear, so I cancelled the programme and we drove back through the fog to the hangar. Nobody really believed that we had jumped. It didn't matter. It was a very personal thing. It was one of those moments that came to mind when a few months later I was offered, for the furtherance of my career in the Service, a permanent commision in the Equipment Branch.

"Stuff it," I said, or words to that effect.

3/ *"Le Lieutenant Anglais a Perdu Son Poignet!"*

" ... Adieu la fille, adieu.
Adieu la fille adieu.
Ton sourire, ton sourire ...
Ton sourire reste dans nos yeux ...

What a lovely way to wake up, I thought. A marching song and the rhythmic tramp of muffled boots, and the early morning throwing bars of light through the shutters. So why was I lying there with my heart beating a lot faster than it normally did at six in the morning? What was I afraid of? And why were they singing in French? Then I remembered. Pau ... I was at Pau, home of "Les Paras". And today we were to make our first free-fall jump ...

Free fall. We didn't know much about it at P.T.S. in 1959. Our world was that of the statichute, which opened automatically, immediately, and with commendable constancy when one jumped. Falling freely through the air, then operating the parachute by means of a ripcord, was the preserve of the unfortunate aviator forced to abandon his aircraft; of the professional stuntman; and of a handful of sport parachutists whom we regarded with respect and grave suspicion.

Not that it was new: people had been tumbling out of flying machines and pulling ripcords since 1919. At that time an alternative to the statichute was being sought as a means of escape from disabled aircraft, which had a tendency to snag the deploying canopy as the airman leapt over the side. The alternative was to fall clear of the aeroplane, then operate the parachute by some inherent mechanism. By many this was considered even more dangerous than the statichute, for medical advice backed popular opinion that a man who fell through the air for any distance at all would rapidly lose consciousness. This theory was not accepted by Leslie Irvin, an American stuntman, who on 28 April 1919 climbed into an aircraft at McCook Airfield, Ohio, to demonstrate a manually operated parachute before an apprehensive audience of military officials. Irvin jumped from 2,000 feet. He was seen to tumble through the air for several seconds, gaining speed and loosing height rapidly until there was a flicker of white silk above him and the parachute blossomed into life, to herald the beginning of free fall.

Irvin's parachutes were soon adopted by airforces throughout the world, and many aviators came to owe their lives to their ripcord. The professional stuntmen soon traded in their static line 'chutes for the manually operated variety. Their job was to thrill the crowds, and what sight more thrilling than a little black speck dropping from a high-flying aircraft, falling closer and closer until it became recognizable to the upturned faces as a tumbling human figure, and then the parachute streaming and cracking open above it? It was in the professional interest of the barnstormers to foster a 'dicing with death' image, a concept that was reinforced by those who diced and lost. Some of those early free-fallers were content to tumble through the sky with their hand on the ripcord until their stopwatch or the proximity of the ground suggested they pull it. Others undoubtedly found that they could exercise some degree of control over their body position as they hurtled earthwards, but being professionals they tended to keep such trade secrets to themselves. Certainly no wide publicity was given to free-fall techniques until Leo Valentin wrote a book about it in 1954. A former French airborne soldier and parachuting instructor, Valentin somersaulted through the sky for 150 jumps before deciding that there was no great future in unstable free fall. He gave the matter thought, and developed a technique based on the premise that a symmetrical convex surface will always present itself to an airflow. He so presented his own body, by arching his back and evenly spreading his limbs in a giant X position, and found that in this attitude he remained face down to the earth as he fell, without turning or tumbling. Valentin's book included photographs of several dashing but dead birdmen, and a sequence of one of the most famous of them − Clem Sohn − hitting the ground at 100 miles per hour under a streaming canopy. Then in 1956 Valentin himself plummeted to his death whilst giving a display at Speke Airport. So we had read his book with an interest that was morbid rather than practical.

Several instructors at P.T.S. had gained a little free-fall experience. Some had trained for and competed in the 1954 world parachuting championships, and with others had continued to pursue the sport with enthusiasm, jumping at weekends from a Tiger Moth at Weston. Then in July 1957 Flight Lieutenant Neil Perry dropped from 2,500 feet for a 10-second delay. He fell in a slow spin and made no attempt to pull his ripcord until he was 500 feet from the ground. It was too late, and his death closed the Abingdon parachute club.

No, we didn't know much about free fall in 1959, and what little we did know was tinged with melodrama. There were plenty of good crewroom stories, but little sound knowledge of techniques. Nor did we try to theorize.

We didn't look on free fall as a science: we didn't think of the body as an adaptable shape that would answer to the basic rules of aerodynamics: although we were acutely conscious of the law of gravity. Free fall was an art, and there was only one way to master an art — to learn from the acknowledged artists. In the late 'fifties, these were the French, so when Wing Commander Eric Brice, commanding the school with great foresight at the time, gained authority for P.T.S. to formulate a training system for free-fall parachuting, it was to France that we turned. With cautious enthusiasm and a vague notion that if we spread our limbs out and kept our head back when we jumped, then all would be well, Flying Officer John Thirtle, Flight Sergeant Alf Card, Sergeant Tommy Maloney and myself found ourselves in an Anson, heading for Pau.

Pau, 20 miles to the north of the Pyrenees, was the home of Le Base Ecole Des Troupes Aeroportees. It combined basic parachute training and instruction in supply dropping with intensive training in airborne tactics and guerrilla warfare. The atmosphere was highly operational. The 'paras' were by 1959 in their fourth year of harsh conflict in Algeria, and prior to that had fought for eight years in Indo-China. Little wonder that they put personal toughness before immaculate liftweb technique.

We were attached to a team of instructors who were about to commence intensive training for the French national parachuting championships. They were led by Lieutenant Auriole, a short, balding man with a wrinkled face and few words. He gave us into the charge of Adjutant Chef Nicolan. Nicolan was a swarthy Clark Gable of a man, with a constant smile that was at its broadest when the joke was on others. He first showed us the parachute that we would be using, and explained how it worked. When the ripcord was pulled, strong elastics would whip open the pack, and a small extractor 'chute would spring into the airflow and drag the canopy after it. As the canopy streamed, the rigging lines would be pulled from elastic stowages by the weight of the still falling body, which would eventually be jerked to a halt at the full extent of rigging lines and liftwebs under the open canopy. It would usually work, Nicolan assured us with a huge smile, provided that one didn't interfere with it by rolling into the deploying lines or snagging the canopy with a foot.

To minimize that possibility, he took us to the 40-foot exit tower to practise the technique for our first jump. The object was to exit the aircraft in a position from which we would be least likely to deviate, and which would at the same time offer as few protuberances as possible to the canopy and the rigging lines as they went about their rightful business. To achieve this, one

stood sideways on the very edge of the aircraft's port door, facing forwards
in the direction of flight with the right foot forward, the right hand reaching
across the chest to grip the red ripcord handle, the left hand holding the
forward edge of the door for balance, and eyes on the despatcher waiting for
the signal to jump – then it was a hard launch sideways and out, snap the legs
together, bring the left arm across the reserve, force the head back, arch
vigorously, shout out the three seconds, then *tac*!! – out with the ripcord. The
'banana' position, it was called. Very apt. We practised it from the tower – a
fearsome device of rattling chains and counterweights – until Nicolan
thought that we had some idea of what was required, then he took us up for a
couple of static line descents with the troops, to acquaint us with the Nord
Atlas and with the large expanse of scrub and heather that was their main
DZ. And so to that early-morning awakening ...

It was like that first jump from the balloon all over again. The unknown. And
a seemingly more hazardous unknown this time. Those pictures of Clem
Sohn kept flickering through my mind.

We went across to the mess to breakfast on a bowl of coffee and a hunk of
French bread spread thick with jam, then swinging our helmets with a show
of nonchalance, we walked through the camp to the instructors' crewroom.
We shook hands with Nicolan, Leguey, Arrassus, Batoufillier, Deniaud.
"Bonjour, mon lieutenant," they said, quite ordinarily, as though there was
nothing special about this particular morning. We waited while they read the
early papers, then walked to the parachute store to draw our parachutes.

In the back of an open truck we bumped away to the airfield. The air was
still cold, and the Pyrenees sharp against the sky. Tall maize was wet and still
asleep in the fields. The truck turned into the airfield entrance. On the wide
concrete aprons, troops were drawn up in long lines, each line an aircraft
load. They were preparing their equipment for jumping. We unloaded our
'chutes from the lorry, laid them like babies on the ground, then sat on a low
stone wall, and waited.

We could hear the Nords running their engines, out of sight behind the
hangars. One taxied round at last, and the first long line scrambled to its feet
and tightened its helmets and filed into the squat, racketing aircraft. A second
one came, and a third. We watched them take off. The sun was up. The
aircraft came back empty, and reloaded. One by one the lines disappeared.
The Pyrenees had lost their sharp edges in the heat by the time the troops
were all gone, and it was our turn.

"Preparez-vous!"

We checked our parachutes. John swore, suddenly and loudly. One of the checks was to give the ripcord a gentle tug to see that it was running clear in its housing, and that the 'pins' were not stuck. John had tugged too hard. The extractor 'chute had leapt out, dragging several fold of nylon with it. "Merde!" observed Nicolan, and with his big fists he rammed canopy and extractor roughly into the pack, closed the covers, and worked the pins back into the grommets. "Voilà, mon lieutenant," he said, and thrust it into John's arms.

We dumbly followed the Frenchman into the Nord. It roared quickly away to 2,000 feet, and levelled off for its first run over the DZ to drop a single man by static line, as a guide to the wind drift from that height, which was hopefully the altitude at which our own parachutes would be open. Auriole watched the descent of the 'siki'* from the open door. Satisfied, he stepped back and the engines roared for more altitude. Auriole waved us to our feet.

I stood up, and looked for my strop, and felt silly and a bit sick because there wasn't one. No hooking up this time. I felt naked without a static line. We moved in file towards the door, John first, then myself, and the others behind. Auriole was leaning out of the door to watch the DZ rolling up underneath us. The slipstream was plucking his cheeks, worrying his overalls. He stepped back. The buzzer clamoured at us. John was a silhouette in the door, facing forwards, crouched, looking at Auriole, then suddenly he wasn't there any more. I followed my feet on to the sill, reached across to grasp the ripcord, and stared into Auriole's goggled face. He jerked his thumb up, and I lurched out, left shoulder leading, into a cold face-full of air ...

Trying to arch ...

Trying to count ...

Sky and ground tilting and turning ...

"and *three ... tac!!*"

... and there I was, bouncing under the big khaki umbrella, staring in some surprise at the ripcord dangling in my right hand. It worked ... it really worked! John was whooping at me from somewhere below and behind. I twisted in the harness and yelled back. What *had* I been so frightened about?

Whatever it was, I was still frightened by it the second, the third, and for many more times to come. It was the mixture as before — fear in the waiting and the anticipation and the early mornings; exhilaration in action; and a satisfying sense of achievement in retrospect.

* 'siki' — 'drifter'.

We made three descents in that 'banana' position. I was never sure what happened to me on any of them, except that somehow I found myself swinging gently in the sky looking across at the Pyrenees with a red handle clenched tightly in my fist. Then we progressed to drops of 5 seconds, in a 'semi-cross' position. The legs were still brought together as we left the door, but the hands were on the corners of the reserve pack with the elbows stuck out sideways like stubby wings. I can't recall that they helped much. Two jumps like that, then Auriole judged us ready to try the 'full cross'. The exit was as before, but the arms and legs were now flung wide into a giant star – the position that Valentin had taught himself in these same skies over Pau some ten years before. The aim now was full stability – to fall spreadeagled on the air, face down to the earth, without turn or tumble. All it required was symmetry and curvature. It sounds simple. But the mind during those early attempts was too preoccupied with the novelty of sensation to consider deeply the relative positions of the right and left legs. Nor were our debriefings always constructive.

"What did I do wrong that time, Nicolan?" I would ask when we were reunited with our tutor on the ground. He would roar with laughter and slap me on the back. Although the French instructors were masterful performers, their teaching of the art followed individual ideas rather than common policy, so that when we made mistakes that were visible from the aircraft, each would make his own diagnosis and suggest his own remedy. Thus what advice we did get was sometimes contradictory.

However, we progressed. John seemed to take to it best of all of us, and it was I who brought the broadest grins to Nicolan's face. Nevertheless, as we advanced to 7-second drops, and then to 10, it was beginning to make sense. The earth usually stayed the right way up. Sometimes it revolved a little below me, like a great green and brown turntable. Just occasionally it would stop still for a few precious seconds, before quietly sliding off again. As we dropped further, we fell faster. At 10 seconds we were almost at terminal velocity of 120 miles per hour. You could feel the airflow building up, becoming more solid. It was pressure, not a whiplash gale. It was not unpleasant.

I was never yet in command. But I was becoming increasingly aware of what was happening to me, even though I was not consciously directing it.

We usually jumped twice each day, sometimes three times. It was mentally tiring, and physically bruising. Simple pleasures became vastly inflated. Food and wine tasted marvellous. A quiet seat on the terrace of the Aragon cafe watching the world go by on a mellow evening was luxury indeed. Letters from home were like blank cheques. Sundays were oases. Those who suggest that parachutists harbour a secret death-wish have got it all wrong: life was never so precious as when we thought we might really be risking it.

On one Sunday John and I went to the bullfights at a little town called Orthez, tucked into the Pyreanean Foothills. We flowed with a noisy throng over a stone bridge where old women sold peanuts and wine and model bulls, and where sunburnt men in black paper sombreros shot at balloons bobbing in the white stream swirling far below. With a litre of local wine we sat on stone terraces on the shady side of the arena, much too close to the ring, I thought. I don't think that the fighting was very good. I don't know. Like provincial boxing in England in the 'fifties, it was perhaps a ring for those on the way up and for others on the way down. Certainly one of the trio of torreros was a young buck full of flash and fire, who collected ears from the bulls and posies from the ladies. Another seemed impressed neither by the bulls nor by the catcalls of the crowd as he did his job methodically, like a butcher, then presumably went home to his wife and kids. The third was tossed repeatedly, bouncing in the sand like a blue-spangled bag of sawdust. But he'd get up, fetch a straight sword, and have another go. I identified with this one, helped by the white wine. His black bull was my wide open door in the side of the Nord Atlas — something that frightened us, challenged us, and had to be overcome. Something which could presumably kill us if we were careless. He sailed through the air again, and we finished the wine.

But the open door became less and less of a challenge as the days and the descents went by. It was becoming more of an invitation. Fear began to lose its grip, and relieved of it, my mind became more receptive to the intensity of excitement and exhilaration, and to the acuteness of sensations. There would still be a flutter of apprehension as the 'siki' went out and the Nord lifted its nose towards our drop height. But we would lean more nonchalantly at the door as we circled out over Pau, gaining height. We would point out the tiny roof of the Aragon where it overlooked the winding silver river, and we would admire the panorama of the Pyrenees which widened into increasing splendour as we climbed higher. Then Auriole would wave us back so that he could crouch in the door to line the aircraft up for its run. Nicolan would grin and make a downward spiral motion with his hand. Then the buzzer, and away we would go, sideways through the door, trying to hit the slipstream square and slide down it with eyes fixed on Auriole's wrinkled face peering round the edge of the door as the Nord lifted up and away ... mentally ticking off the seconds ... turning a little on the slippery cushion of air, and tightening up the body position to hold it, pressing the head back ... face down to the ground now, feeling the speed and the air pressure building up, riding it ... stable ... chequered fields and the tiny red roofs perfectly still, not even seeming to come closer, but they were – 170 feet closer each second as the count reached twelve and the arms and legs came in ... a glance for the red handle ... "*tac*" ... shoulder hunched for the shock, and the harness would grab the body with a cruel but welcome jerk as the canopy banged open above.

It was like stepping in from a storm and closing the door, that sudden transition from the exhilarating rush of free flight to the gentle descent under the canopy. I would ease up my goggles and grin across at the Pyrenees as I tucked the ripcord handle under the elastics of the reserve. Look around for the others, some below, some above. Look for the DZ. Look for the little white cross in one corner of it. Haul down a liftweb to steer for the target. It was hard work, steering the big shaped canopy down from 2,000 feet, and I would loop the rigging lines under a corner of the reserve, watching the drift, and changing liftwebs if the canopy started to rotate. A gentle touch down in the soft heather, then walk the rest of the way to the target to watch the team of instructors dropping in around it.

Those were the good ones. There were others.

There was the time I hit the rear edge of the door with a lazy exit, to spin away from the aircraft like a loose propellor, with the earth and sky flicking before my eyes, chasing each other round and round, until I yanked the ripcord to end the kaleidoscope.

There was the time that I pulled the glimpse of red handle and things seemed a long time happening. Hunched for the shock that didn't come and thinking of going for the reserve, I started to somersault forwards and was head down when there was a sudden ripple of nylon close to my legs and the parachute opened with a bang that cracked my body like a whip beneath it. Little points of light were flickering all over the sky, and the Pyrenees were dancing up and down, laughing at me. I looked up, and I had several canopies, and each one had a hole in it, with loose nylon flapping busily. Unable to steer all those canopies, I spiralled down to land in an uncomfortable bush. The little lights stayed with me all day.

There was the time when the handle didn't come at the first tug. So inspired was my second attempt that my arm flew up and back with the ripcord, which was wrenched from my grasp as it tangled with the flowing rigging lines. On the ground I reported my loss to Nicolan, expecting commiseration. He beamed with pleasure. "Le lieutenant anglais a perdu son poignet!" he bellowed. There were cheers, and a sudden hurrying to climb aboard the truck. Anyone who lost a handle, I discovered, had to buy a full round of champagne in the crewroom before lunch.

But the bad ones became less frequent, and less bad. I certainly hadn't tamed the air yet, but I was beginning to make friends with it. I was achieving a cautious sense of balance. I was a toddler in the sky. And we must have been improving, for Auriole despatched us one day with an uncharacteristic grin on his face, the reason for which was apparent as soon as we left the aircraft and looked for the familiar oblong of the DZ. It was about two miles away. I landed in maize, 10 feet tall. It is a difficult crop from which to retrieve a parachute.

"Vous avez faites une petite promenade, mon lieutenant?" grinned Nicolan when we reached the DZ, munching our corn cobs. But they wouldn't have pulled a trick like that on us if they had thought that we couldn't take it. I don't think they would ...

When Auriole took his team to Biscarosse to try out their paces on the DZ that was to be the venue for their forthcoming championships, he deemed us fit to accompany them. Biscarosse was then one of the two national centres for sport parachuting in France. The other was at Chalon. They offered subsidized courses for young enthusiasts in all stages of parachuting. Much of what was known about free fall in Europe and America came from those centres, which then and for many years to come were the Meccas of sport parachuting devotees. We flew a hundred miles to the north, over Les Landes – a green cloak of pine forests patched with occasional yellow and brown fields. The 'siki' hooked up, and jumped. We went next, from 4,000 feet, stable enough to admire a new landscape. A narrow strip of sand and a sparkle of surf separated the green forest from the blue of the sea to the west. Immediately below us was a large white target cross, in the middle of concentric circles drawn in the sandy DZ. It was a gentle ride down into soft, warm sand. We bundled our 'chutes and carried them across to the target area where bronzed young men in shorts and jumping boots watched the instructors from Pau pitch themselves out of the blue sky at the cross, then politely shook hands with them and wished them "Bonjour". Pierre Lard, the winner of the first world parachute championships in 1951 and one-time compatriot of Leo Valentin, showed us around the centre. Then we drank cool beer and ate a good lunch in a wooden mess hall that was set amongst pine trees that were silently filling little cups with their resin and the warm air with its scent.

Our training was nearly over. At 15 seconds we tried turning in free fall. When stable and flat to the ground in our spreadeagle position, we were to lean to the left to start a flat turn in that direction. It worked. It worked so well that I couldn't stop it. The turn became several, and the several became a spin, and the spin a wild cartwheeling tumble through space as I tried to fight it. I yanked the ripcord early and high, and the Pyrenees revolved around me as I unwound from the twists of my rigging lines. Deniaud said that my right leg was bent; Arrasus thought it was the left. Auriole said "Arquez ... Arquez." Nicolan laughed.

On the next jump, the turns worked well, but as I was tucking the ripcord under the elastics of the reserve after the 'chute had opened, I fumbled and dropped it. In horror I watched the handle fall, dwindle, and disappear. I tried to steer for the area over which I had released it, and on the ground poked with little hope amongst the long grass and heather. From afar my search was observed and correctly interpreted.

"Le lieutenant anglais a perdu son poignet!" rang out the cry over the DZ, and I was transported jubilantly to the crewroom once more.

For our last jump at Pau, Auriole took us to 5,000 feet, for a 20-second drop. We were still without stopwatch and altimeter, but counting was second nature now. It may have been rather fast counting. But it seemed a long, beautiful time, hanging in the rush of air over Pau which kept quite still for me to have a last look at it in free fall. As I tucked the ripcord away – carefully, for I was broke – I grinned across at the Pyrenees, half expecting them to smile back. For a month they had watched me struggle in the sky, but then they had watched Valentin and a thousand others before me, so they probably weren't impressed.

We shook hands with the instructors, and wished them luck. "Au revoir, mon lieutenant," grinned Nicolan, "et merci pour le champagne ... "

The Commandant of B.E.T.A.P. presented us with French airborne wings, certificates of competence, and a parting glass of wine.

Thus fortified, we turned our faces and thoughts back to P.T.S.

4/ Trials and Errors

We left Pau as novices. At Abingdon we were hailed as instant experts. Our immediate task was to train more of the P.T.S. staff, then to plan and implement a training programme for tactical free fall for Army personnel. Vaguely aware of our inadequacies in this role, we hid them with modest airs, and tried not to look too apprehensive when a few days later we boarded a Beverley for our first free fall in England. Weston looked very green and British after the rugged operational DZs of Pau, but the air wasn't any different.

We had, however, returned to certain luxuries other than a dubious fame — a blank-gore canopy; sleeve deployment; and instruments.

The blank-gore canopy was not new. During some supply-dropping trials in the 1940s, one of the canopies being used had split on deployment. It was observed to have an inbuilt drive in the direction opposite to the now gaping hole. From this accident was developed the blank-gore principal, which is based simply on the control and calculated redistribution of the air pressure inside an inflated canopy. Some of the air trapped under a canopy needs to escape, and that escape can be controlled to a limited extent by hauling down the liftwebs to distort the canopy and spill air from one side — hard and not very effective work! Now we returned to a parachute that incorporated the standard 'X' type 28-foot canopy, but with one of its twenty-eight segments or 'gores' removed. Through this 'blank gore' escapes the majority of trapped air, giving a ram-jet effect and imparting thrust in the opposite direction. With the blank gore positioned in the rear of the canopy, the parachutist had an inbuilt forward drive, of about 3 miles per hour in this case. A pull on the bottom corner of the blank gore via a toggle attached to that particular rigging line would angle the direction of the escaping air and cause the canopy — and parachutist — to rotate. Rotation plus drive — steerability! Luxury indeed.

Even more welcome was sleeve deployment. My shoulders and upper thighs still bore the bruises of those cruel canopy-first openings of Pau. By stowing the canopy inside a long sleeve and allowing the rigging lines to deploy first — as in conventional static line deployment — this opening shock was greatly reduced. When the ripcord was pulled and the pack opened, the extractor parachute dragged out the sleeve with the canopy inside it. With the sleeve and its contents fully extended and already inducing some deceleration, the rigging lines paid out from their elastic stowage loops, and only when they were fully extended and the mouth of the sleeve 'unlocked' was the canopy allowed to escape and take in air. The whole business of deceleration was thus lengthened and controlled. Also, the canopy was kept well clear of possible interference from a flailing limb. A very humane innovation, we thought.

And instruments too! On the top of the reserve pack were two small canvas pockets into which one fitted a normal type of stopwatch, and an altimeter of the same size and of doubtful accuracy, designed for mountaineers. It was very nice, but we thought that there would be no harm in continuing to count as well.

Before we could settle fully into the task of training others, there was the question of a free-fall display. "Whereabouts?" we asked. "Australia" we were told.

We were to jump at an air show near Brisbane as part of the Royal Air Force representation at the Queensland centenary celebrations. Sergeants Keith Teesdale and Pete Denley, who both had experience of sport free fall, were added to the group. We stuck union jacks on our helmets, borrowed some groundcrew white overalls, and felt very dashing. We flew in jet comfort to Singapore, thence to Australia in a Beverley. Not a long-range aircraft, it took short and fascinating hops to Queensland. There was a stop at Djakarta where there were MIG 15s lined up beside the runway, then a night-stop on Bali. We arrived there in darkness, and left at dawn, so that Bali remains a fairy-tale land of deep shadows and soft orange light, coppery bodies and warm smiles, carved gateways and steep thatch. The hotel rarely catered for Europeans, so the lads took over the kitchen and fried their own eggs. Then, led through narrow tracks by the sound of cymbals and drum, we and a mangy dog watched delicate girls dance out their folk stories on a floor of trodden earth. Whenever the music stopped the dog threw up its head and howled at the stars.

At Darwin we ate steaks for breakfast, and swam in hot water at Fanny's Bay until someone told us of the sea-wasps and the salt-water crocodiles. As we flew at night across northern Australia there was a bush fire crawling over the land like a red caterpillar. Townsville, Amberley, then on down to Williamtown to visit the Australian Parachute School. We drank a lot of their cool beer, jumped once with them on to their DZ of fine sand, then flew north again to Amberley, close to Brisbane.

We jumped only once at the air display – from 4,000 feet in strong and variable winds on which the blank-gore parachutes made little impression and barely got us on to the DZ. We received far more publicity than we were worth, enjoyed receptions, parties and conducted tours, then flew home.

"Hell of a long way to go for a couple of fiddles," said Alf Card.

Hardly were we back with our Balinese carvings and toy koalas than John was sent round the world again, this time with another hastily raised team for a series of displays in New Zealand. I stayed at Abingdon to start the free-fall training programme.

Because we knew of no other, we accepted almost in its entirety the Pau system of free-fall progressions and techniques. To it we added a more rigorous method of equipment checks, and a system of individual observation and debriefing. Our own experience as trainees suggested that in those early and brief free falls a pupil is rarely aware of his actions and body positions between leaving the aircraft and pulling the ripcord: he is more concerned with self-preservation and the peculiarity of his situation. He needs to be closely observed in his free fall, told what he did or did not do, and advised of the points to concentrate on when he next jumps. Fortunately the Beverley was ideal for observation of the shorter 'delays', for the aperture in the boom of the aircraft made an excellent gallery from which to witness the antics of those jumping from the side doors of the main fuselage.

I felt a little uneasy at the enormity of the step I was taking – straight into Auriole's shoes. I was trying to teach what I did not fully understand myself, and had certainly not fully mastered. However, I endeavoured not to show it. I tried to smile reassuringly at the men sitting quietly and rather pale in the Beverley as we flew out to Weston for their first free fall.

"Nothing to it lads ... lots of arch, keep your eyes on the aircraft as you fall away, and don't forget to count ... nothing to it!"

I would try to grin like Nicolan, then leave them with the despatcher, and climb up into the boom. The air would rush cold through the big rectangular aperture as we laid on our bellies looking over the edge, watching the well-ordered fields slide into view then disappear aft as though on rollers. Over the Bicester road ... the edge of the DZ and the peri-track and the windsock and little figures with their feet on firm ground and their white faces upturned ... then out would come the first stick, falling below and behind us, their goggled faces straining to keep the aircraft in sight, bodies rolling, tumbling, writhing in space, then the white flash of escaping nylon ... Ken Kidd, Bluey Lambirth, Pete Quinney, Jim Davies ... We would write it down on the pad with cold fingers before we forgot it – "Number one – rolled on exit. Good

Parachutist

arch but dropped head on pull. Clean deployment ... "

Then we would climb higher for those who had advanced to the full spreadeagle position, and again watch them as they swooped away from the aircraft like great birds, falling towards the patchwork of fields, dwindling beyond critical vision. And when they had all gone we would close the aperture, and blow on our fingers, and it was a relief to fit our own parachutes and to launch ourselves out of the Beverley's big door. Free fall was a far better thing to do than to watch ...

Being responsible for others, and facing questions to which we did not always have answers, we began to look more critically and constructively at the methods we had so readily adopted. Certainly the training that we had received had been the best available in the Western world. But did that mean that it could not be better suited to our own requirements? That it could not be improved upon? Until we found ourselves in the role of tutor rather than pupil, we had not given the question much thought. We now began to do so.

One of the first things we considered was the body position for the initial free-fall descents. On the first course of P.J.I.s that we took, all of them experienced lateral rolling as they struggled to maintain the classical 'banana' position – just as we had done in France. It looked even more frightening than it felt. We still accepted that for those first jumps the parachutist needed to have his hand clamped firmly and reassuringly on the ripcord handle as he left the aircraft, and throughout his fall. But did he still have to keep his legs together? Now that we had the canopy safely stowed in its sleeve and less likely to be snagged by the body, couldn't our first-timer part his legs as he made his exit, and wouldn't this give him some lateral stability to stop the rolling? There was only one way to find out.

The result was rather alarming. I jumped with arms across the chest, the right hand grasping the ripcord on the left suspension strap of the harness, but with the legs spread wide apart instead of being snapped together into the 'banana' position. The aircraft disappeared instantly, to be replaced by Weston as I went straight into a vertical dive towards its familiar surface. The other trialists experienced a similar reaction. In fact, this was the head-down position in which the Italian ace Canarrozo had learnt to hurtle earthwards many years before. It might have been all right for Canarrozo, but it was no position for beginners. But at least nobody had rolled – we were on the right track. If only we could balance the position by giving more 'lift' to the upper part of the body ... but how could we do that without taking the hand away from its grip on the handle? Simple! Why not shift the ripcord to the right side of the harness, so that still gripping it with the right hand, the arm would extend sideways in a bent position like half a wing – with the left arm in a similar position to maintain symmetry and balance? It was not only simple: it was sacrilegious. No one had ever heard of a manually operated parachute with the ripcord anywhere but on the left side of the harness. But why not? Well, we wouldn't be able to get a strong enough pull from that bent-arm position, we were told. We shifted our handles to the right suspension strap, put on our 'chutes, and pulled them, all over the hangar floor. Ah yes, but we wouldn't be able to do it so easily in free fall ... Again, there was only one way to find out.

It worked beautifully. There were no problems with the ripcord, and the position itself – although it gave no great measure of control – was inherently far more stable than acting like a banana. So the 'banana' disappeared from our initial training syllabus, to be replaced by the 'half spreadeagle', and the ripcords stayed on the right. There were some who shook their heads and opposed it – then and later – on the grounds that everyone else, including the French, used the left-side ripcord. To them we suggested with some pomposity that this was evidence of our progressive attitude. The right-side ripcord is now almost universal.

Another major realization at this time was that one didn't have to be a gymnast with a particularly flexible spine to achieve stability. Certainly we had accepted and tried to honour the principle that a falling object with one surface concave and the other convex would present the latter to the airflow. Indeed, we used to demonstrate this most effectively to trainees with a rubber model of Bugs Bunny who, with limbs well spread, ears tucked symmetrically behind his head, and with an alarming curvature of the spine, made many a stable fall from the hangar roof, although nobody really liked the way he bounced.

Then on one occasion when we were jumping as a stick from 7,000 feet, I suddenly found myself on a level with and about twenty feet away from Alf Card. It was quite by chance, for we had no idea then of how to purposely achieve such proximity. Other than for an occasional and distant glimpse, it was the first time that I had seen another person in free fall with me. It was fascinating! There he was, hanging like some great hawk in the sky, seemingly motionless, with only the ripple of his overalls to show that he – and I – were hurtling earthwards at 120 miles per hour. When I got over the pure aesthetics of the sight I realized with some surprise that Alf's body was by no means in the classical, straight-limbed arch that Auriole and Bugs Bunny had always insisted upon. In fact he looked quite sloppy, with his legs bent at the knee and his arms slightly flexed too, and his head down ... But he was stable!

So fascinated was I by the spectacle of his floating body that I quite forgot the slow creep of the altimeter needle and the rapid approach of earth until Alf suddenly reached for his ripcord and was whipped from my sight under a flash of white nylon. I grabbed and pulled. Swinging gently under the opened parachute, I trembled in a cold sweat. Just suppose that Alf had been watching me, equally absorbed ... It was the first and only time that I have not been mindful of altitude.

When the impact of that lesson had sunk in, we analysed the other. I described Alf's bent-legged position to the others. He seemed quite hurt. "But you fall like that yourself," he said, having also seen me in flight at some time. "In fact your boots stick up in the air like bloomin' great rudders." Well, I surely hadn't been aware of it. We had all realized that we relaxed a little after the rigid ride down the slipstream, but not to what extent. Before we had heard of the 'frog' position we had automatically adopted it, as I am quite sure had most stable free-fallers at that time. It was a natural progression – a natural relaxation as confidence drained the tension out of mind and body. As for the theory of 'convexity', the bent legs and the high carriage of the shoulders provided the overall curvature that kept us face down to the earth.

If we, the instant experts, were falling like that, shouldn't we be teaching it? Whilst we continued to stress the classical star position for exit, we began to cautiously suggest that once trainees had achieved initial stability in this position, they might consciously relax it just a little – not too much! Just eeeease out of that stiffness.

Our own performance was improving all the time, albeit slowly. Opportunities to jump were not as frequent as we would have liked, for there were a limited number of parachutes available for free fall, and a growing number of P.J.I.s keen to use them. When we didn't have enough 'chutes for our own use, we would despatch our pupils, then make static line descents from 2,000 feet, trying to steer the 'X' types for precision landings close to the target flare.

One free-fall skill that evaded me for too long was the most critical of all – opening the parachute in the correct attitude. The requirement is for the parachute to deploy cleanly from the back-pack, with no interference from the parachutist himself and with a clear passage into the airstream. We had been taught in Pau to close our legs and 'hunch' for the opening shock of the canopy-first deployment when we pulled the handle. With the lesser shock of sleeve deployment, one could now operate the ripcord in the full spreadeagle position, remaining face down to the ground and even keeping the legs apart. We had tried it, adopted it, and now taught it to more advanced pupils. But I found great difficulty in doing it myself. I was quite unable to lose the habit of rounding my shoulders and hunching as I reached for the ripcord. The more I thought about it and the more I prepared myself as I watched the ground coming closer and the altimeter needle quivering down to 2,000 feet, the more I hunched. Perhaps my reflexes had been irretrievably conditioned by some particularly cruel opening shocks. Or perhaps I was particularly prone – as Alf Card suggested – to that inherent instinct that advises a man to curl up in times of stress, the better to protect his genitals. Whatever the reason, whenever I went for the handle, I hunched. The result was a tendency for the body to roll forwards. The outcome was inevitable. During a display for visitors at Abingdon, I somersaulted straight into the deploying rigging lines, which grabbed me painfully by one ankle and suspended me under the canopy in a position both undignified and dangerous. My reputation and back would have suffered serious damage had I not been able to untangle myself. Even after that I couldn't hold my arched position on pulling. Instead I perfected a reasonably good front somersault: as I hunched and felt myself going over, I would hold the handle until the earth came into view again, and *then* I would pull. But this was no way to continue. Mike Reilly – the leading figure in British sport parachuting at that time and a useful if somewhat unorthodox source of parachuting lore – gave me the tip that achieved the breakthrough.

"Stick your belly against your reserve, think of nothing else, and keep saying 'belly button' all the way down," he advised.

So on my next jump I fell all the way from 5,000 feet with my eyes on the altimeter and muttering "belly button, belly button, belly button ... ", and it worked. My front loops became a thing of the past.

Actually, I was not alone in my 'pulling troubles'. No one would readily admit to embarrassments of this nature, but all was revealed when for the first time we had our descents recorded on camera. We were engaged in trials on Larkhill artillery ranges to measure the distance that the body was 'thrown forward' when it fell from the aircraft. Our flight through the air was radar tracked, and also filmed from the ground – from exit to parachute development. Although the film was distant and indistinct, it was quite good enough to cause some red faces amongst the instant experts, by showing that I wasn't the only one who had been protecting my genitals.

But as we logged the jumps through that first autumn and winter of free fall at P.T.S., the sky gradually became a more friendly place. It stopped throwing us around so much. Stability became something that we no longer had to strive for, and consciously think about. As children learn to balance on their feet, so we were learning to balance on the air. Like them, the frequency of our tumbles lessened. Only when we were trying some new and adventurous movement did the horizons sometimes slip and chase the sky round for a moment or two before we arched out of the tumble and got back on our bellies again. What had once required conscious effort was now a reflex action – balance.

Fear had long since gone. Oh yes, the adrenalin still flowed as we waited with fingers on the stopwatch button for the green light to come on, but it was with anticipation and excitement, not fear. It was waiting for the starter's gun – waiting for the whistle to start the match. And the jumps themselves were pure exhilaration. So many new things to try. We couldn't get enough. We were hooked ... And with more skill came a gradual and long-overdue realization that free fall was not, after all, just an art. There were a few elementary scientific principles that it was as well to be aware of.

They were very simple. A body released in the earth's atmosphere is dragged towards the surface by gravitational force: that we were well aware of as a starting point. If there were no air, the body would accelerate at 32 feet per second per second. Accelerate it does, but as it picks up speed through the atmosphere the pressure of air on the body also increases until the two forces are balanced at a steady falling speed – terminal velocity. Terminal velocity will vary with altitude (greater in the less dense air of high altitudes) and in accordance with the area of body surface presented to the airflow. In a full spreadeagled position the body offers about 10 square feet of surface and in the lower atmosphere falls at approximately 176 feet per second. In a head-down dive, presenting less than 2 square feet of surface, speed would increase to 225 feet per second. Conversely, when he is suspended beneath 800 square feet of nylon, our parachutist will descend at a more sedate 18 feet per second.

At 176 feet per second in free fall, the dynamic pressure acting on the body is about 35 pounds per square foot. As we have seen, this pressure is evenly distributed over the body surface, and if that surface is itself evenly presented, stability will be achieved. Change the distribution, and that stability is lost, either in a vertical or a lateral plane, or a combination of the two – a tumble, a spin, or a cartwheel. A problem, of course, in the early stages of learning. But what about when our free faller has achieved his balance? All that dynamic pressure, quite literally in his hands – can't he do something with it? Can't he find a use for all that latent energy? Of course he can: he can now intentionally do what he has been trying so hard not to do for some time – he can lose that precious stability at will. He can turn, somersault, roll, or adopt a different free-falling attitude, all by offering uneven or inclined surfaces to the air pressure.

What a simple fact. Yet it took us so long to fully grasp and apply it. The most obvious and useful application was in turning the body in a lateral plane. This we had already achieved by a simple lean of the upper body in the direction in which we wanted to go. Now we found that the turn could be speeded up and more precisely controlled by dropping the shoulder in the direction of lean, and raising the lower leg on the same side. In fact we were turning the body into a simple propellor and spinning it against the airflow.

And with the ability to face in whatever direction we chose, we now began to move in that direction. From the basic stable position, the arms were swept back towards the sides in a delta-wing position, and the legs were straightened and brought closer together. This redistribution tilted the body into a slightly head-down attitude, and the deflection of the airflow from this inclined surface imparted thrust in the opposite direction – forwards. Vertical speed also increased in this head-down position, as anyone who operated their parachute before pulling out of the delta soon discovered. So now we could turn, and move across the sky as we fell. We could steer ourselves through the air.

Less productive but very exhilarating was the back loop – more correctly a backwards · somersault. By thrusting the arms forwards from the basic position and at the same time drawing the knees up towards the chest, the air pressure became concentrated on the upper part of the body, which was thrown upright and over as the momentum continued. Early attempts were far from stylish, with recovery from the loop presenting more problems than its initiation. But it was an exciting sensation to throw yourself up and over, see the sky sweep your vision and the earth come swooping back as you flared out into the full spread again ...

We also tried falling in other positions. At some time or other in our training most of us had found ourselves lying inadvertently on our backs looking up at the clouds and wondering where all that good green earth had gone. Now we purposely directed ourselves into a position of back-down stability by reversing the curvature of the body – pushing the head forwards and rounding the back instead of extending it. Physically it was a comfortable way to travel through the sky, like lying back on a well-cushioned rocking chair. There was always that niggling impulse, however, to look over your shoulder to see where you were going, and to assure yourself that the ground really was as far away as your stopwatch suggested that it should be. The position was not one in which to operate a back-mounted parachute, and well before opening height one needed to extend the limbs and arch the back to flip over into a normal and reassuring face-down attitude.

Whilst we began to feel our way around the sky in free fall, our skill under the canopy was also improving. Not that there was a great deal that one could do in terms of pin-point accuracy with the single-blank parachute. But we were becoming increasingly aware of drift distances and angles of approach; we were beginning to read the windsock and the smoke signs on the surface as well as the weather forecasts; and usually we knew where we ought to be in relation to the target, even if we weren't always there. Early on we had worked out the basic mechanics of 'bombing' a free-fall parachutist into a target area, based on the French system. The wind of course was the major factor, and with a knowledge of its mean strength and direction one could estimate the correct position in relation to the target in which the parachute should be opened at 2,000 feet – known as the 'opening point'. The same principle was then applied to the free-fall part of the descent. The faller had to be bombed on to that opening point by taking into account the throw forward from the aircraft and the drift effect of the upper winds. The 'release point' would thus be determined. The procedure for guiding the aircraft over that release point was known as 'spotting', but at that time we were not accorded the privilege of telling pilots which way to go, so the navigator gave the directions while we waited patiently for him to switch on the green light, then obeyed it.

We were improving our equipment, as well as our techniques. There were a number of teething troubles with the parachutes. The incidence of canopies being torn on deployment was high, and 'blown peripheries', whereby the canopy is divided by a rigging line over the top into a fair resemblance of a giant brassiere, were more common than we would have wished. We soon had our ideas as to what was wrong, but we were still at a stage when parachutists weren't supposed to have ideas, so it took a long time and a few anxious moments before the kicker-boards were removed, and the mouth flap of the sleeve extended, and an apex tie added. Then our peripheries blew far less frequently.

Our advance was by no means independent. At P.T.S. we were developing techniques and equipment in parallel with many others at home and overseas, and learnt much from them. We heard more about French methods from those who paid their way to the centres at Chalon and Biscarosse. The Americans too were coming more into the scene. They coined the term 'skydiving' and published avidly read information between the adverts in a magazine of that name. Also there was useful advice to be gained from the growing body of sport parachutists in this country – particularly the British

Skydivers Club, operating at Thruxton. Comprising Norman Hoffman, Geordie Charlton, Mike McCardle, Jake McLoughlin and Dennis Lee, this group was a major source of information, based on their own experience and on their contact with continental parachutists.

And so after six months of trial and error we at last reached a stage where we could begin to apply our free-fall skills to a military context.

If free-fall parachuting was to become a viable means of delivering soldiers to a destination, those soldiers would need to carry with them the equipment necessary for their task, and they would need to jump under cover of darkness. We turned our attention to these new areas.

In evolving a method of carrying additional equipment, we were looking for a system that would not restrict bodily movement for exit from the aircraft nor in free fall; that would not jeopardize stability; and that would offer the least possible hazard to parachute deployment. We considered thigh bags and leg pockets: too small, and a hazard on landing. We tried to stuff as much as we could inside a jumping smock, beneath the harness: not enough, and it also obstructed the reserve parachute. So we eventually developed a canvas wrap in which 25 pounds of equipment could be stowed, and which could be fastened to the leg straps and carried across the loins below the reserve. We jumped cautiously with it at first. It had no adverse effect on stability — just a tendency to cause a slight buffeting motion with the more bulky loads. We then subjected it to unstable exits, back loops, rolls and spins, and it all stayed in place. Later we were to progress to larger loads, culminating in the bergen rucksack, but the first time we went 'operational' it was with 25 pounds of kit in our home-made canvas wraps, fastened across the front of our thighs.

Apart from the P.J.I.s normal reluctance to hit the ground when he can't see it, we envisaged no great problems with free-fall parachuting at night. But it seemed to worry some who weren't going to be doing it. These theoretical free-fallers were concerned that with no visual references and without attitude-indicators we would become disorientated in free fall to the extent that we would spin without being aware of it, and lose consciousness. We tried to explain that we were well aware of the sensations of instability, and didn't need horizons — real or artificial — to tell us if we were spinning, or whether that 120 m.p.h. wind was blowing in our faces or up our backsides: there are those who believe that people who choose to jump out of aeroplanes should be protected from their foolishness. The wise ones eventually gave in, and we were told to go ahead. It was planned that we should demonstrate the feasibility of military free fall to an audience of gentlemen who would presumably determine its future. A date was fixed in May when we would jump at night on to an unmarked DZ on Salisbury Plain, carrying enough equipment to mark a DZ for a conventional airborne assault.

Our main problems were with navigation, not free fall. The aircraft had to get to an unmarked release point in a reasonably clandestine manner, and when we reached the ground we had to find each other and subsequently the rendezvous point in the darkness. It was decided that the drop would be made from a timed run from a recognizable feature – in this case the centre of a hamlet 6 miles from Fox Covert DZ. While Flight Lieutenant Jack Richardson took his Beverley off to practise his timed runs, I took the team up on to Boars Hill to practise finding each other in the darkness, armed with a two-shilling, tri-coloured torch and a poor imitation of an owl.

We had a practice drop on a moonlit night, which was cheating a bit, then one evening when everyone else had gone home we flew from Abingdon to demonstrate our unsure skills as airborne infiltrators. We had time in the Beverley to watch the earth grow dark, and to ruminate on our lot. It seemed a daft thing to be doing, leaping into the night with your life wrapped up in a parcel on your back, when everyone else was watching tele. Sergeant Nicholson handed round cold chicken legs and cardboard cups of coffee as though it was the Last Supper. With twenty minutes to go we fitted up, then sat with the lights out to accustom our eyes to the darkness. The runway lights of Boscombe Down slid past the open door as we swung on to the heading for the DZ. Salisbury was spread out like spilt jewels in the distance. We stood up, tightening the containers across our thighs. The red light glowed, which meant that the navigator crouched in the nose of the aircraft was starting his countdown. We turned on the little pocket torches that were fastened to the harness where they could shine on to the stopwatch on top of the reserve. Green light ... jab the stopwatch button, and out through the door into a cold black slap of air. The shape of the Beverley lifted away, and a scatter of distant lights swung across the darkness as I turned, then there was nothing but the thin hand of the stopwatch jerking off the seconds, which seem so long when you watch them go one by one and when you can't see the ground beyond them. When the hand finally reached the red mark pencilled on the torch-lit dial, I pulled fast and carelessly, rolling a little so that I saw the sleeve snaking white above me for a moment, like a shroud, before I was jerked upright beneath the canopy.

It was extraordinarily quiet. Just the sound of my heavy breathing and a buzzing in the ears as I tucked the ripcord away. Salisbury plain lay grey and black beneath my feet. I twisted in the harness to look for the shapes of other canopies, and could see nothing. I looked for familiar landmarks, and saw none. That black stain down there must be a clump of trees ... that grey thread drifting under my boots was a track I didn't recognize. Where the hell was I? I landed fast, going sideways, in long dry grass that was comfortably soft. I fought down the canopy in the darkness, bundled it quickly, then listened. Not a sound. Where were the others? Worried and lost, I shone my two-shilling torch in short red flashes, and made owl noises, and they came up like shadows, one by one. Alf Card knew where we were, and we single-filed with our kit to the rendezvous at the Covert where men in trench coats and big scarves said that it was a jolly good show, and they hadn't seen a thing, yet here we were, and that was what it was all about, wasn't it?

"They don't believe we jumped at all," grumbled Alf as we drove home through the night, but a month later the first batch of S.A.S. troopers arrived at Abingdon for military free-fall training.

The first jump, from the balloon cage. The static line tautens and the rigging lines snake from the bag. " . . . my stomach rose into my chest and my boots appeared before my disbelieving eyes and the cold air rushed past me . . . " (*page 17*)

"Rigging lines front!" Anti-entanglement drill in the hangar, 1957
(*Crown Copyright*)

"Get-yer-feet-an'-knees-together!" Forward landing practice from the slides, 1957

Sliding down the slipstream from the door of the Beverley. The rigging lines are fully deployed, the canopy about to be pulled from the bag (*Crown Copyright*)

Jumping from the Beverley boom, over Weston. "One just kept walking towards the rear of the upper deck until you fell through the large rectangular hole in the floor" (*page 36*)

Pau, 1959. Left to right: John Thirtle, Tommy Maloney, Nicolan, Alf Card, and myself

"The first long line scrambled to its feet and tightened its helmets and filed into the squat, racketing aircraft" (*page 44*)

The P.T.S. free-fall team in Australia, 1959, waiting for take-off at Amberley. Left to right: Alf Card, Keith Teesdale, myself, John Thirtle, Pete Denley, and Tommy Maloney (*Crown Copyright*) (*page 52*)

(*left*) Leaving the Beverley in the classical 'full cross' position, complete with collar and tie. Before I learnt to relax; (*right*) . . . like this – stepping off the sill, with smoke, a year later

Moussatchevo, 1960. Left to right: Myself, Geordie Charlton, Mike Reilly, a lonely Italian, Alf Card, and Dennis Lee

The French canopy

The American 'Conquistador', with Loy Brydon touching down (*page 69*)

The 'six' in training. Sometimes it went well . . . *(Crown Copyright)*

. . . other times, not so well! *(page 82)*

The first Royal Air Force parachute display team, 1961. Left to right: Myself, John Thirtle, Tommy Maloney, Doug Peacock, Snowy Robertson, Jake McLoughlin

" 'Way . . . hayyyyy,' we shouted as we all stepped backwards" (*page 85*)
(*Syndication International*)

5/ Moussatchevo

We had learnt much, in those days of trial and error, from our involvement in sport parachuting, and from its devotees.

Competition jumping was born in 1926 when a barnstorming parachutist called Joe Crane suggested to the organizers of the Pulitzer Air Races in Philadelphia that instead of the customary exhibition jumps by a number of professional skymen, a 'spot landing' competition might attract more attention. This was agreed, and for the first time parachutists competed with each other in an organized event to see who could land nearest to a given spot on the ground. Many air displays in the U.S.A. were soon featuring such contests. "It was a pretty rough sport," reminisced Joe Crane. "We used to try to kick each other out of the air to get in the pay-off circle." Neither the pay-off nor the accuracy were outstanding. At the 1928 National Air Races in Los Angeles, George Wheeling recorded an average distance of 66 feet $9\frac{1}{2}$ inches for three jumps to win the 350 dollar prize. It was in an endeavour to improve the status and the financial lot of the American pro jumper that Joe Crane formed the National Parachute Jumpers Association in 1932. The movement to introduce safety regulations and competition rules became international when the Federation Aeronautique Internationale created its International Parachuting Commission, and shortly afterwards sponsored the first world parachuting championships – in 1951, in Yugoslavia.

Britain was represented in 1951 by Chuck Thompson and Dumbo Willans. The competition comprised three accuracy events, including one into water. Dumbo survived a vicious 30-second spin and a mangled main parachute to win round one. He further increased his lead in the next event, and with only the water jump to go, seemed a sure winner. He dropped into the lake only a few yards from the marker buoy. All he had to do was swim a few strokes to reach it. Alas, before he was fully clear of his harness, an over-zealous retrieval crew grabbed the parachute and dragged a spluttering Dumbo away from his world title.

For the next world championships in 1954, Sir Geoffrey Quilter, the parachute manufacturer, sponsored and equipped a team of five P.J.I.s from Abingdon, and his test parachutist Arthur Harrison. Most of them arrived in

France with no more than the twenty jumps required for their licence, and although armed with the first blank-gore canopy to appear in international competition (a single blank, positioned in the side of the canopy), they were no match for the French, Russians and Czechs. The championships became a bi-annual event, and in 1956 and 1958 were again dominated by the Czechs and Russians. Accuracy standards improved rapidly. A four-man team accuracy jump was introduced, and the style event now required four 360-degree flat turns. Our own standards lagged behind. Lack of sponsorship, of natural recognition, and of any further development of British equipment left the initiative to the enthusiasm of a dedicated few – like Norman Hoffman, Jake McLoughlin, Sue Burgess, Peter Lang, Dennis Lee, Geordie Charlton, and Mike Reilly.

Mike was the leading figure by 1960. There was no direct governing body for sport parachuting in England at that time. The Ministry of Aviation laid down certain guidelines as to what and who could be dropped out of aeroplanes, and Mike headed a small and informal committee loosely affiliated to the Royal Aero Club, where we held vociferous and usually inconclusive meetings. Mike would then go away and make the decisions. He lived for parachuting. The little money he made on displays and publicity was ploughed straight back into his jumping, and he seemed for ever and cheerfully in debt. He combined the reckless enthusiasm of the old barnstormer with the new awareness that if parachuting was to succeed as a sport it must have central control and a respectable image. I jumped with him once at Kidlington when he had his reserve tied to his main harness with a piece of rigging line – which he would never have allowed anyone else to do. It was perhaps this willingness to accept risks from which he sheltered others that later cost him his life when parachuting into the Channel during the filming of *The War Lover*.

Mike had jumped for Britain in the 1958 championships and in lesser international meetings, and now in 1960 he was raising another team to go to Bulgaria for the fifth world championships. As a result of a few sport jumps that I had made at Thruxton and Kidlington, I was invited to compete in the final team trials at Woburn Abbey.

We jumped twice, for accuracy, on to a DZ complicated by majestic oaks, a lake, and a wandering herd of bison. I had little experience of 'spotting', but I watched Alf Card closely when he jumped before me. He seemed to go out when we were above the near edge of the lake. On the next run I clambered on to the lower wing of the Rapide, clinging to the strut and looking down between my legs until the shining water crept into view under the wing, then I let go. I landed 170 feet from the target centre – my first recorded accuracy jump. On the second try, aiming for the same release point, I misjudged it badly and found myself over the far side of the lake when the parachute opened. The wind, however, had risen considerably and now carried me kindly over the water to dump me only 70 feet from the target. All the others, better spotters than I, came out where they intended and were blown out of the scoring area to land amongst the oaks and bison. I had won, though I don't believe anybody recorded the fact.

I certainly didn't take it very seriously, until two days later when Mike called to say that he wanted me as reserve for the British team – which would be himself, Alf Card, Geordie Charlton and Dennis Lee. I bought a pair of decorator's white overalls, and Ed sewed a union jack on to them, and I felt very proud.

"You'll need a bit of cash ... " Mike had said as an afterthought. We would be the only team competing that had no government backing or diverted military aid: true British amateurs. Through his own efforts Mike raised enough for the air fares from the Society of British Aircraft Constructors and the Irving and GQ parachute companies. For the rest we had to dip into the housekeeping.

And so to Bulgaria. Or nearly: my parachute went astray at London Airport, and since there was little point in going without it I waved goodbye to the rest of the team and eventually set off after them a day late and by a route that seemed to take in half the capitals of Europe. The last leg was at night from Zagreb to Sofia in an aircraft of Bulgarian Airways. There was only one other passenger – a tall, silvery haired American. We sat together. The hostess brought us smiles and free samples of Slivovitz. The American asked what I would be doing in Bulgaria. I told him. "A parachutist, huh?" he prompted, and I proceeded to fill his ear with tales of daring. The hostess, with nobody else to give her Slivovitz to, brought more of the deadly stuff, and the American continued to listen with great interest.

"Have you ever seen a parachute descent?" I eventually asked.

"Well ... actually I done one or two myself," he said, apologetically. "My name's Joe Crane ... "

"Oh hell," I said. "Have another Slivovitz ... "

The championships were to be at the airfield of Moussatchevo, some ten miles out of Sofia in a sunlit plain of maize and tomatoes and flocks of sheep. Women in white headscarves bent in the fields, and shepherds and their dogs slept in the shade of the trees that lined the road. There were dusty villages with red-tiled roofs. Mountains dozed in the background. It seemed a friendly, unhurried place.

All the teams were accommodated in a hostel belonging to the Bulgarian Aero Club, built alongside the grass airfield. It was a modern building, well adorned with portraits of Party members and Masters of Sport, but not well blessed with modern conveniences. Everything, we were to find, was tepid: the showers, the shaving water and the wine were all of a' constant and similar temperature. But the place was kept spotlessly clean, and the food and cordiality were plentiful. Each team had its own room. The Americans were next door to the Russians.

Each team also had its own interpreter. Ours was George. He had been co-opted from his full-time job of translating extracts from British railway journals for use in Bulgarian publications, and seemed a little put out that none of us were engine drivers. He was a darkly handsome, intense young man, with no humour in him. We puzzled and frightened him. He didn't understand parachutists for a start, and British ones added to his problems. He woke us next morning, early.

"Where's the tea, George?"

"Tea?"

"Yes. British people can't get out of bed until they've had a cup of tea."

"I was not told ... " He worried deeply for a moment, then brightened. "Perhaps a glass of wine ... ?"

"That'll do nicely, George ... "

On the first day, each team was allowed two practice jumps, to familiarize themselves with the DZ, its surrounds, and local conditions. The Bulgarians, as hosts, would jump first. We were drawn to jump towards the end of the practice programme, so we walked out on to the airfield to watch the other teams perform. Spectators, officials, team coaches and other competitors were grouped around the circle of sand, 9 metres in radius, with its white target cross and the little disc in the centre. I thought that everyone was standing far too close to it.

There was an air of great expectancy as we watched the Russian-built Antonov bi-plane winding up into the blue sky with its first load of jumpers. In the development of the blank-gore parachute, 1960 was a period of innovation and experiment. Different 'cuts' in different types of canopy were being tried, all with the object of achieving maximum forward drive and speed of turn with the minimum loss of descent rate and stability. In many cases the 'cuts' were being made in standard main canopies rather than the canopies being designed around the blank gores — this was certainly so with us, with our single or double gores cut out of 28-foot flat 'X' type or American C9 parachutes. It was now whispered that the Americans had a parachute with remarkable forward speed, and that the French were coming out with something new too. And what about the Russians? Nobody knew. We all waited by the target like Christmas morning children, waiting for those nylon parcels to be opened.

Heads were craned back and eyes shadowed from the sun to watch the Antonov pass slowly above the target at 7,000 feet. Out they came, little black specks falling for 30 seconds, then "Aaaahhhhh" we all went as four big, shaped canopies in the Bulgarian national colours with a large, bowed blank gore in the rear blossomed into pretty life. They descended slowly, steady as mushrooms, to drop their riders into the sand one after the other with no apparent effort. Then the American team unveiled for the first time in world competition the 'Conquistador' – a double blank gore joined at the bottom of the canopy by a horizontal 'cut' to form what became known as a TU configuration. "Formidable!" muttered a Frenchman as the white and red chequered canopies chased each other across the sky. They had tremendous drive, we thought, but the Americans seemed to hit the ground rather hard. The Russians opened up an unusual double blank, which they handled with methodical efficiency. The French had an inverted V cut, which drove well but had a tendency to swing wide on the turns, with a certain *élan* that seemed nationally characteristic, but not good for accuracy. Coaches and technicians were scribbling frantically in their notebooks as each team revealed its secrets, while we became increasingly glum as team after team thudded into the sand and the time approached for us to display the latest from Britain – an assortment of patched canopies of different colours and with nothing more startling than a standard double-blank.

I made up a stick of four with three Canadians. We watched Mike lead our British team out at 7,000 feet. As we circled for our run we watched their canopies collapse to the ground near to but not in the circle of sand, which looked so tiny from up there. Then it was our turn. I jumped fourth, giving the Canadians plenty of space, and turned to watch them falling below me. When I came in for the ripcord, I did so carelessly and my right shoulder dipped so that I slipped off balance as the white nylon hissed out above me. I was straightened out with a tremendous wrench and an unusually loud crack. A broken rigging line trailing across my face suggested that all was not well. I looked up. The single blank gore had been converted into a far more interesting configuration. Several torn panels were flapping with annoyance, but the peripheral band was intact and the tearing didn't look as though it would get any worse. The rate of descent was not alarming, and the parachute still turned in response to a tentative tug on the toggle, and seemed to go where I pointed it. So I took my hand from the handle of the reserve, where it had rested for the past few seconds, and turned my attention to the target. It appeared to be in the right place. With an occasional upward glance to make sure everything was still there, I watched the three Canadians below me, and followed them as best I could. I saw them miss the sand pit one by one, then to my surprise the target was getting much larger and coming straight towards me. I crashed into the sand 3 metres from the centre of the white cross and tried desperately to appear nonchalant as I brushed myself down.

"Man, you ought to take out a patent on that!" said one of the Canadians, as I dragged my 'chute on to the grass and examined it ruefully. It wouldn't take another opening. It was the only one I had. Mike very nobly and with some concern lent me another assembly for our second practice jump. He wanted us to try out a style sequence of turns and loops, with accuracy as a secondary consideration, but I had high hopes that if I could hit the sand again and the others should miss it, he would have to put me in the first four.

We were joined in the Antonov by some of the Polish girls. We were to jump on separate runs with Mike spotting for the first four. He put me out first. I skidded through a semblance of turns and a back somersault, then looked for the DZ. It was miles away. I pointed myself towards it but had no chance of getting there, and landed in a stubble field, with a surly looking canal between me and the aerodrome. Brown, bare-footed children came to listen attentively to my curses. On the next run I was joined in my field by a puzzled Polish girl called Zza Zza who I believe had never been off a DZ in her well-trained life. Mike didn't do it on purpose though, for he was the next to land there, apologising profusely — while still 50 feet above us — for his poor spotting. That evening at dinner we made him recompense Zza Zza with a bottle of wine. She left the dining room without a word, leaving Mike worried that he had unwittingly insulted her, until she returned some minutes later to shyly present him with a peacock blue neck-tie and a Polish sausage. All was forgiven.

On the following day, a Sunday, we paraded for the opening ceremony. I had never considered parachuting as a spectator sport, but a hundred thousand flocked to Moussatchevo in coaches and lorries but very few cars, to swirl colourfully amongst the marquees and the roped-off arena. I had borrowed blue track suits from the R.A.F. athletics team for our uniform. It was the only kit we had in common, but we had stitched Union Jacks on them and wore them proudly as we marched past the rostrum and took our place in the line-up of teams. Comrades made speeches, which George said were of welcome and of praise to sport. The welcomes and the praises went on for a long time in the sun, while the crowd studied us with interest and we looked with interest at the crowd. The speeches over, we exchanged penants with the other teams, smiled for photographers, and were each given kisses and bunches of white flowers by 'young pioneers'. As we marched off we threw our bouquets to the fairer ones in the crowd while George walked ahead pretending desperately that he was nothing to do with us.

The competition should have begun that afternoon, but a warm wind of 20 knots had sprung up, so we sat on the broad windowsills of our rooms watching the crowds and the dust eddying around the marquees. The wind and the people stayed all day. There were displays of gliding and aerobatics, then towards the end of the afternoon a tight formation of military aircraft flew over the airfield and spilt several hundred paratroopers into the air. The square-shaped parachutes flew across the sky like sheets of white paper, and we winced for the troops as they were hammered into the ground and dragged over the grass behind their billowing canopies. "That's a hell of a way to earn your jump pay," said one of the Americans.

It was bright and calm the next morning.

The championships began with the team accuracy event. This required all four team members to jump as a stick from 2,000 metres and to delay for between 23 to 30 seconds before opening their 'chutes. All four would then aim for the same target – the 9 metre cross in the centre of a scoring area of 100 metres radius. The average landing distance of the four would be recorded and converted to a numerical score. Each team would jump four times, and their three best team scores would be added for a final total.

I sat on the dry grass out by the target, saying "British coach!" to the officials and policemen who periodically tried to move me back into the crowd who thronged the barrier just beyond the 100 metre line. The sun was warm and the little white specks fell out of a perfectly blue sky. The parachutes mushroomed and swung, turned and tacked to and fro, four at a time, 'stacked' on the approach line above and slightly behind each other, queueing up for the final dash at the target. The Americans whistled in hard on their fast-moving Conquistadors. "Shit!" yelled Arter to the world in general as he overshot at 100 feet. The young Russians, tanned from their three months in a Black Sea training camp, tacked to and fro across the wind line with military precision, then turned to sweep down on to the target one after the other in a flurry of sand, with the judges diving beneath the swinging bodies to peg the first point of impact. The Frenchmen gave cries of despair as their skittish canopies swung them wide of the target as they made their final turns. The Czech girls took off their helmets and shook out their long hair before they bundled up their 'chutes and trooped over to their stern-faced coach. The Bulgarians dropped gently into the sand to loud "Bravos" from the crowd, and the Austrians landed with delightful regularity over the far side of the canal.

The Russians won the event, with a 4-metre average. We were tenth out of eleven teams, with 47 metres. We told George that we would probably be shot if we didn't do better in the other events, and he wasn't sure whether or not we were joking.

With the skies still blue on the following day, the style event was begun. Competitors were to jump, singly, from 2,000 metres. In response to a signal from the ground they would then in free fall perform a sequence of five flat turns followed by a back loop. Turns and loops had to be precise, starting and finishing on heading. The panel of judges, watching through telemeters, would award points on the basis of speed of the whole sequence and accuracy of the individual movements. Each competitor would jump twice, and total his scores for the final result.

I lay on my back, shielding my eyes from the sun to watch the white dots leave the aircraft and grow steadily bigger, until the signal panels would crash into place to show the sequence to be performed, and the white dots would flicker into action. On his first descent Dennis Lee broke the monotony for the watchers by hurtling earthwards all the way to 700 feet. He lost all points for that jump for exceeding the maximum free-fall time allowed. In the judges' enclosure around the telemeters there was much animated discussion, consulting of stopwatches, and comparing of notes. They seemed surprised at the performance of the Americans, and indeed when the final scores were totted up, Jim Arender of the U.S.A. was the champion, with sequences of 14 and 14.5 seconds. Afterwards, in the packing hangar, Jim was on his belly on a packing table showing the Russians how he had beaten them, working from a tight 'frog' position and initiating fast flick turns by arching sideways into the direction of turn, drawing the knee on that side forwards and dipping the opposite arm and shoulder. It was an improvement on the classical French style of outspread limbs. Geordie Charlton was our best, twenty-seventh out of forty-two competitors.

It wasn't all jumping. In fact, for me it wasn't much jumping at all. I sat getting browner and wishing unkindly that one of the others might hurt himself – not too badly, but enough for the team reserve to be called for.

Occasionally there was a lift for judges and coaches, but I usually didn't find out about that until they were airborne, and then I would blame George for not telling me. George was our constant and increasingly nervous shadow. In the morning he would translate the national papers for us — they being the only ones available. He would tell with pride how well the tomato harvest was doing, and that the steel workers of Plonk had been granted an extra week of Black Sea holidays for increased output, and that a new statue to George Dmitrov would be unveiled in Sofia tomorrow.

"What about train crashes, George?"

"Trains," he announced, "do not crash in Bulgaria."

We were taken for well-chaperoned trips. By coach we wound up through the mountains to the Stalin Dam, that provided water and electricity to the plain below. The Bulgarians looked proud and the Russians looked bored; the French took photographs and the Austrians stripped off and swam in the lake; the Americans retired to the cafe and ordered wine.

We went several times into Sofia, always with George, who informed us that the city had been largely rebuilt since the glorious revolution of 1944. The massive bold lines of the buildings were impressive, and the streets were wide, with little traffic, like constant Sunday.

In the warm evenings, after dinner at the hostel, the teams would gather outside to sit on the steps with bottles of white wine and to exchange parachute badges and stories, and a guitar would pass from nation to nation, and the politicians seemed very far away. Then Storchenko, the portly Russian coach, would look significantly at his watch, and without a word his team would file indoors, followed a little later by the Bulgarians and the Poles, then the Hungarians and the Czechs, later still the French ... leaving us and the Americans to finish the wine.

The final event was the individual accuracy competition. It provided high drama.

Competitors jumped individually, again from 2,000 metres, each one selecting his own release point and doing his own spotting, then free falling for the mandatory 23 to 30 seconds before opening his 'chute and steering for the target. Two hundred points would be awarded for a dead centre, and correspondingly less for every metre and centimetre away from the disc. The best three scores out of four would give each competitor his final total.

The standard of accuracy was such that anyone not landing consistently in the sand was out of the running. In the first round Dick Fortenberry of America slammed his foot on to the white disc to score the first dead-centre in world competition. Shortly afterwards Monique Gallimard stepped daintily out of the air on to it to show that women could also hit the button.

The second round took place in perfect conditions of light and steady wind, and the top placers were all scoring within a metre. The Americans were improving all the time, worrying the Czech and Russian aces, but they were sweeping in hard under the Conquistador, and suffering for it.

For the third round, on the next day, the surface wind was high and close to the limit. Fortenberry was leading on the score sheet, and we watched for his third jump. His fast descending parachute gained rapidly on the Russian who had jumped from another aircraft shortly before him. Both were steering for the target. Shooting past the startled Russian in a fast turn over the cross, Fortenberry crashed in heavily – for another good score, and a dislocated elbow. For him it was the end of the competition. But when the scores were added up at the end of the third round, the points for his three jumps, together with his sixth place in the style event, put him in the lead for the title of overall champion, just ahead of the Czech Kaplan and the young Russian Anikiev. If they were to beat him, their final jump of the whole competition would have to be within one metre.

The elements then took part in the drama. The wind was too high for the fourth round that afternoon. All next day the windsock stayed horizontal. The Czechs were fretting, and the Americans jubilant. The calmest of all was Dick Fortenberry in his brown sling. There was only one more day to go, but the windsock fell asleep that night and didn't wake up in the morning.

The final round began at 6 a.m. Anikiev jumped. He made a good approach, but mistimed his final turn and swung in 5 metres wide of the disc, and the Americans smiled again. Just Kaplan to go. About 50 feet up, well set, a slight change in the direction of the surface breeze wafted smoke from the signal flare across the target. He touched down about 2 metres out, to a whoop from the Americans. But they whooped too soon, for the Czechs were in deep consultation, gesticulating, calling for judges. A rejump was demanded, on the grounds that smoke had obscured the target and ruined Kaplan's attempt. The judges agreed. The Americans immediately filed a counter protest to the jury of appeal. Even before the predominantly Eastern bloc jury upheld the rejump decision by four votes to three, Kaplan was airborne again. In utter silence he zigzagged in from 2,000 feet, then came in on a curving final approach, with a last second turn into wind and a casual stand-up landing 3 centimetres from the disc. Dick Fortenberry was the first to congratulate the new world champion. When the final placings were announced, Geordie Charlton was our best at twenty-fifth with Mike twenty-seventh.

Before the closing ceremony there was to be one more organized trip – to the Golden Sands of Varna, on the Black Sea coast.

This was before international tourism broke through the Iron Curtain and Varna was the place the good workers went to – hotels taken over by whole factories or communes. There was no commercialism; no tinsel. There were no partitions or private beaches, but miles of unspoilt sand with free deckchairs for Mum and free camel rides for the kids. The only advertisements were vast posters of stern-faced young men and rosy-cheeked girls urging higher steel production and bigger tomatoes. All was clean and functional, and the sea and the sun were allowed to rule the place with the minimum of interference.

We ate on a hotel patio overlooking the Sands. The food was magnificent, the wine as it should be, and swallows flew beneath the tables. There was a convention of world-wide communism taking place in the hotel. I was pointed out by a waiter to another apparent Englishman. Obviously we were rarities. The man in the tweed jacket came curiously across.

"Hello old chap. I'm Battersea. Which branch are you?"

"Physical Fitness ... " I replied in all innocence, and he retired in confusion to his fellow delegates.

After lunch we went on to the sands. I enjoyed a swim, and was drying in the sun when a small man with a nervous moustache came over to me. He spoke in French. Was I a Frenchman? No. I was English. He looked more worried, but summoned courage. Would I care to go for a swim with him?

Hello, I thought, but didn't want to be impolite, so followed him into the water. We swam out beyond the in-shore splashers, out of range of the dog-paddlers.

"Now ... " he said, treading water, "we can talk."

He was a Bulgarian doctor. Was I a communist? Not on his life, I tried to say in French. Then I must be a sportsman. How did he guess? Because only sportsmen could travel to other countries. Couldn't he travel to other countries? He sank a little as he laughed. He asked about life in England. I really had my own car? And a television? I must be a highly thought of sportsman. And how about the workers – did they get enough to eat?

Treading water and speaking bad French, I sensed confusion, fear and an unspoken thirst for truth. The Golden Sands lost some of their glow.

The crowds turned up again for the closing ceremony. It began with the 'friendship' jump, with all the competitors in a mass drop from as many aircraft as could be got into the sky at the same time. I managed to borrow a Russian plain canopy, and climbed aboard one of the biplanes to find myself with Akiev, Sam Chasak the one-handed Frenchman, a Roumanian girl, Glen Masterson of Canada, an Austrian, and a bearded Italian greatly worried because nobody could tell him from what height we were to jump and at what height we should open. At 7,000 feet Akiev slipped casually out of the door and we piled out after him, the Italian's beard still wagging. Other aircraft were spilling their loads alongside ours, filling the air with spreadeagled bodies and goggled grins ... figures were weaving and gliding, some looping, two holding hands ... then the whooosh of opening parachutes, and people shouted across at each other as they swung in their harnesses. Glen Masterson was yodelling somewhere above me, and the loudspeakers and the crowd and then ourselves were all singing 'Volare' in a dozen languages as we drifted down like coloured confetti on to the airfield.

We lined up again in our track suits. We had nobody to translate the speeches for us. That morning George had woken us five minutes late. "We'll report you to the Party, George," we had jested, and hadn't seen him since. No sense of humour at all. There were national anthems as the prizewinners stood tall on the rostrum. Then, in our teams, we marched quietly away.

That evening we wore our crumpled suits and cleanest dirty shirts to a banquet in the Balkan Hotel in Sofia. We drank much wine, ate much good food, danced the Hora very badly and drove back through the night with Storchenko occupying a whole seat and leading the coach in a passionate rendering of 'The Volga Boatmen'.

6 / "Got the Cards, Snowy?"

Following our displays in Australia and New Zealand in 1959, we had continued to give occasional demonstrations on Abingdon airfield to visiting groups of military personnel, and had also jumped at a number of other R.A.F. stations on such occasions as Battle of Britain days. We would jump as a single stick of six from heights up to 12,000 feet, with the sole intention of trying to land as close to the prescribed area as one could with a single-blank parachute.

Demonstration required that our free fall was visible from the ground. We bought a sack of talcum powder, and used it in bags tied to our lower legs to create a trail as we fell. The bags had a tendency to leak inside the aircraft. On one occasion, as we waited at the open door of a Twin Pioneer, ready to jump, we could see through a thin white haze the pilot leaning from his seat, wiping his goggles and making rude gestures to suggest that we left his aircraft and took our talcum powder with us. Geordie Charlton, ever a perfectionist, thought that powdered fertilizer might give a better flow. We only used it once. We eventually replaced the powder bags with smoke flares, which were worn on a metal bracket fixed to the boot.

But display was still a part-time and very minor part of our free-fall work, just as free fall itself was but a subsidiary activity at P.T.S. Indeed, there were some who considered us a luxury, but they were usually those with no inclination to join us. John Thirtle was fully occupied in training S.A.S. personnel in basic free-fall skills, and I had the trials flight — working not only on free-fall trials but on static-line projects as well. Then in 1961 we were told that our part-time display activities were to be given formal recognition: an official Royal Air Force Parachute Display Team was to be established that summer, and its debut was likely to be at the Farnborough Air Show.

So we looked more closely at this display business.

The sight of people descending from the sky, with or without support, has always intrigued those with their feet on the ground. Since its earliest days, parachuting has been associated with display. Certainly the intrepid aeronauts of the nineteenth century who pioneered the art in their semi-rigid parachutes, borne aloft beneath giant gas balloons to cut themselves loose high above the incredulous crowds, were motivated by a sense of showmanship as well as by an undoubted spirit of adventure. Thomas Baldwin, an American showman, had by the end of the century introduced the flexible, folded canopy, stowed in a container attached to the balloon basket, whence it was dragged by the falling weight of the parachutist when he leapt over the side. Charles Broadwick, another showman, took the next major step by attaching the parachute to the body and having it pulled from the pack by a line attached to the balloon car – the fore-runner of the modern statichute. Then the aeroplane arrived. Albert Berry was the first to jump from one, in 1912, a feat that was recorded by the parachuting historian, Glassman: "Albert Berry's jump boasted no scientific premeditation. It was conceived by a showman and executed by an actor as an interesting variation to the more common sight of balloon jumping."

Well, Glassman wouldn't have had much parachuting history to write about were it not for the showmen and actors. Almost every major advance in parachuting to that date had been achieved over the tea-gardens of Europe and the fairgrounds of America, and the exhibition jumpers were for many years to be the ones with the bright ideas and the guts to try them out. It was showman Leo Stevens who conceived the idea of the manually operated parachute; stuntman Leslie Irvin who publicly displayed it for the first time; and the "gypsy moths" who further used and developed it at air shows throughout the world.

Those barnstorming birdmen sold danger to the public. Some inevitably lost the gamble with gravity, and they made the best news – men such as James Newell, Curly Wells, Clem Sohn, James Williams, Vassard, Bolhelm, Valentin, Canarozzo ... It is little wonder that parachuting was awarded a 'dicing with death' certificate during the heyday of the air circuses. It was an image that still lingered when we came on the display scene. In popular opinion the free-fall parachute was still an instrument of dare-devilry, and those who used it were death-defying idiots. It was an image that we had no desire to foster. In fact, we would try to dispel it, by presenting parachuting as an activity that was surely exciting and exhilarating, but that was also safe and quite respectable when well regulated and organized. There would be no dicing with death.

So what exactly were we going to do, now that display was to become a serious business? There were two basic skills that we wanted to demonstrate – the ability to control the body and move across the sky in free fall, and the capacity to land under the canopy in a small, predetermined area. Because we ourselves were greatly preoccupied at that time with movement through the air, we tended to emphasize that particular aspect. Much thought was given to possible ways of demonstrating this movement. We could all delta across the sky now, but to make it apparent, we would have to move in relation to each other. We hadn't yet the skill to all fly towards each other for a massive link-up, but if we started off all linked together, we could move *away* from each other. Thus it was that John Thirtle came up with the 'bomb burst' concept: if six of us left the aircraft holding on to each other, fell together, then split up and delta'd in different directions, our diverging smoke trails would appear from the ground as an inverted bomb burst. Marvellous. "How the hell are we going to do it?" someone said.

We took stock of our tools – our skills, our equipment, our dropping procedures. Up to that summer of 1961, our standards had matured slowly, yet surely. We had read with awe of the first baton pass performed in the U.S.A., in 1960. It was the beginning of relative work, in which man no longer flies in isolation, but puts together with others his control over rate and direction of fall to manoeuvre in relation to them – to meet with them in mid-air if he can. The passing of a baton from one free faller to another was considered the height of achievement. In 1961 we had begun tentative attempts to reach that height. Our opportunities were limited to those occasions when we had enough 'chutes and enough altitude to jump after we had despatched our trainees or trialists. One such chance came for John Thirtle and I on a July morning. We rolled up a sick bag and ringed it with elastic bands. I carried it as the first man out. Our techniques for mid-air meetings were as rudimentary as our baton. Spreadeagling myself as wide as I could on the airflow to keep my rate of fall down, I watched the Beverley lift away and saw John fly out of the door and swing towards me. His hands went back towards his sides into a delta position, and down he came, swooping out of the sky. On previous occasions we had usually undershot, but suddenly here we were, level with each other, five feet apart, goggle to goggle almost – closer than we had ever been before! With a sort of involuntary swimming motion we closed the gap. Then in my eagerness I made the mistake of thrusting the baton at him. His hand was actually closing over it as I slid off balance and rolled away beneath him, taking the sick bag with me.

He called me many names, and when we went up for another go that afternoon there was no mistake. John came down on me like a full back. In mid-air we grabbed each other, and as we somersaulted over and over together we made absolutely sure that the sick bag changed hands before we pushed each other away and tumbled off into our own airspace.

It was the first all-British baton pass – a skill of no great value in itself, but a landmark in our development, and an event which then became commonplace. What was important was that relative work of this nature put free-fall skills into perspective: one moved not for the sake of the movement itself, but as a means to an end. As those movements became subordinate to a definite objective, so they became easier and more natural. Body movement became an automatic response to a situation, so that one turned and flew with no more conscious thought than it takes to walk round a corner on the streets below.

What about landing accuracy? Farnborough was going to offer a very restricted dropping area. Could we hit it? Those of us jumping in trials and free-fall training were developing a nose for accuracy. Our parachuting was constant and varied, free fall and static line, with differing types of parachutes in all manner of conditions. In addition, some of us were also sport jumping. I had bought a candy-striped American C9 canopy, and took a pair of scissors to it to cut a double-L blank gore configuration. The first time I used it was in competition against 22 S.A.S. on Hereford racecourse. We jumped twice each, from an Army Beaver, aiming for a white cross on the grass. The double-L seemed to known its own way there. I scored 4 feet 6 inches and 2 feet 6 inches, which in 1961 added up to a British accuracy record. Others were achieving similar results. To the horror of the more conservative P.J.I.s Weston's green surface was desecrated with a centrally placed sand-pit, 15 yards across. Sergeant 'Snowy' Robertson christened it, and thereafter it received regular visitors. Some who landed nowhere near it were known to rub a little sand on their boots before returning to P.T.S. on the coach.

But it was not just canopy control and pin-point accuracy that we needed. Landing in a target area required more than the ability to delta in free fall and to work the toggles of a steerable parachute: one had to know in which direction to delta, where to point the canopy, and when. Awareness was the basic skill of accuracy — an immediate and constant appreciation of position in relation to the ground and in relation to drift conditions. Those of us who had sport jumped had been better able to develop this instinct for accuracy. The necessity to think for ourselves, make our own calculations, guide our pilot to the release point, then find our way to the target in free fall and under the canopy gave us a level of experience and confidence that our jumping-on-the-green-light military system could not at that time offer. It was no coincidence that our first display team were all P.J.I.s who had such experience — John Thirtle, Doug Peacock, Tommy Maloney, Jake McCloughlin, Snowy Robertson and myself.

Our own ability, however, would be of little use without certain back-up skills. We had to be put within striking distance of our opening point, and that opening point had to be calculated with reasonable exactness. Our single-blank gore could cope with nothing more than a 250-yard error, and less than that if we were off the wind-line. We needed an aircrew well practised in our particular requirements, and we needed a better parachute to extend the margin of acceptable error. We said so, but nobody believed us. Then in June we jumped at Farnborough for the Royal Aircraft Establishment's open day. It would serve as a useful pointer for the big show in September, in which our participation was yet to be confirmed. For major air displays one can rarely drop a streamer to determine drift distances and to plot the opening and release points, so as usual we received our instructions from the DZ based on forecast wind conditions. The forecast and the drop were both inaccurate, and the stick of six was scattered widely over the western end of the airfield. Some landed in the high-security enclosure, and had great difficulty in explaining their presence to the gate guards. We repeated our case, with feeling, for a regular crew and for new parachutes, and were promised both.

To improve our method of drift calculation we equipped our DZ party with their own mini-kit for wind measurement – cylinder of hydrogen, supply of met balloons, and theodolite. Accurate wind speeds and directions, and thus a precise opening point, could then be passed to us in the aircraft ten minutes before drop time.

With less than two months to go before Farnborough, official recognition of the team and our participation in the Air Show were confirmed. We set about learning how to jump as a group.

Fortunately the Beverley was perfect for a linked exit. By removing the large clam-shell doors at the rear of the freight bay, there was an ideal platform on which all six of us could line up and step off together. But should we all face forwards, backwards, or some each way? We were used to forward facing exits for individual jumps, so we tried that first, in threes. We lined up on the sill, the centre man gripping harnesses of the men on either side of him, all facing into the aircraft, and took one step backwards. The wing men swung in a bit on exit, and the centre man took a bit of a pull on the arms, but the trio fell reasonably stable and parted company at the predetermined height with no bother. We thought, however, that a line-up of six all facing the same way might be a little too elongated – that it might crack in the centre like a whip. Perhaps the line would be more compact if alternate men faced aft. We tried it in threes again, the centre man in this case facing out of the aircraft. He didn't like it, because he was on his back all the way down, but we thought we would try a line-up of five like that, with numbers two and three facing aft, the others forward. It was like fighting with an octopus. We shook our dizzy heads and went back to try another five, all facing forwards this time. It worked. We tried the full six, and that worked too, and that was how it was to be – line abreast, facing forwards.

But it needed practice. Whenever we could get the altitude, we were up there, taking that backward step into space that had to be made with the precision of a chorus-girl line-up, for anyone caught lagging on the sill would be dragged off forcibly with the others, probably throwing the whole group into a confusion of arms, legs and curses. Even with a good step off, the first few seconds of fall through the turbulence behind the Beverley and at sub-terminal velocity were always precarious. The group tended to fold in the middle, or to wag at the ends – the sensation depended on where you happened to be in the line-up. Sometimes we would sweep away in a gigantic cartwheel, but we learnt that as long as we had a good harness-hold and a tight leg lock on each other, and as long as we didn't try to fight it, the line would settle down as speed built up, and by ten seconds we would be falling stable, slightly head down, with time to grin sideways at each other before preparing for the break.

Jumping from 9,000 feet, we planned to break at 6,000, after 20 seconds of free fall. In some of the less stable groups it was forced upon us before we could get that far down. Grips would be torn loose, boots would fly, and six bodies would scatter through the air like black spiders shaken from a paper bag. On the intentional breaks we first of all went for a simultaneous split, but a kick or two behind the ear persuaded us to change to a staggered break, peeling off from the wings. Each man would then delta outwards from the group for ten seconds to give the bomb-burst effect, and then it was up to him to get back to the opening point, keeping a sharp eye out for other streaking bodies as we all converged into one area to operate our parachutes.

Whilst we worked on the group techniques at every opportunity, Flight Lieutenants John Leary, our pilot, and John Taylor, our navigator, were sorting out their own problems – how to get us over the release point with the split-second timing required for a Farnborough Air Show. There was no aiming device in the Beverley to give the navigator a direct overhead position. It was all eyeball work from his little window in the nose of the aircraft. John Taylor was quick to pick it up, so that we were soon stepping off the sill without that nagging worry of where we might finish up on the ground. Very important, is that relationship between aircrew and jumpers.

To accustom us to the size and shape of the Farnborough DZ, we marked out with white tape at Weston a replica of that tiny area that was to be our haven, and thoroughly investigated the reasons for any of us missing it.

Our new parachutes arrived with less than a month for us to practise with them. They incorporated a TU blank-gore cut — an adaptation of the American 'Conquistador' pattern. We were impressed by the speed with which they took us around the sky, but not at the rate with which they dropped us out of it. By cutting yet more 'holes' into the long-suffering 'X' type canopy, we had sacrificed rate of descent in the interests of more drive. I was the first casualty, with a bruised heel that kept me from jumping for a couple of days. Watching the group from the aircraft was terrifying and I was glad to get back in the middle in time for press day and the final rehearsals.

The press flew with us on a sortie over Weston, and when we ducked under the retaining tape and lined up on the edge of the sill, we faced a battery of cameras and nervous faces. We were the only ones laughing. It wasn't one of our best jumps, but they weren't to know that.

"With a roar and a wave curiously like the last salute of the gladiators, six young men leap backwards off an airplane into a nine thousand foot void. Linked arm in arm they rotate in a grotesque back somersault. Then spreadeagled in a terrifying swallow drive, they plummet earthwards for forty-five seconds — about as long as an average traffic light takes to change ... " wrote Victor Blackman in the *Daily Express*, with suitable photographic evidence. "Grotesque back somersault" indeed!

We had two final rehearsals at Farnborough. The sceptics who had watched our dismal performance ten weeks earlier came with knowing smiles, expecting us to scatter ourselves about the airfield again. I must admit to being worried. The shape and dimensions of that patch of grass that was to be our sanctuary amongst the runways and the crowds and the car parks and the scatter of expensive aeroplanes were imprinted on my mind. I studied the aerial photograph daily, like a prayer book. I dreamt of it. I can still see it perfectly. But we hit it on both of the rehearsals, and it grew bigger with each jump, until we knew that we couldn't miss it.

And so to Farnborough week. For the first five days the cloud base was low and the winds sometimes high. We managed to jump on three of the days, but from low altitudes where we were unable to demonstrate our much publicized group jump, and had to be content instead with a normal stick of six. It was well received, and confirmed our accuracy. The two remaining days — the public days — were the important ones.

The Saturday dawned clear. I watched the sky all morning. The clouds stayed away, and the leaves on the silver birches outside our window on Boars Hill stirred but lazily. It looked good for a high one, and the met man had a smile for me at the early afternoon briefing. I took his wind forecast and plotted the provisional dropping instructions on the aerial photograph. They would be confirmed or altered by the DZ party ten minutes before we were to jump. In the hangar, strangely empty and echoing on a Saturday, the lads gathered round for the preliminary briefing.

" ... normal line up, and let's keep it tight ... weather looks good and we should have no trouble getting nine thousand. It looks like a run in track from north to south ... little bit of wind up top will give us a mean of about fifteen and an opening point somewhere over the terraces here – easy to pick out. There's a dog-leg in the wind, so don't be fooled by the surface smoke – don't go racing to get up-wind of it. Remember there are no overshoots coming in from the south ... the Lightnings will be on the pans and then you've got the big hangar, so no high pulls ... should be crossing the runway just below a thousand ... if you're dropping short, the only undershoot is this car park ... "

" ... and if you land in there, pick a cheap one," someone added.

We checked our 'chutes, altimeters, stopwatches. Picked up our helmets, goggles, gloves, smoke flares ...

"Don't forget the cards Snowy ... "

We looked again at the sky and the windsock as we walked out to the Beverley. It still looked good. Twenty minutes before take off, then another thirty to drop time. I didn't join the card school. Snowy always won anyway. I sat looking at the Farnborough photograph, going through the jump, mentally anticipating every part of it. I went through it with everything going right, and I went through it again with everything going wrong, ticking off the emergency procedures in every case. There was no fear. Just a gently welling excitement. A touch of tension. An adrenalin-fired quickening of the whole system that gives marvellous clarity of thought and quickness of reaction. With twenty minutes to go before the green light I fitted my kit and stepped carefully between the engrossed card players to join John Taylor where he squatted in the nose of the aircraft. We had 9,000 feet on the altimeters, and only a wisp of thin cloud in the sky. I watched the Hog's Back revolving slowly below us as we circled in the holding area. Fifteen minutes to go.

"Kit up, lads ... "

"Can we just finish this round?"

John Thirtle came to lean over my shoulder, to double-check my calculations. The headsetted navigator was scribbling on his pad. I copied the instructions on to the aerial photograph – wind speeds and directions at various heights, run in track, release point, opening point. I translated it all into concise symbols on the map, and called the team around me, trying to keep it basic, just the main points – release, opening, 1,000-foot check mark, no overshoots, and watch the dog-leg. They passed the map between them, studied it, nodded, and finished fitting the smoke flares to their ankles.

I moved aft to the yawning end of the fuselage, and looked out. The ground below seemed less real than the wispy clouds around us. There was that smug feeling you can get from two miles high, looking down on thousands of ordinary people doing thousands of ordinary things. You don't have to be a parachutist to feel that way, but it helps.

We checked each other's equipment for the last time. John Taylor gave me a thumb up – no change in instructions. We were clear to drop. The Beverley was steady on its run in. We watched Bagshot and Frimley sliding below us.

"Two minutes," signalled the despatcher.

We lowered our goggles, and ducked under the restraining tape. I clenched my fists round the harness straps on either side and felt with my right foot for the edge of 9,000 feet. All heads were turned half right, eyes on the jump lights, time standing still, with just the roar of the engines and a cold wind licking our ankles ... red light on, ten seconds to go ... green light ...

"Way ... hayyyy ... " we shouted as we all stepped backwards.

A cold slap of air and no more noisy engines ... a sudden pull on bent arms as the line wavered and we grappled for leg locks ... the horizons swung and tilted as we spiralled away from the aircraft in slow cartwheels ... we clung tight to each other, and as the speed built up and the earth settled down underneath us, we relaxed just that little bit because we knew we had it, and laughed at each other along the row of wind-whipped faces and perfectly aligned instrument panels, then all eyes down on the altimeters. The needles crept to 6,000 and right on the dot John and Tommy went from the wings, then the grips on my harness slackened and I was alone in the sky, already sweeping my arms back and my legs closer together and diving away into clear air. From the ground, one thick trail of orange smoke had broken into six, radiating outwards like spokes from a hub. As I counted off the seconds on the stopwatch I was picking up the Aldershot Road and Queen's Parade beyond it, knowing where I was and where to go next as the aerial photograph came to life, and at ten seconds from the break I was leaning left and swinging round in a wide banking turn, without losing the delta, and with twelve seconds remaining to get back to the opening point ... no time to really think about it but just enough to hear instinct saying " ... over there, a little more left, about four hundred yards ... " and to dip the shoulder a touch and straighten out again and drive in for the edge of the terraces ... the pattern of runways was coming closer ... aware of other orange smoke trails streaking for the opening area and easing off a little to the right to keep from getting above them ... arms forward to brake for the opening, watching the altimeter and the ground beyond it, relating the two, pulling ... and swinging down beneath the canopy ...

I reached for the right toggle and turned to face upwind before I tucked the ripcord away and lifted my goggles. It wasn't over. That triangle of green grass was still 800 yards of drift away. I watched the signal smoke, and the wind, the altimeter needle and the ground and my movement over it — and put them all together in another gentle pull on one toggle or the other, reading all the signs like a printed page ... over the upturned faces of the crowd now, hearing the loudspeakers telling them all about it ... across the main runway at 800 feet, then steering for the flare with a sudden exuberance,because it was there ... we had got it ... nothing could go wrong ... it was just a matter of how close. I swung into wind for landing, hit, rolled, and dodged the others as they came in around me, all within twenty yards of the target. I loosened my helmet.

"How did it look?"

"Not bad," said Ron Ellerbeck, our DZ Sergeant.

That was praise, coming from Ron. I unbuckled the harness, and removed the smouldering smoke flare from my boot. A Vulcan flew low and slow over our heads and the upturned faces followed it as we carried our bundled 'chutes off the landing area.

"Bloody marvellous ... "

"Steady as a rock ... "

"Spot on the release point ... "

"Who kicked me in the crutch?"

We climbed aboard the waiting coach, and dumped our kit. It was all over, until tomorrow.

"Got the cards, Snowy?"

7 / North America

Trial and error is a fine learning process. It is also a painfully slow one. Thus although our free-fall skills advanced steadily, it had soon become apparent that the process would be greatly hastened by some further lessons from those more knowledgeable than ourselves. Our frequent requests for further factfinding tours to France or to the U.S.A. were turned down with a certain pomposity that suggested that we British had nothing further to learn from foreigners.

The Army had no such reservations. The free-fallers of 22 S.A.S. Regiment, after receiving their basic free-fall training at Abingdon, had furthered their own skills through their unit sport parachuting club, with the energetic backing of their commanding officer, Lieutenant Colonel Dare Wilson. At French and American centres they learnt advanced techniques from some of the foremost free-fall parachutists in the world. The R.A.F. Parachute Jumping Instructor, who should have been giving the lead in free fall as he had done in every other aspect of parachuting, was slipping behind. Nobody would listen to our cries for help. "But you're a Parachute Jumping Instructor!" they would say, as though a brevet was worth a month at Biscarosse. Brevets certainly didn't help us in the 1962 national championships at Goodwood, where our former pupils of the S.A.S. thrashed us and made up the entire team that represented Britain in the world championships that summer.

Those championships also showed the wealth of expertise and technical knowledge that had now developed in the U.S.A., who provided the overall champions in both the men's and the women's events.

The news that four of us were to visit Canada and the States that Autumn was therefore welcome, if somewhat overdue. Squadron Leader Dick Mullins, Sergeants Dave Francombe and Paul Hewitt, and myself, were the lucky four. The programme for the three weeks looked rather ambitious. "When do we sleep?" asked Dave Francombe as we looked through it.

In early October we packed our bags. That wasn't easy. The same directive that allowed us sixty pounds of baggage also listed a hundredweight of essential items. We compromised, and to further keep the luggage weight down we wore our jumping boots with our number one uniforms for the journey. The boots had yellow elastic laces, which raised the eyebrows of the very senior officer on the flight to which we were assigned. "We're parachutists, sir," I explained to the eyebrows. "Aaahh!" he said, apparently accepting that anyone strange enough to leap from fully serviceable aeroplanes was entitled to wear yellow laces.

We refuelled at Gander, which shivered under a dirty blanket of cloud. Further west the cloud thinned, then cleared, and the land below was red and yellow with maples. Supper at Ottowa. Night flight to Winnipeg. Train across the prairie lands to Portage La Prairie, then a staff car to Rivers and the Canadian Airborne School, and a party to welcome us.

We cleared our heads the next morning with a couple of jumps from the C 119, the 'Flying Boxcar'. It took to the air with a rattling roar. The Canadian soldier sitting next to me grinned.

"Nice aeroplane," I shouted, politely.

"This is no aeroplane," he yelled back. "This is two thousand loose rivets flying in close formation ... "

But it was a friendly aeroplane. Or perhaps it was the people. It was all very informal. Ash-trays were passed round instead of sick bags. The 'command-response' system of aircraft drills that they had adopted from the Americans was heartening too.

"Get ready!" bellowed the despatcher.

"Get ready!" we all shouted back, and got ready.

"Hook up!" he bawled.

"Hook up!" we echoed, and did.

"Check equipment!"

"Check equipment!"

"Everybody gonna jump?"

"YEEEAAAHHHH!!"

The stick departed slowly, almost leisurely. We tagged on the end, trying not very successfully to imitate their hunched-up style of exit. The big T 10 parachute yawned slowly, and drifted almost aimlessly down through a sky that was so blue and fresh, to a DZ that was comfortably soft and appeared to have no boundaries. We rushed back to do it again.

We dozed in the back of the car that took us 150 miles to Winnipeg along a highway running broad and straight through the glow and smell of stubble fires, then we flew east into the dawn with a breakfast-tray of pancakes, bacon and maple syrup.

Low cloud was scudding over Boston, and Mohawk Airways had cancelled its local flights to Worcester, so we took a taxi. The driver was fat and voluble. "It's de jooveniles what's de trouble ... " he was saying as we fell asleep, and was still talking when we woke, seventy miles later, " ... you can even get money on credit over here ... "

In a swirl of wet leaves we drove into Orange. Orange, Massachusetts, had been the venue for the 1962 world parachuting championships. It was the home of Parachutes Incorporated. The home of Jacques Istel, who as competitor, coach, and administrator had become known as the father of American sport parachuting. In 1957 he and Lew Sanborn had founded Parachutes Incorporated, to sell parachutes and parachuting. Two years later he had opened the sport parachuting centre at Orange, and also the Inn.

It was at the 'Inn at Orange' that we were to stay for two days. A converted New England farmhouse, it stood amongst birch and pine on the side of a hill, looking out over the airfield a mile away. On the downhill side of the building was a small clearing into which, at weekends, parachutists were invited to jump at the close of the day's sport. A steak dinner was the award for the winner of these impromptu accuracy competitions. Although we had no pretensions to the free steak, we had looked forward to adding our names to the impressive list of those who had 'dropped in', but the low cloud and the strong winds stayed with us at Orange for the weekend, and we didn't even get off the ground.

Time was not wasted, however. Lew Sanborn showed us reel after reel of his films, shot air-to-air in free fall with a helmet-mounted camera, some of the earliest of its kind and the first that we had ever seen; Billy Jolly, designer and workshop manager, talked some of the best sense we had heard on parachute design and function as he showed us round the Company's technical area; Daryl Henry, Canadian champion and one of the ten yellow-overalled instructors, showed us the training facilities and explained the teaching policies of the centre.

"We sell gravity," Sanborn had said, and their main money-maker on the training side was the first-jump course. Instant parachuting, for thirty dollars. Clients registered at the well-appointed administration building, and proceeded with a fistful of tickets to the equipment room to be fitted out with boots, overalls, and helmet. From there they would go to the class room for a film and lecture on parachuting theory, thence to the training area for instruction in exit, canopy control, and landing techniques. Next they would be fitted into main and reserve parachutes in the fitting area, then straight into one of the Company's three aircraft for a static-line descent from 2,500 feet. A friendly voice over the loud-hailer would advise them which of the two steering toggles to pull next, and guide them down to a landing in the soft sand of the DZ. The successful tyro would be picked up, dusted off and driven back for a debrief and the presentation of a first-jump diploma. Next please ...

Orange had been criticized by some for commercializing the sport. But if the Company could make a profit out of a service to parachuting and to the spirit of adventure, then why not? And although profit may have been the motive, safety was the overriding consideration. The records of the centre spoke for themselves: 16,000 jumps in three years, with no fatalities and no major injuries, and that included 2,000 pupils who have travelled on the first-jump conveyor belt. We were impressed, and wondered if our own training progressions were perhaps a little cautious.

Our education continued during the evenings at the wind-buffeted inn. It was all parachuting. Parachuting with the T-bone steak; parachuting with the lime-sherbert ice cream and the cherry cheesecake; parachuting with the cold beer in the pinewood bar that was decorated with framed photographs of Jacques ...

"First time I flew that old Hustler, I just got on those front risers, and wheeeee ... !"

"Well, I surely wouldn't jump now without those twin extractors ... "

"You remember that crazy guy who was making a charity jump into Boston and he eyeballed the wrong stadium and landed in the middle of a ball game ... ?"

"Yeah ... and do you remember ... ?"

Until Bev Galloway — professional troubador until he took to the sky — produced his guitar and Daryl Henry warmed his bongo drums over a candle, and then for an hour or so Appalachian maidens would lose their true loves, dust storms would blow and moonshine would flow, Tom Dooley would hang down his head and the Wabash Cannonball would roll again.

The wind was still worrying the red and golden woods of New England as we drove back to Boston — in another taxi, as Mohawk Airways were still grounded. I had known an American called 'J.T.' who lived in Boston. I idly scanned the pavements for him. Everyone looked like 'J.T.'

The British liaison officer from Fort Bragg met us off the aircraft at Fayetville, and took us straight to someone's cocktail party. "I could do with a cup of tea," said Dick Mullins.

Fort Bragg. One of the major bases of United States Airborne, in the flat lands of North Carolina. A worried escort officer was assigned to us. "Lootenant Jenkins, Major," he greeted Squadron Leader Mullins. He had a several-page programme for our education and entertainment. Bragg was vast, and our hosts were determined that we were going to see most of it, by day and by night.

We spent a day with the 82nd Airborne Division. The U.S. airborne soldier received his basic parachute training at the main Airborne Training School at Fort Benning, but the subsequent instruction was the responsibility of each major unit's own training centre. Lieutenant Tom Olsen, commanding the 82nd Airborne School, showed us round. Watching a group of trainees at work on the outdoor apparatus, practising flight and landings, we had the usual argument — whether it is best to watch the ground for landing, as we do, or to keep the eyes on the horizon, as taught by the Americans. They reason that the sight of rapidly approaching ground causes trainees to tense in apprehension. We argue that there is a tendency to tense up when the ground *can't* be seen. As always, we agreed to differ.

The training was supervised by well-built, crew-cut instructors wearing torso-tight T-shirts, immaculate combat slacks, and highly polished jump boots.

"Leroy!" bellowed one, "that was a godawful parachute landing fall! Give me twenty ... " Leroy fell to the ground and counted off twenty push-ups. Attitudes towards parachute training reflect national character: our system of gentle persuasion would not have suited the Americans, any more than their method of aggressive salesmanship would suit us. We left Leroy to his push-ups, and the men in the flight harnesses gazing at their horizons, as Lootenant Jenkins suggested that we might just have time for a shower before the next cocktail party.

The next day he led us to the 7th Special Forces. The 'Green Berets', specialists in counter-insurgency, were the nearest equivalent to our Special Air Service, and of particular interest to us was their HALO School. HALO — High Altitude, Low Opening — was a technique devised to drop men from altitudes above 20,000 feet, where an aircraft would be less likely to be seen or heard, and less likely to be associated with people jumping out of it. The training techniques used to bring a man to high altitude competence were of special interest. One of the arguments against military free fall had always been that it took so long to train a man to the necessary standards, and the HALO system seemed to offer an acceptable short cut. The training philosophy was one of rapid progression to long free falls. Within five descents pupils would be free falling for 40 seconds, whereas in the classical step-by-step progression he would still be on 5-second delays. It was a bold philosophy. The case against such rapid advance had always been that should a novice fail to sort out his problems he would be likely to pull his ripcord too early if he panicked, or too late and possibly not at all if he became preoccupied with his actions. This valid argument was now countered by the use of a barometric triggered automatic opening device (AOD) which would automatically open the parachute at a pre-set altitude should the faller fail to do so with his own right hand. This built-in insurance policy gave a man confidence, and the system gave him time in the air to practise the basic requirements of stability and control.

We discussed the concept eagerly with the training team and with the trialists who were still evaluating the system and its associated equipment. The idea was still young, but full of exciting potential. We crammed our notebooks and heads with ideas, and rushed off to another party.

Next, we met the Golden Knights, the U.S. Army Parachute Team, who had that season established twelve world records for individual and group precision jumping, and had provided five out of the six men in the national team. Without a doubt they embodied the greatest concentration of precision landing and demonstration expertise then in existence.

We were a little over-awed, but had no need to be, for their friendliness was as exceptional as their skill. Dick Fortenberry in particular was liberal with advice and information. We spent a day jumping with them on one of the five huge, sandy DZs amongst the pine woods around Bragg. We all went over the tailgate of a Caribou at 14,000 feet. I had never before engaged in relative work of such a standard: they flew their bodies with effortless control and precision. Dick Fortenberry came smiling up to me, nodded, and glided off to look at someone else ... there was a hand on my ankle, spinning me round, and there was big Duffy, grinning through his goggles, then he was gone too ... I lay there, turning slowly, just watching them in mid-air fascination. Instead of using a delta position to increase speed and lose relative height, they were 'tucking' – reducing the effective body area by bringing the hands in close to the shoulder, and drawing the knees up. I had heard of it, never seen it, and had rarely practised it. I tried it now, and slipped ignominiously on to my back.

The Golden Knights drew most of their talent from the Army sport parachuting clubs. Tom Olsen made us honorary members of the 82nd Club and we spent the next day happily jumping with them from a Huey helicopter, which seemed to take us up almost as fast as we came down.

"What next?" we asked Lootenant Jenkins. He leafed through his programme. Next was Sunday. "Personal recreation," he said.

"Come on up to Winston Salem with us," offered Tom Olsen. "We got a little show on ... "

"But it does say personal recreation," worried our escort.

"It *will* be recreation," promised Tom.

So we went, in a C123, to Winston Salem. At the airfield we sat on the grass in the sunshine, drinking grape juice from plastic cups while Tom Olsen scurried around looking for organizers and an aeroplane and a programme. It was nice having someone else do it. Parachuting conditions were ideal: a cloudless sky, and just enough breeze to give a definite wind-line. A good crowd, too. A smiling, friendly crowd of mums and dads and juniors, strolling slowly and rather aimlessly, or sitting to eat their picnics in the shade under the wings of parked aeroplanes. Such a pleasant, relaxed atmosphere, with none of the neck-stretching urgency of a British air-display, where what you do sometimes seems less important than doing it precisely on time. There was just a lone aircraft doing slow rolls up and down the length of the airfield, not too close to worry anyone with its noise.

The word got around that there were English jumpers guesting with the American team.

"You-all from old England?" asked pleasant people, and shook our hands warmly when we told them that indeed we were. A wartime merchant mariner asked if we knew someone called Smith from Liverpool. We were sorry that we didn't. Someone bought Miss Winston Salem, with raven hair and a throaty voice.

"You all jump?"

"Jump? Oh ... yes ... rather."

Her publicity man produced a photographer. I pinned a P.T.S. badge on the all-American bosom, and had another grape juice.

Tom Olsen returned, and suggested that we have a look at the dee zee. We stood outside a small air terminal building and looked across a wide expanse of concrete to the grass airfield beyond. I wondered which part of all that greenery we were going to use as a landing area. "That'll do fine," said Tom, and pointed to a patch of turf about the size of a tennis court, in the centre of the concrete apron. We looked at it thoughtfully, nodded as though we approved, then ran shifty eyes around the horizons for soft undershoots. Twelve men in there ... ?

Small boys insisted on carrying our reserve parachutes to the aircraft – a Caribou. We thanked the small boys, and climbed aboard.

"What would you like us to do?" asked Paul Hewitt of the team leader.

"Just tag on the end."

"How high?"

"High as we can get."

We got as high as 15,000 feet. On the run in someone gave us each a hand-flare, and someone else shouted "Let's go!" and everyone disappeared over the tailgate. We followed at a run. I tumbled through the air in slow somersaults as I held the smoke flare in front of my goggles to read the instructions, as there was no readily apparent method of igniting it. Smoking nicely at last, I stabilized and looked down at the main bunch. Bodies were zipping to and fro across the Carolina landscape like bees. I moved off a little to one side, dropped the smoke flare when it started to burn through my glove, and pulled the ripcord when I saw the flicker of the first extractor 'chute.

I was trying out a T10 canopy with a double blank-gore. It was lazy – not keen to go anywhere. Not even downwards. It followed the others at a respectful and gradually increasing distance, and was still dawdling at 800 feet as the leaders started to land on the little green island in the middle of all that dazzling white concrete. In a mean sort of way I was hoping someone would miss it so that my eventual arrival would be less embarrassing, for I had no faith in the ability of my machine to get me there. But one after the other the gaily coloured canopies spilled over the grass until it was obliterated by nylon, and then to my surprise and relief the big parachute deposited me not unkindly amongst them. All twelve were there.

"WOW!" everyone was saying to everyone else as they unclipped their harnesses. "How about *that*, man!!"

Early the next morning I left the others at Bragg and flew west, to Charlotte, then across the green waves of the Appalachian ridges to Chicago, and on over the squared prairie lands, the brown wrinkles of the foothills, and the cloud-covered Rockies. There was hazy mist at Los Angeles.

A short, slim man, chewing meditatively on a toothpick, met me at the airport. He had shrewd, knowing eyes that made me decide straight away not to add even one jump if he ever asked me how many I had done.

"I'm Jim Hall," he said. "Welcome to Para Ventures."

In the early 'fifties Jim Hall, a graduate mining engineer, had worked as a 'smoke jumper' for the U.S. Forestry Service alongside a former paratrooper called Dave Burt. The two of them decided to establish a commercial parachuting firm, and in 1959 they formed Para Ventures Incorporated, based in Hollywood, and offering services in any aspect of parachuting –

display, advertisement, stunt work, filming, supply dropping, rescue missions, pathfinding jumps for geological surveys, sport parachuting, and development work under government contract. It was an aspect of their development work that I had crossed the continent to see — the 'Buddy System'.

In an attempt to reduce the numbers of fatalities and major injuries sustained by bale-out aircrew, the U.S. Air Force had submitted an operational requirement for a parachute training programme. They sought the maximum benefit in the shortest time, and to meet this need Para Ventures had evolved a twelve-hour training programme to include stabilization in free fall, correct parachute operation, canopy control, and landings. The principle feature of the programme was the use of a 'buddy system' whereby an instructor would leave the aircraft with the pupil, gripping his harness, and so controlling him during free fall. He would stay with his pupil until the latter had operated his own ripcord, and if he failed to do so, the instructor would pull it for him before dropping away below. An automatic opening device provided the ultimate safety precaution. In this way, a first free-fall descent was made from 8,000 feet, and a second from 12,000 feet. This was even more promising than the military HALO system, and I was beginning to believe in such things.

Jim drove me to the Company's office and parachute 'loft' in Hollywood Boulevard. I met Dave Burt, and Bob Sinclair, who in a varied career had also been a paratrooper, smoke jumper and barnstormer, and was now to be my immediate guide during this short visit. I found myself in the midst of a parachuting professionalism that I had not dreamed existed. I put my notebook away in despair, and opened my eyes and my ears to a flow of parachuting know-how, technical expertise, well-founded opinion, and dramatic story, in the hope that some of it would stick. These men had lived parachuting, in all its guises; their approach to it was imaginative and fearless, and they inspired a confidence that was absolute. I listened to Sinclair and watched his films for hours, and would have listened and watched all night if he hadn't finally growled that even if I wasn't ready for a steak he surely was.

Somewhere down the Boulevard under a picture of Alan Ladd we ate steak and drunk lots of cool Budweiser, and the stories rolled. There were Dave Burt's jumps for the mining companies in Alaska and Mexico; his descent at the Hermosillo Fair with a Coca-Cola banner when he narrowly missed the big-wheel to crash instead through the roof of a refreshment stand; their para-scuba jumps into canyon rivers up in the mountains; Bob Sinclair's capers with his helmet-camera when filming the 'Ripcord' television series. I said nothing at all about the first all-British baton pass. I just listened.

Late at night, or perhaps early in the morning, Jim drove me slowly through mellow streets, up and away from the Boulevard. The white bungalows grew larger and more extravagant with altitude.

"This is dancing girl level," said Jim. "The most beautiful girls in the world live right here." I couldn't see any. I supposed they were all in bed, or dancing. "And this is private secretary level," he added, and the Thunderbird glided to a halt. I was too tired to really believe it all.

Bob Sinclair picked me up early in the morning. "Better strap in," he said. We drove out on the southbound freeway with a smoothness that belied the speed, and swooped up through the Ortega Hills, and down again into a broad valley of dry slopes and green orange groves. I had heard it said that Californian jumpers knew it was time to reach for the ripcord when they could distinguish the oranges on the trees. "Who picked the goddamn oranges?" was the famous cry.

"I'm Bud Kiesow," said the big man at Elsinore as he crushed my hand. I had heard of Bud too — one of the wilder jumpers of a few years ago but now reformed, I was assured. He showed me round the parachute training centre, and told me more about the 'buddy system' and its application.

The programme had already been evaluated by the U.S.A.F. Director General of Safety, who had completed the twelve-hour course himself, with several members of his staff. There had been no problems at all, Bud said. All descents had gone according to plan, and the instructors had found no difficulty in controlling another body in free fall.

"Not that we had to do much once we got 'em stable," said Bud. "Jest hold 'em tight and give 'em a big smile. Get a body relaxed, and free fall comes easy."

Several of the U.S.A.F. trainees had in fact 'gone solo' from 12,000 feet on a third jump, with an instructor falling alongside them, but not in contact, and they had fallen stable all the way and operated their ripcords smoothly at the correct height. "Grab a rig, and I'll show you how it's done."

Bob put on his helmet with the big cine-camera mounted on it, and we wedged ourselves into a Cessna 172. The DZ was a dried lake-bed, giving some 6 square miles of soft, unobstructed landing area, with the mountains rising 2,000 feet alongside it. "When you can't see the top of the plateau, it's time to unpack!" yelled Bud as we circled for altitude, my legs getting cold in the open door. We flew to 9,000. I clambered into the air blast, holding the strut, one foot on the step. Bud filled the door beside me, gripping my left harness strap with a huge right fist. He gave me a shove, and away we went.

I felt that had he needed to, Bud could have controlled my fall with ease — could have held me had I started to slip from balance, stopped me had I started to turn. And how reassuring it must be for a beginner to have that strong hand on the harness and that big comfortable grin just the turn of a head away! Bob had dived out behind us, had positioned himself up-sun, and was now dropping down to our linked bodies, his camera taking it all in. Although he spread himself as wide as he could on the air, he was unable to stay with us and dropped slowly away and below with a sad shake of his head. Bud hung on until I opened, then fell away to operate his own parachute. I strolled into the sand pit under the big 32-foot steerable canopy they used for "First timers, heavy-weights and very valuable people."

I went up again, for Bob to shoot a film of me solo. I went first, keeping my head up to watch him dive from the Cessna after me and swoop down to my level. I slid in close to meet him, smiling for the camera, looking at Bob's mouth all puckered up by his chin strap and his hands moving like the fins of a lazy goldfish. He stayed in close to film my pull and the deployment of my parachute, and was waiting on the ground for me when I landed.

I took off my helmet and stood for some little while looking around me at all that soft DZ, and a sky with nothing but sunshine in it.

Back to Hollywood; more films in the Para Ventures offices. More stories with the steak and the Budweiser. More stories yet in a dimly lit bar, Bob Sinclair crunching the ice out of his vodka-eights, almost embarrassed at the profusion of his tales.

I fell asleep at private secretary level wondering if Para Ventures had a vacancy for a Flight Lieutenant, retired …

The dream ended, and Bob came in his baseball cap and Thunderbird to drive me down past the still-sleeping dancing girls and through quiet morning streets to the airport. We had time for another drink, and another story.

He was barnstorming once in Alaska, where one of his acts was to ride the top wing of a Stearman biplane through a series of loops, and to drop off as it went over the top for the third time. He was giving his show at Palmer, on an airfield flanked by a gorge through which flowed the Matanuska river. He hung on to his perch for the first two loops, and at the start of the third he unhooked his feet from around the guy-wires and as the plane became inverted again, let gravity do the rest. He fell for several hundred feet, then opened his main 'chute. Without any warning, rigging lines were suddenly falling around him and he was tumbling through space again — having completed its third loop the Stearman had levelled out and torn straight into his canopy, completely severing it from the lines. Bob tugged the reserve handle from its pocket. Nothing happened. The rigging lines of his main parachute were tangled round the reserve pack, preventing it from opening. Somersaulting earthwards, Bob reached into the end of the pack and started to manually drag the canopy into the air flow, until at last it streamed above him and cracked into life. As he bounced to the end of his rigging lines he was looking straight at a brown cliff: he had plummeted right into the gorge. Nor were his troubles over, for the Matanuska was flowing fast below his feet. Fortunately he dropped into waist-deep water where he was able to fight down the canopy and struggle to a sand bar. "Guess not many guys have opened up below ground zero," he said.

It was time to go.

"You ought to write a book, Bob."

"Naw ... " he swilled the beer round his glass and looked embarrassed. "I got a few more chapters to live yet."

8 / The Day We Nearly Saw the King of Siam

"Let's go men, let's go!! First call ... let's go ... "

His boots echoed loudly on the wooden floor as in the half-light he picked his way between the stacked carbines and the piles of field kit and the humpy shapes under the mosquito nets.

"Okay men ... let's go ... "

Grunts and hawkings of a hundred waking men, voices muffled and thick under the nets.

"That top-sergeant – he sure got a mean voice ... "

"Every man got a mean voice at five and a half in the morning!"

Grey light and the rotten-sweet smell of wet jungle were creeping in through the large unshuttered windows.

"Where'd I put those friggin' boots?"

Shapes were moving, softly cursing. Torches went in search of strayed kit.

"You got my goddamn mess kit!"

"I have not got your goddamn mess kit!"

"You have too! You got my goddamn mess kit!"

"So I have *not* got your goddamn mess kit!"

The goddamn mess kit faded down the wooden steps. When a little more light drifted in, I got up. I put on my shorts and jumping boots, and went down the steps. I borrowed an airborne helmet, filled it with chlorinated water from one of the jerrycans at the foot of the stairs, and walked across to the outdoor toilet area. Men were squatting on the ground, shaving with cold water and instant-lather, talking softly.

"You get any pam-pam last night?"

"Sure thing."

"How much it cost?"

"Cain't remember. Sure weren't free though."

I shaved as best I could without a mirror, then crossed to the latrines. "Wash your hands," said a big notice. Inside sat two negroes, smoking, taking their time. I wondered if there was anything against sharing latrines with negroes, but they didn't object.

"Man, this whole operation is a pig's ass ... There I was, jest finishing settin' up those dummies out on the range when KEEEEEBAMMMMM – all hell started comin' down. Nobody told me they was gonna change the firin' time ... "

I washed my hands like the notice said and went back to the billet to get my mess tins. Snowy Robertson was coming down the steps, and I knew I wasn't dreaming after all.

But it was all very strange.

A week before I had still been in Abingdon, making final and frantic preparations for our posting to Singapore. "One thing about this job, Ed – I won't be off on displays every weekend," I had promised.

"We'll see," said Ed. She wasn't convinced. She was quite right.

Within a week of arriving in Singapore I was carrying my parachute and a rucksack on to a Hastings at Changi, bound for Thailand to take part in a military display at the close of the annual SEATO exercise. Snowy Robertson and Dai Hurford, both Sergeant instructors at the Far East Parachute and Survival School at the time, made our team to three. We were, we understood, to jump with Americans and Thais. Squadron Leader Douggie Brown, the Command Parachute Officer, was with us for DZ safety.

The Hastings had brought us to Kokethiem, a hundred miles north of Bangkok, where we were met by a burly colonel of the U.S. Airborne. He was carrying shaving gear in a little plastic bag.

"I'm so busy movin' my goddamn ass around this place I don't even get time for a goddamn shave," he announced. We crowded ourselves and our gear into his dust-covered jeep. As we bounced down the roads between summer-dry paddy fields, he told us about the display. "Nine of you – you three, three Thai boys, and three of my men from Okinawa, right at the end of the show, from nine thousand, lots of smoke, and each one of you with a SEATO nation flag in your overalls, so that when you land right there in front of the King, you just all line up and hold them goddamn flags right out ... How does that sound Major?"

"Did you say the King?" said Douggie.

"Sure I did."

"What about some practice?" I asked.

"All the goddamn practice you want, Lootenant."

"And what's the dropping zone like?"

"Fine. Fine. A fine dee zee ... "

The jeep ground to a halt in front of a long wooden building, open sided, raised from the ground on pillars.

"My boys are living here with the artillery. Not much goddamn room left. Just squeeze yourself a bed space ... "

He reversed into a cloud of dust and shot out of it again like a rhino. The American team met us. There were six of them wearing big blue baseball caps. They were led by a rangy lieutenant.

"Nice to have you with us."

"Nice to be here."

After we had found space for our sleeping bags, and strung our mosquito nets over them, the Americans produced cold beer, and we talked about the display. As we would be using an American aircraft, rangy lieutenant would be overall leader and would do the spotting. Some of the Thais, he thought, were rather inexperienced. They had a dozen to choose from, however, and as the Americans themselves needed to select three out of their six men, there would be about twenty of us jumping during practice. He suggested that there was no need to decide the final format of the display until we had all jumped together a few times: after all, we were going to get plenty of practice. We drank a few beers to that.

And woke next morning to the sound of the top-sergeant's boots on the wooden floor ...

We ate breakfast in the open-sided mess hall, then swallowed our paludrin, washed our mess tins, and went back to the billet to wait for the Thais. We sat on the verandah watching the artillerymen fall in, then roar away in their armoured carriers for a day of practice on the ranges. The Thais came for us in an open truck. They were pleasant, dapper men, who shook hands shyly but meaningfully. Some had trained at Fort Bragg, and spoke English well. Others didn't speak it at all, but too polite to admit it, they smiled and nodded understandingly when addressed. We overcrowded the truck, and jolted away to the airfield. There wasn't an aircraft in sight: just the Colonel and his shaving gear.

"Looks like we don't have a goddamn bird today boys, so why don't you all drive on out to Pulon to look the zone over?"

So we headed for the hills, followed by a long plume of red dust. We left the paddy land. Jungle closed in on the track. The slopes steepened around us. The jungle thickened. The lorry climbed. At the summit of a particularly steep incline, it stopped, and everyone got out. Standing in the sun, we looked down at the Colonel's fine dee zee in a respectful silence, that was finally broken by one of the Americans.

"Jeeeeeesus!" he said.

We were on the almost precipitous side of a mountain. The jungle had been scraped from its face, terraces bulldozed, and wooden stands erected. There was a prominent royal box, to which an awning was being fixed. Immediately below there was a cleared and levelled space, the size of a football pitch. Beyond this, secondary jungle stretched for a mile up a gentle slope, thinning into scrub as it climbed. It was on that slope that the fire-power display and the armoured assault would be launched. The clearing was for helicopters and us. Its size was no cause for concern: we had jumped into smaller areas. It was the surrounds that added a sporting touch. The crag on which we stood suggested that with an approach from this direction we would be able to carry on a reasonable conversation with the spectators on our way down. On the other side the jungle looked prickly and uninviting, and along two edges of the clearing – as though specially prepared for the deterrence of an airborne assault – rose extensive clusters of six-foot spikes where bamboo thickets had been incompletely cleared. We looked down at the fine dee zee for several minutes, drawing mental maps, with the bamboo spikes marked in red.

"You'll be allright, lads," said Snowy as we at last turned away. "Just keep your legs together."

There wasn't a 'bird' for us the next day either, so we took another trip in the lorry. The Thais invited us to their airborne training school at Erewan. It was organized and equipped on U.S. Army lines. Painted in prominent red letters along the length of one wall in the training hangar was the motto of the Thai Airborne – "Never mind is the way to die". Quite so.

Still without an aircraft on the third day, we stayed at the airfield, sprawling in the shade until a Hastings or a C130 or a Dakota landed. Then we would stir ourselves to accost its pilot, but none of them could take us up. We went back to the billet and played volleyball on a makeshift court, against the agile negroes from the artillery unit. They thrashed us. The evenings were spent sitting on boxes of compo rations in the mess hall, drinking canned beer by the light of hissing tilly lamps, enjoying being dry while a tropical deluge hammered on the corrugated tin roof. Snowy would get the cards out.

"Poker? Not sure how to play it. But I'll give it a go," he would say, and two hours later would pocket his winnings with a grin.

At last, an aeroplane! The Colonel gave a magician's smile, as thought he had produced the C130 from his plastic bag. The first drop was to be a practice on the airfield at Koketheim. Like children on a picnic, we fitted up and clambered aboard.

"What are the sticks?" we asked.

"Well, I guess we'll just all go over the tailgate on one pass," said rangy lieutenant. Eighteen of us. Well, that was all right. He obviously knew what he was doing. We strapped in. The Thais were all smiling broadly. Rows of white teeth under big helmets. We smiled and nodded back. Some of them appeared to have no instruments. Others had only a stopwatch.

"Why no stopwatch?" Snowy asked of one.

"Not my turn for stopwatch," he smiled.

At 9,000 feet the ramp at the rear of the aircraft was lowered. Rangy lieutenant crouched at the door, eyeing the drop zone. We lined up with the smiling Thais. I was one of the first off, and banked through the slipstream to face the airfield. It was a little too far away — the drop was deep. I decided that I would pull a little high rather than track for the opening point, so that I could spend my free fall enjoying the cool rush of air and making slow, leisurely turns to look at the panorama below, where the brown and yellow plain washed up against hills dressed in jungle green. I pulled a little above 2,000 feet. The familiar rustling thump of my own canopy was followed immediately by another but more unusual whoosh as a body hurtled past, about 10 feet away. He was on his back, like an upturned beetle. I swear he was still smiling. I watched for the puff of his parachute far below me, then turned my attention and my canopy towards the distant drop zone. I landed gently in the dust alongside the cross. Most of the others made it, but a few of the Thais were scattered widely about the countryside.

In the afternoon we made a practice descent on to the display DZ at Pulon — just nine of us this time. There was little wind, and the visibility was good. The DZ looked much better from 9,000 feet: they always do. The drop was deep again, but we had plenty of time to track back to the opening point. The approach was well clear of the terraces and of the spikes. Most of us landed in puffs of red dust around the target, to find the DZ party distracted by the performance of one of the Thais. Having opened his main parachute, he for no apparent reason disconnected it at about 1,000 feet over the jungle and dropped for a further 500 feet before operating his reserve. Douggie Brown demanded that the stuntman be immediately barred from further jumping with the team. He was advised, politely, that this would not be possible as the gentleman was an officer, and was, moreover, related to Royalty. "Well if he keeps pulling tricks like that he won't be related to them much bloody longer," said Douggie.

More practice would have been useful, particularly for the spotter, we thought. But two more frustrating days passed without an aircraft and without jumps. Our volleyball improved though.

So, with only two practices behind us, we came to display day. In the morning we were to perform for the local population on the airfield, followed by the royal performance at Pulon in the afternoon. An American general had offered a 50-dollar prize for the man nearest the cross at Koketheim, and the King had offered 100 for the afternoon jump. As good as ours, we thought.

It was to be another mass drop for the Koketheim jump. Mindful still of that hurtling body that had nearly taken my canopy with it, I asked to go last in the twenty-man stick, so that I had the smiling faces below me. It was a bad mistake. When rangy lieutenant gave the "Go", nobody seemed in any hurry to leave. I herded them from behind, like chasing sheep over a cliff. By the time I eventually got out, the airfield was on the horizon. It had been another late drop, as well as a slow stick. I tracked, and pulled high again, hoping to drift in the extra distance. But we hung as helpless as wet washing in still air, with no hope of making it. Even the crowd, who had never seen parachuting before, could see that most of us were going to drop short. A flood of white-shirted figures came swarming off the airfield towards us, trickling through the scrub like spilt milk. I picked a clear spot amongst the thorn, and steered for it. I had to drive in hard to reach it, swinging my feet over a bush to land heavy and fast in a scurry of dust and children and curses. I bundled up my 'chute and was escorted back to the airfield by gleeful brown children. Snowy had wisely gone number one in the stick. He was the only one to have reached the DZ and was smiling broadly at his 50 dollars. "Where you been?" he said.

We were a little concerned about our chances that afternoon. We suggested to the Colonel that it might be a wise precaution to pre-position the nine flags on the DZ at Pulon — or at least have a duplicate set — just in case one or two didn't quite make the target area. But he was a supreme optimist. He wasn't jumping.

The artillery was crumping away in the distant hills as we climbed into the C130. We sat sweating, waiting for the take-off and the cool air of altitude. We couldn't think what the Thais still had to smile about.

As we ran in at 2,000 feet to drop a streamer, there was a pall of black smoke drifting lazily over the display area. "Hope the Colonel's got his timings right," muttered Dai Hurford. Streamer away! Normally we would have circled it, watching it all the way to the ground to see the precise drift direction and distance. However, the pilot had no intention of circling a fire-power display, and the aircraft lifted its nose and roared away, so that we soon lost sight of the yellow strip of crepe paper wriggling in the haze. "No sweat", said rangy lieutenant. "Dee zee will tell us where she goes ... "

Just above 7,000 feet we ran into cloud. We ducked below it again. Seven thousand feet it was. Less time to track, should we need to. Cloud could also mean turbulent winds, if it was the underside of cumulus that we had hit. Five minutes to go. Time we were briefed.

Rangy lieutenant was talking on the intercom by the door. He looked worried. "Can't get the dee zee ... " he yelled over the engine roar. "Play it off the cuff," and he stuck his head into the slipstream to line us up.

Ah, that well-worn cuff. Every display jumper wears them. So we tightened our chinstraps and did a quick mental appreciation of the situation. The drift of smoke had told us that the wind was from the north. Not much on the surface, probably more at 2,000. Drift would be parallel to the mountain face, with perhaps a bit of turbulence close in. If he dropped us just north of the clearing, and a touch to the west, we could come in from that corner, giving us the full diagonal of the DZ to play with; and well away from the bamboo ...

"Running in!"

Goggles down, last check of the altimeter, nod and smile at the three Thais, and off the tailgate at a run as rangy lieutenant dropped his hand.

Just sometimes you get the feeling that you want to climb back in and start again — like a bad dream that you want to rewind and run through once more to get it right. It was one of those. The sinking feeling in my stomach as I swung on the slipstream to seek the DZ was not caused by the acceleration of my fall but by the sight of the smoke from the signal flare blowing TOWARDS us ... rangy lieutenant had dropped us south of the DZ ... down-wind ... a long way down-wind. There were one or two seconds of disbelief, then I glimpsed a white figure with his arms close to his sides and head down streaking away beneath me, and I sucked my belly in and took off after him. But it was too far. The DZ came nearer, but not near enough. Pull high and hope to drive in? Not with a double L — not into wind. Even the TUs would have a job. So I kept tracking all the way down to 2,000 feet, flaring out at the last second and paying for it with a wrench at the shoulders and a kick in the back as I opened.

I was still down-wind, the smoke blowing slowly and mockingly towards me. I looked across at the stands and wondered if the King had a sense of humour.

Then I started to study the foliage below, looking for a spot that appeared less dense and painful than other spots. Fortunately there was beneath me a narrow track carved through the jungle for the tanks to use. It was barely wide enough to accept a 28-foot canopy, but self-preservation is a fine incentive to accuracy, and I slid silently between the green walls of foliage for a gentle stand-up landing in the centre of the track.

With my 'chute bundled in my arms I reached the DZ some ten minutes later. Nobody had landed on its carefully raked surface. They had found one of the Americans first, and rushed him in a jeep to the royal presence to collect the hundred dollars. Most of the others were still trying to get down from their trees. The Colonel had despatched searchers for the flags. By the time they were gathered in, the King's helicopter was an echo in the hills and the spectators were a cloud of red dust on the road to the plain. The Colonel, game to the end, lined us up. To the empty terraces and to the cleaners in the royal box, we presented the sweat-stained, thorn-torn flags of the nine SEATO nations.

"Someone's gonna have my goddamn ass for this ... " muttered the Colonel. We rather hoped that someone would.

9/ *Jungle Rescue Team*

Although my primary job on posting to Singapore in 1963 was as Physical Fitness Officer at Royal Air Force Seletar, I was not without parachuting opportunities. On welcome occasions I was attached to the Far East Air Force Parachute School at Changi to assist with the basic parachute training of Gurkha troops.

For them, leaping out of aeroplanes was an even more unnatural and momentous undertaking than it was for us. So anxious to do well, so terrified of failure, their efforts were magnificent. They had the mental will to overcome extreme fear, but couldn't always get the message through to their legs — even up in the roof of the hangar when jumping from the 'fan' their knees would sometimes fold as though on uncontrolled hinges, and in the aircraft for the first descent there would be one or more physically unable to get to their feet when called to "Stand up", or unable to direct one foot in front of the other towards the open door when the green light shone above it. Knowing what it meant to them, the despatcher usually helped them on their way. By the end of the course they would be flinging themselves into the air like happy children. Armed with a loud-hailer and Ghurkali for "forward liftwebs" and "back liftwebs" I would stand in the hot sun on the DZ at Sembawang and watch them tumble from the Argosy above my head.

"Number two starboard ... *agari ko phita* ... *AGARI*, you fool!"

They would bounce up off the hard ground, broad grins with helmets on, and scamper off to the Flight Sergeant for debriefing.

"How do you feel now, Bishnabahdur?"

"Very happy, saab."

"Well, next time keep your legs together old son, and we'll all be bloody happy ... "

And then, there was the Far East Air Force Jungle Rescue Team ...

In 1952 Flight Lieutenant Stan Kellaway had been posted from No.1 P.T.S. to take up an appointment as Physical Fitness Officer at Royal Air Force Changi. Although physical education is our basic trade there are those in our branch who, having sampled parachuting, would rather not return to ground-level appointments, a sentiment that is shared by most aircrew. Thus Stan Kellaway was no doubt delighted to find, as soon as he arrived in the Far East, that he was required to run a parachute training course for Special Air Service personnel then engaged in counter insurgency operations against the Communist terrorists in the jungles of Malaya.

A month later, fifty-five men parachuted into the Belum Valley near the Thai border, where some isolated Kampong Malays were being forced to grow food for the terrorists. The DZ was a small area of cultivated paddy, surrounded by tall jungle. The drop was successful, and after a brief battle, the Malays were brought out for resettlement in a safe area. It was a good start to parachute operations against the jungle-based enemy, and the requirement to give basic and continuation training to the growing S.A.S. force in the Far East was confirmed.

To meet this task, Stan Kellaway was joined at Changi by Sergeants Ken Kidd and Ron Smith. What they lacked in official support and equipment was compensated for by improvisation and ingenuity. In an old Japanese hangar that had originally been built by British prisoners of war, a ground training area was set up. Threadbare coir mats, two home-made ramps and some ammunition boxes served as landing aids; a single flight-training harness was suspended by ropes from the roof; a 'fan' descent machine was installed on a wooden table-top that nestled on the hangar beams twenty-five feet above the floor. For the last period of each day, stick-exits were practised off the high board in the station swimming pool – non-swimmers included.

The parachuting techniques and their application also came under review. To achieve surprise and to avoid the long and exhausting approach marches over rugged jungle country, the S.A.S. needed to parachute as close as possible to their area of operations. Cleared areas suitable for DZs were rare in the jungles of Malaya. Belum Valley had been an exception, and even there each parachutist had jumped with 100 feet of rope, in case he should land in the tall trees that bordered the DZ – a wise precaution, as it had turned out. Attention was now turned to techniques for parachuting intentionally into the tree-tops, which would give the S.A.S. almost complete freedom in their choice of landing area. The inventive mind of Stan Kellaway was much exercised by the development of a piece of equipment that would enable the parachutist to lower himself and his kit safely to earth after he was 'hung up' in the tree-tops, which in the tropical forests could be 200 feet above the ground.

The S.A.S. themselves carried out much of the initial trial work on the various ideas, and between them and Stan Kellaway, a form of abseil gear was eventually evolved, comprising 200 feet of webbing that was channelled round the body and through a metal retarding ring. It was known officially as a 'tree lowering device', unofficially as the 'bikini', from the canvas sling worn round the loins to provide a friction channel for the webbing tape. It was not foolproof, and tree jumping remained a hazardous activity that was to claim several lives.

Later, to the parachute training task was added the job of teaching aircrew the basic principles of survival in the jungle. The unit became the Far East Air Force Parachute and Survival School.

A by-product of this dual role of parachuting and survival training was the F.E.A.F. Jungle Rescue Team, established in 1956. Its purpose was primarily to bring rapid aid to those in distress in areas not readily accessible to more conventional forces, and then to help with their recovery from those areas. Obviously the jungle was the most likely area of potential operations, and an aircraft crash was the most likely reason for the rescue processes to go into action. Speed of arrival at the scene of an emergency was essential. With overland travel through the jungle often being measured in days, the parachute and the helicopter were favoured means of transport, backed up by a good pair of legs. The first occasion on which the team was fully committed to a rescue attempt was in August 1957.

On the 22nd of that month a Valetta aircraft of the supply dropping force based at R.A.F. Kuala Lumpur was reported two hours overdue from a leaflet-dropping sortie over the jungles of north Malaya. Members of the rescue team were hurried from their lunch at Changi to collect their kit. Equipment was checked, extra rations issued, and weapons drawn from the armoury. They were flown that afternoon to Kuala Lumpur, where a crash rescue team of No.22 Special Air Service was also waiting to go into action if required, for there was still no sign of the missing aircraft. The following morning the combined teams moved forward to an airstrip at K K Bahru, where they flew as extra 'eyes' in the aircraft that were sweeping the dense jungle for a sign of the missing Valetta. It was found late that afternoon. There was no sign of life near the burned-out wreck, and little hope was raised of there being any survivors from the crew of seven. Low cloud prevented the team from parachuting to the wreck that evening, but at dawn on the following day twelve men – six R.A.F. and six S.A.S. – leapt from four Whirlwind helicopters into the jungle to the east of the crash scene. Squadron Leader Dick Mullins was the first to jump:

As I sat on the sill ready to push myself off into space I found myself worrying about the whole situation. Partly because this was the first time the team had been committed but mainly because our superiors were reasonably convinced that no one could have survived the crash and they were therefore reluctant to allow us to jump. We on our side had argued that it was incumbent upon us to go and see. Success was very much needed for the future standing of the team and here we were on the verge of trying to prove ourselves. But the background worries soon disappeared as I launched myself; I was on my way.

Following the usual check on my canopy I lowered my fifty-pound pack containing explosives, food and medical kit to a position immediately under and touching my feet. The idea was that the equipment protected the parachutist as he entered vertically into the trees and this it certainly did. I crashed through the twigs and branches of one of the 200-foot Malayan giant trees and came to rest dangling unceremoniously 150 feet in mid-air with the trunk of the tree at least thirty feet away.

So far so good — not even a scratch. Out came the lowering line, which was attached to the snagged parachute, and this was lowered into the jungle below, and very quickly I was sliding down it through the dense undergrowth and finally on to terra firma. Later I discovered that many of the other team members had similar experiences with hang-ups varying from two feet to 150 feet above the ground; six members actually crashed straight through the trees and landed directly on the jungle floor; two of the less fortunate ones came to rest upside down in the trees!

Having assembled, luckily without any injuries, we were all very quickly at the scene of the crash.

They found the aircraft concertinaed against the ridge, the front portion badly burnt, and no immediate sign of survivors. However, a few hundred yards away, lost in the dense vegetation, they eventually found two of the injured despatchers. Two others who had previously set off to seek aid were tracked down and brought back. Strapped in their rear-facing seats, these four had survived the impact, and had fled the aircraft just before it exploded with the aircrew still inside. It took two days of exhausting work to clear four acres of primary jungle and construct a platform on the side of the ridge for a Sycamore helicopter to land and to ferry out the survivors and team members, one at a time.

Much was learnt from this operation, particularly in matters of basic organization, communications, and resupply. Perhaps, even more important was the lesson learnt at Command levels that the team existed, and was viable. In 1959, when 22 S.A.S. Regiment returned to the United Kingdom and its crash rescue team was no longer available in north Malaya, the role of the F.E.A.F. team became even more important. That same year an operation of happier consequence was undertaken. It involved a birth, instead of death.

On 20 March, the Commander in Chief at Headquarters F.E.A.F. received a signal from the Governor of Sarawak: "Most grateful your assistance to parachute a R.A.F. doctor to Bario to attend wife of government servant critically ill. Reported may die giving birth, due in two days, without medical care. Bario is 03°43'N 115°33'E."

By ten o'clock the next morning a Valetta was circling between jungle-smothered mountain ridges on the high border of Sarawak and Indonesia, seeking a possible drop zone close to the Pa Mein longhouse where lay the expectant mother – Bulan Iwat. A drop into the trees near Pa Mein itself was discounted as being unacceptably hazardous, and it was decided to jump into a small cleared area close to the longhouse at Bario, twelve miles away. The six men prepared their kit. Squadron Leader Glen Thomson was the doctor, with Senior Tech Mike Hanson as his medical assistant. As interpreter and adviser they had picked up at Kuching Mr John Seal, the operations officer of the Civil Aviation Department of Sarawak. Sergeants Frank Gavin and Paddy Keane were there from the F.E.A.F. school, and Squadron Leader Dick Mullins was leading the team. Frank Gavin recalls the drop:

Two hours after the plane had taken off from Kuching, there was the clearing in the dense jungle down below. Such a small clearing. Shades of Weston on the Green! Mr Seal looked pale. The Valetta made its first pass over the DZ at 600 feet – a dummy run to recce the clearing and the surrounding jungle. On the next pass, Squadron Leader Mullins and Paddy Keane jumped. We watched their parachutes float to the ground. Doc Thomson and Hanson jumped on the second pass, and Mr Seal and myself on the final run. My job was to jump out as quickly as possible in pursuit of Mr Seal so that I would be close to him on the way down, to offer instructions during flight and immediately prior to landing. I saw his canopy open after his somewhat unorthodox exit. When my own canopy had developed I shouted to him to keep his legs together and look down at the ground. Then I looked at the ground myself. Below and not far away lay rough, uneven terrain, littered with deep trenches, ditches, huge logs, and tree trunks. I looked across at Mr Seal. He seemed to be holding a reasonable position, and I wished him luck. I touched down dangerously close to a water hole. I released the harness and ran across to help Mr Seal with his canopy. We were all safe.

The Kelabits of the Bario longhouse had watched the drop with excited interest, and there was much handshaking and drinking of 'borak' before the team set off through the hilly jungle country, on the five-hour trek to Pa Mein. The welcome was warm, and Doc Thomson was soon with his patient. Bulan Iwat appeared to be in premature labour, with the baby in a dangerous transverse position, which with some difficulty the doctor was eventually able to rectify, undoubtedly saving the life of the unborn babe, and probably that of the mother.

There were celebrations that night in the Pa Mein longhouse, and the following day, leaving Bulan Iwat in the reassured charge of a Kelabit midwife, the team began its walk-out to the coast — 400 miles of jungled mountains and turbulent rivers. Twelve days later they emerged at Anduki, where an aircraft waited to return them to Changi. On the 23rd of that month, Bulan Iwat gave birth to a baby girl. She was named Valetta.

At the first opportunity I had volunteered for a place on the Rescue Team.

The team of twenty comprised the P.J.I.s of the School as general members; medical officers and orderlies for obvious reasons; technical personnel to carry out initial and immediate examination of any wreckage; and signallers to maintain radio contact with a rescue control centre. All were volunteers, and it was, of course, but a part-time duty, unlike the fully professional pararescue teams maintained and so excellently equipped by the United States Air Force.

As basic training for the team, one had to complete the two-week aircrew survival course. I joined some twenty aircrew in various stages of apprehension at the Survival School, well sited along a stretch of sandy, palmy shore to the east of Changi airfield. In the cool, attap-roofed huts we were lectured on the theory and psychology of survival, on the principles of jungle navigation, on the search and rescue organization and on the methods of attracting its attention. Outside, stripped in the sun, we improvised items of survival equipment, constructed simple shelters, and for our lunch killed and cooked chickens in earth-ovens on the beach. Then in the second week we put it all to practice in the Malayan jungle. For five days we carried our improvised packs, ate improvised meals, and slept in improvised shelters. We were drenched most of the time, either in sweat or tropical rain. We thought of beer and baths and a steak in Fosters', but in a perverse sort of way it was enjoyable. It was particularly enjoyable getting out.

After the basic course, there was more for me to learn that was specific to rescue team requirements. I was classed as a 'general member'.

"That means you'll be swinging an axe with the rest of us," said Dai Hurford.

But clearing jungle to make a landing zone for a helicopter wasn't all axe work: explosives and a power saw were usually more expedient, and I was taught to use both. The system for 'blowing' trees was to place a 'cutting charge' at the base of the trunk, and a 'pushing charge' further up to give the tree a nudge in the desired direction. We practised at Seletar, and by choosing trees with a definite lean, I usually got them to go the way I declared they would.

I learnt too how to use the lowering gear that we would carry for parachuting into trees. It comprised a 200-foot length of webbing, coiled tightly in a canvas bag strapped to the side of the thigh. The loose end of the webbing was threaded through the canvas 'bikini' round the loins, and then through a metal ring at waist level and in front of the body, to be secured firmly to the parachute harness. One would land in the tree-tops with the bergen rucksack lowered to a position just below the feet where it would take the initial impact of the foliage. The canopy would snag in the branches, and when one was dangling securely, the immediate action was to make another tie if possible to a nearby bough, as canopies had been known to become dislodged from their 'snag' during the subsequent descent. The roll of webbing was next dropped clear to hang below, hopefully all the way to the ground. The harness was then undone and gingerly vacated, and by lifting the webbing and allowing it to run through the friction ring at an easily controlled speed, the parachutist abseiled to earth. It was quite simple in the hangar.

The team made regular practice parachute descents, sometimes from Whirlwind helicopters in the early mornings on Changi airfield, or from Twin Pioneers at Sembawang, or from Hastings and Argosies at Kuantan, a large DZ on the east coast of Malaya, where I landed once far too close to a greeny-gold, four-foot-long snake that slithered off in one direction almost as fast as I moved in the other.

And there were, of course, periodic team exercises. On the first in which I was involved we were to parachute at dawn on to a disused airstrip in central Malaya, trek to a supposed crash site, take a resupply of heavy equipments and explosives, and in the shortest time possible construct a landing site from which helicopters could recover the 'casualties'. It was the classic rescue situation.

We were a little worried about the DZ. It was only 60 yards wide. Squadron Leader Jim Davies, commanding the F.E.A.F. School and leading the team at that time, assured everyone that it would be all right, but with a certain lack of logic also reminded us constantly of the stumps and rocks and other hazards that lurked in the high grass and fern that had crept out of the jungle to surround the old airstrip. It was some small relief to see Flight Lieutenant Jack Huntingdon standing by the Hastings when we arrived at the 48 Squadron pans, burdened with our rucksacks and parachutes.

"Are you still jumping out of bloody aeroplanes?" he said.

Jack was one of the most experienced 'droppers' in the business. But I was still a bit edgy. For those who have free fallen, there appears a certain lack of independence about static-line jumping. They don't mind coping with parachuting problems of their own making, but there's not much scope for initiative from 1,000 feet with a plain canopy. So the adrenalin was flowing nicely when I leapt out into the early sunlight – certainly there was a great clarity of perception and speed of reaction. I noted the rivets on the underside of the tailplane as I slid below it on my ride down the slipstream, and I had the rucksack away before the 'chute had taken a second breath, and the drift figured out and a liftweb down before the load had stopped bouncing on the end of its suspension rope. But there was no need for frantic steering. Jack put us right down the centre of the strip, even though there was a cross-breeze. We laughed at our worries as we bundled our parachutes.

We hoisted our bergens and followed Jim Davies through the high fern, where the heat lay like a wet, suffocating blanket, then on through tangled secondary growth into deeper, darker jungle, where after three miles we arrived at the 'crash'. The resupply was radioed for, and whilst some organized its reception, others of us set up our base camp. Hammocks made of parachute canopies were slung between trees, with poncho capes strung above them like gabled roofs to keep off most of the inevitable rain. Fortified by a brew of tea and a can of steak, we then went to work on the landing zone.

It began to rain. Torrentially. It was like working in a lukewarm shower bath as we hacked away the undergrowth, blew over trees, and sawed and dragged them. The power saws gave up, drowned. But we could already see a grey circle of sodden sky over our heads. Then we came to a great hump of tangled roots and earth.

"We'll blow it," said Jim.

Nobody was quite sure how much plastic explosive was needed to remove a mound such as that, but there was no shortage of advice and willing hands.

"Just a bit more in this side, I think ... "

We withdrew a short way into the undergrowth, and the fuse was lit. With a thunderclap the mound leapt up and came tearing through the trees at us, in large lumps. We picked ourselves up and crept wonderingly back to the clearing. The hummock was gone. In its place smoked a crater that was worth at least four hummocks.

"Well, don't stand there looking at it – fill it in!" said Jim.

We shovelled and levelled, hacked and chopped, until sudden darkness was upon us, then we went back to the camp site to coax a fire into life and hang our sodden clothes around it. Another can of steak, a drink of Oxo laced with a tot of rum, then into the hammocks, and it seemed only a moment later that I was waking to the repeated kee-kee-kar of a dawn bird and the occasional and sudden splat of water drops in the poncho as they fell from tree-tops wreathed in mist. We ate our porridge, drank sweet black tea,. laughed unkindly at Dai Hurford who had mosquito bites like pigeon eggs on his forehead, and went back to the clearing.

There was no rain this time, but soon came the sun, who seemed to concentrate all his attention on this new hole in the jungle, as though curious about it. But at last the job was done — a clearing 30 yards across, with an approach line also carved through the taller trees, regulation size for one Whirlwind. We radioed for the helicopter, which said that it couldn't come until the next morning, so we bathed naked in a brown stream, then burnt off the leeches, and dried in the sun. We spent another night with the mosquitoes, then the Whirlwind came to lift us out, and back to Changi.

"Go home and do the washing up now," said Jake McLoughlin as we tramped across the hot tarmac with our bergens.

On the only major operation in which I was involved, we in fact left our parachutes on their racks, where they were always maintained, fitted and ready for instant use. The parachute was already becoming a less likely form of transport for the rescue team. There were few anticipated areas of operation that could not now be reached by helicopter, which provided a safer and usually quicker means of entry. If the helicopter was unable to land, it could use its winch to lower men into the tree-tops, whence they could continue their journey to the ground with their own tree-lowering gear, exactly as they would if suspended under their parachutes. The parachute capability was still retained, however, for that unforeseeable occasion that might be out of range of helicopters, or for which helicopters might not be immediately available.

The team was likely to be called out at any time, day or night, from work or from home. I was well fed on steak, and thinking of bed, when the landrover came.

"Rescue team call-out, sir," said the driver.

My bergen was ready packed on top of the wardrobe. I stuffed extra socks and a couple more tins of sardines into a side pocket, kissed Ed goodnight, then hurried down the Tampines Road, to join the rest of the team in the Changi transit mess, eating bacon and eggs.

"Army helicopter — a Scout — gone in somewhere near Kluang. They haven't located it yet. We can't do anything until daylight, so we're going up by truck," said Flight Lieutenant Kip Gilpin, second in command of the team.

We motored up across the Causeway and through Johore, the headlights shining silver on the ranks of rubber trees as we wound through the plantation country. We had two hour's sleep at Kluang, and were standing by when the horizons turned grey. A rescue control centre had been quickly set up in the Army Air Corps offices. The Squadron Commander and the R.A.F. rescue controller were marking off areas on a large map – areas of higher and lesser probabilities. The Scout, flying east out of Kluang, had sent out a 'mayday' distress call only seven minutes after take off. It may have left its planned route slightly in order to skirt heavy storm clouds that had been in the area at the time, but even so, if it had crashed immediately after making its call, it couldn't be more than ten miles away. No flares had been seen during the night, and there was no sound from the 'sarah' distress beacons that all aircrew carried in their survival kit. Perhaps the two men were already walking out, hoping to make it for lunch. Or perhaps they were injured. Anyway, it shouldn't take long to find them ...

The first search helicopters clattered away into the dawn. We sat leaning against our rucksacks outside the ops room, ready to board the stand-by helicopters as soon as word came through on the radio that the Scout had been spotted. We could hear the reports coming into the ops room.

"Nothing in sector charlie five ... proceeding to charlie six ... "

One hour passed. Two. The sun was up. We took our shirts off, enjoying the warmth. Someone fetched coffee. The helicopters had returned, refuelled quickly, and headed back over the rubber plantations to the jungled hills beyond. Three hours. Surely if they were all right they would have put up some flares by now? They must have heard the search aircraft. Then through the ops room window we heard the radio crackle urgently.

" ... tail rotor ... got a sighting on the tail rotor ... south of the Mersing Road, about one mile ... hold one for co-ordinates ... "

Within ten minutes a Naval Wessex was putting six of us down on the road. We went in on a compass bearing through thick, wet secondary growth, until we could hear the Whirlwind hovering as a marker over the spot where the red and white tail rotor had been glimpsed through the foliage, then we slithered and sweated as fast as we could towards the sound, until the racket of the blades was directly above us and the trees were whipping in their downwash. We spread out, searching ... searching for wreckage, for men. Instead, we found a red and white boundary post lying half throttled in vines where it had been left by some survey team. We tramped out to the road, swearing.

More aircraft joined the search, extending now into areas of lesser probability. We took it in turns to fly as observers, adding more eyes to the quest. The helicopters swept their own allocated stretches of jungle, hovering and darting like dragonflies over a vast green pond. We lay on our bellies, looking out of the open door. There was the occasional glitter of water through the laced branches, a flurry of startled gibbons in the tree-tops, the brown and white swoop of an eagle across a clearing – and mile upon mile of grey-green leaves swimming and swirling before our eyes. But no Scout. The jungle had swallowed it, and closed over it like still waters. By nightfall there was still no sign.

As we fell into our bunks we could hear the monotonous drone of the Shackleton, coming and going as it flew in long sweeps high above the search area, its radio receiving gear patiently waiting for a bleep from 'sarah'.

We were roused early. A police post had received reports of lights in the forests just to the east of us. Five of us drove out in a landrover, along a logging track where there was elephant dung like footballs. We took to our feet and splashed and tore our way round a three-mile sweep of the area. Nothing. We drove back, dropping iodine on the leeches and plucking them off.

None of us knew the two men we were looking for, but they were constant in our minds. Were they trying to walk out still? Were they lying injured? Perhaps unable to move, listening to the choppers flying in search over their heads? Or dead?

The ops centre was full of frustration and dirty coffee cups. The next morning, up early again, thick mist kept the pilots fuming on the ground for two hours while we dozed with our heads on our bergens. They got airborne at last, to start the third day of the search.

The message came crackling into the ops room at about eleven o'clock.

"I've got it ... I've got it ... stand by for position ... " and everyone was grabbing for kit and lacing their boots and waking up and saying, "Wha's happened ... wha's happened?" then running for the helicopters on the pans.

The pilot of an Auster had spotted the fuselage of the Scout with a lucky angled sighting through the trees as he was banking at the end of a run – in a part of the jungle that we had flown over a dozen times before without seeing it. There was a logging track close by. The Wessex slithered gingerly down between high green walls to land us on it, and we walked in, less than a mile. The Scout was lying very quietly on its side, like a strange alien creature asleep amongst the vines and broad-leaved tropical plants. Both men were dead, still strapped in the cockpit of shattered perspex. The Doc thought that they had broken their necks on impact, and died instantly. For that alone we were glad.

We carried them out to the logging track, in impersonal canvas body bags, then sat quietly in the rain eating the last of our glucose sweets as we waited for the helicopters to come and take us all away.

10/ Free Wine

There was a lighter side to parachuting in the Far East, although at first it was not easy to find.

Sergeant Keith Teesdale had made the first free-fall parachute descent in Singapore in January 1961, when he jumped from a Beverley at 12,000 feet above Sembawang, to land closer than intended to the swimming pool. The following year, parachutists of 22 S.A.S. had jumped from the same height in Malaya, but there was as yet no specific military requirement for free-fall parachuting in the Far East, and following our Thailand venture, Douggie Brown's recommendation that an official display team be formed had not been adopted.

So, unable to free fall on a military basis, I sought permission from the Civil Aviation Authority in Singapore to jump as a private parachutist, and at the same time wrote to the Royal Singapore Flying Club to offer my services as a display jumper for any shows that they might be planning.

Nobody in the Civil Aviation offices actually said that I was eccentric, but their opinions were not well disguised. The dark man in the white shirt spoke of insuperable difficulties in finding air space for parachuting on such a small island. I persisted. He changed his tack.

"Do you have a permit, sir?"

"No. That's what I've come here for. A permit."

He went away, looked through several drawers, and came back. They didn't have parachuting permits. I showed him my F.A.I. international licence. Would that do? He sent for another man in a white shirt. They examined my licence with interest, agreed that the photograph was a very good likeness, but the licence did not constitute an authority to fall out of aeroplanes over Singapore, on purpose. I still persisted.

"Are you a pilot, sir?"

"No. I keep telling you – I'm a parachutist."

"Ah! Well, sir – you cannot possibly go falling out of aeroplanes unless you have a pilot's licence," was the final edict, delivered with triumphant smiles as they at last found a good reason to prevent me from killing myself. I decided to give up for a month, by which time they might have forgotten me, and I could start again.

Then Malaysia happened. This union of Far Eastern States was declared in August 1963 and celebrations were called for, including an air show at Paya Lebar, the civilian airport. The Royal Singapore Flying Club looked around for suitable items to attract and entertain the crowds. I was asked if I would jump. I mentioned the insuperable difficulties. They would be overcome, I was assured. Would I jump? Would I jump!

I asked Snowy Robertson to join me. "I might have known!" said Mrs Snowy.

It was not quite the same as our well-regulated display team days. There was a different atmosphere. Free fall was unknown in Singapore, and we were curiosities. Although I tried to publicize us as reasonable people displaying a safe but exhilarating art, they would not hear of it. We were foolhardy stuntmen. Dicers with death. They wouldn't have it any other way, and when I protested that we were certainly no stuntmen, that we weren't getting paid a Singapore cent for it, that we were doing it for fun, then they took that as sure confirmation of our idiocy. Rudi, a mid-European who was to pilot the Cessna 172 for us, kept shaking his head and muttering, "You are crazy, bloody crazy ... "

As we sat in our white jump overalls in the clubhouse before the show, people were surprised to see that we had wives and children, like normal folk; that we drank fresh lime and read the sports pages of the *Straits Times*, just like them. They were puzzled. They couldn't reconcile our normalcy with leaping from aeroplanes. "And they don't look a bit frightened!" you could hear them thinking.

We were very much on our own too. No DZ party to work out the dropping instructions; no navigator to get us over the release point and switch on a green light. It was all ours. It was quite exhilarating, though not without difficulties. We spread a white cross just in front of the crowd barriers, and showed someone how to light the signal flares when we dropped. I spoke with the met man who assured me that the wind might be from the north or it could be from the south, and then with the air traffic controller who said he was running an international airport and not a circus, and that he wasn't going to hold up PANAM for anybody, that he would let us drop when he was good and ready, and would we please keep off his runway.

We kitted up, and walked out to the Cessna through bright sunlight and curious stares. I briefed Rudi. " ... nice flat turns Rudi, and don't forget to put the brakes on when I yell CUT so that I can get out on to the wheel ... " He said that yes, he would do all that, and that we were bloody crazy. We climbed in, and waved to the brown faces and white shirts that lined the fences as we taxied out over the grass. There was a long wait at the end of the runway, and we thought that they had forgotten us, but at last we were away and the prop-wash came like air-conditioning through the open door. We ran in over the airport buildings to drop a streamer at 2,000 feet, and watched it wriggle earthwards to land some 500 yards down-wind of the white cross. We visually measured off the same distance up-wind to mark the opening point on our minds — a spot right on the palm-fringed edge of the airfield.

"Take her up Rudi ... "

"Okay. You are crazy, bloody crazy ... "

I watched the island spreading out below, and traced the roads I knew, and filled in with interest the gaps between them. We circled at 5,000 feet, waiting for a DC8 to land and a Boeing to take off. We could see them down there, like toys on the model airport. It was getting cold, and we felt forgotten again.

"Turn off the air conditioning, will you, Rudi ... " shouted Snowy.

"Bloody crazy ... " said Rudi.

Then the tower was calling us in, and Rudi banked us round, suddenly and steeply. I sorted my legs out, and knelt in the open door, tapping Rudi on the shoulder to give him the directions that would bring us over the DZ, to the opening point.

"Cut!"

The engine faded. I tugged the pin from the smoke flare on my ankle. My right foot battled through the slipstream for the wheel, where I would perch for a moment while Snowy followed into the door. I found it, and swung out. As I put my weight on the tyre, it spun like a treadmill, and pitched me backwards into space. I caught a glimpse of Snowy laughing in the door, then a mouthful of acrid fumes as I somersaulted through my own smoke trail. But we were in the right place, and it was a smooth ride down, both of us coming in slow and easy on to the target. The 10,000 people we had forgotten all about applauded wildly, as though we had done it all for them. Rudi taxied up in the Cessna as we were bundling our 'chutes.

"Sorry about the brakes. I forgot," he shouted.

"I know you did."

"You are crazy. Bloody crazy ... "

We repacked our parachutes on the grass outside the clubhouse, with the sun hot on our backs. Small boys asked technical questions, and small girls tripped over the rigging lines. Small men watched, in silence. They wanted to say something, but weren't sure what it should be. One intrigued Malayan summoned courage as I jammed the last ripcord pin into its grommet and snapped the elastics on.

"Will it ever open again, sir?" he asked politely.

"Come back tomorrow and find out," I said, with an eye to business.

We jumped five times during the three days of the air show. Not without incident. On the second jump, the TU canopy that Snowy was using blew up when he opened it. He flew his reserve, and came in smoothly, accurately and to the great delight of the crowd, under the reserve and the tattered remnants of his main parachute. It was Dai Hurford's parachute, so he wasn't terribly worried.

On another jump, Rudi remembered the brakes, but he forgot to keep his turns flat, and his vigorous banking on the corrections I asked for completely threw my spotting out of line. We couldn't afford to go round again, so I gave what I hoped was an expressive shrug of the shoulders to Snowy, and dived through the door. Instead of being over the corner of the airfield, we were above a kampong of palms and corrugated iron roofs, and track as we did, we couldn't make up for the error. "Sorry," I said, as we walked back across the runway with our 'chutes bundled in our arms.

"So you bloody well should be — sir," said Snowy.

We were thanked for our small contribution to Malaysia Day, and then the insuperable difficulties returned. Occasionally we were able to jump as 'civilians' from a hired Cessna into Service sports meetings and charity events, and then in 1964 the Army and the Royal Marines — the latter inspired by Lieutenant 'Ram' Seeger — began to lay the foundations of what was to eventually become a thriving Joint Services parachute club in Singapore. At the same time, in Malaya, the Australian Army began jumping regularly at Kluang, and in August that year they organized the first Malaysian skydiving championships, in association with the Royal Flying Club of Singapore. We jumped on to the sun-baked airfield at Kluang in winds that seemed to change direction every 400 feet, and with more luck than skill I became the first Malaysian parachuting champion.

By the time of the first anniversary of Malaysia Day, Singapore had withdrawn from the federation, so our services were not required at Paya Lebar. Instead, we were invited to jump at celebrations in Kuala Lumpur.

We had by then been joined in the Far East gy Sergeants Jake McLoughlin and Andy Sweeney, and also by Squadron Leader Mike Stamford who was campaigning energentically for official recognition of a Far East Air Force Parachute Display Team. It was he who arranged for the Royal Malayan Air

Force to drop us at Kuala Lumpur, as part of their air display. We were offered the services of a Single Pioneer, a high-winged communications aircraft. I had been involved in the free-fall clearance trials of the 'Single Pin' at Boscombe Down two years earlier, but had forgotten the various limitations put on its usage for that purpose, and the Royal Malaysian Air Force had never heard of them.

"How many of you?" asked Squadron Leader Mike Norman, a Royal Air Force pilot seconded to the Malayans.

"Four," we said hopefully, although there were only seats for three.

"Squeeze in," he said. We did.

"How high do you want to go?"

"How high can it get?"

"I don't know," he said, and started up.

We all thought him an excellent Squadron Leader. We dropped the streamer, then up went the nose of the Single Pin, to circle out over the sprawled city, and the brown scars of the new development areas cutting into the green hills, and the rubber plantations beyond. We climbed up through wispy cloud, skirting a few scattered puffs of cumulus. We levelled out at 13,000 feet, and tumbled through the door into all that beautiful sparkling air like kids coming out of school. Then came one of those fleeting magical moments that happen once in every hundred or so jumps. When I looked below I found myself falling towards a patch of cloud, on the glistening white surface of which I could see the giant shadow of my spreadeagled body, framed by a complete rainbow. We hurtled towards each other, my shadow and I, mesmerized, until I burst through the halo into total greyness, taking the shadow with me. I flew through the cloud and dropped suddenly from its belly into sunlight once more. We tacked in over the runway, and all landed well. And that was just the rehearsal!

The show itself seemed to be in jeopardy, for as we ate our steaks in the friendly atmosphere of the Flying Club, turbans of cumulus were building in the skies. We went outside to repack on the grass. When the rain started, we had all finished except Snowy. We covered him and his half-folded 'chute with ponchos and canvas, beneath which he burrowed up and down for several minutes, to eventually emerge dripping with sweat but with parachute packed.

"It'll never open," we assured him.

The tropical storm lashed the airfield for almost an hour. The palms bent before the wind, and the monsoon drains gurgled happily. But it was our lucky day. The rain stopped, the runways began to steam, and a big blue gap came and sat right over the airfield, waiting for us. The Squadron Leader spiralled the Single Pin up into it. I kept one eye on the dwindling airfield, the other on the towers of cumulus around us, not only because they were magnificent, but also because they could do strange things to the winds if they came too close. At 13,000 feet we grinned. At 14,000 we laughed out loud, and at 15,000 we levelled out as the engine started to protest. It was cold, and Andy Sweeney was turning blue, but it was magnificent. I knelt in the door to spot the drop. The slipstream was a blast of icy exhaust fumes, which I only cared for in small doses, but the Squadron Leader's run needed hardly any correction − until the signal flare winked into life far, far below and the smoke drifted off at right angles to the expected line. I called for a hard left, held it for a few hundred yards, and dived, into 75 seconds of free air. For much of it, I flew down the face of a great cumulus mountain, with the sensation of falling from a cliff, and the rest I gambolled away with loops and a final swoop to where I thought the opening point ought to be. It was a new Malaysian altitude record. There were soft landings around the cross, and another steak before we were flown home. "Long live Malaysia," said Jake.

While Squadron Leader Stamford pursued official recognition for us, and at the same time sought a quota of Service parachutes for us to use, we continued our 'civilian' jumping whenever there was an opportunity − as at R.A.F. Tengah, where we put on a Father Christmas drop for the children. I jumped as Santa, with cloak and beard pinned well down, while Andy Sweeney and Jake were dressed as snowmen, in bulky white suits borrowed from the cold storage refrigerator rooms. The jump was no trouble, but we hadn't realized what we had let ourselves in for, as we were whisked straight before the yelling hordes to present their gifts − more than 200 of them, and us still in our gear, panting for a cold shandy.

"What do you mean, am I real? 'Course I'm bloody well real ... "

At last came the authority to form an official team − two months before I was due to leave Singapore and return to the U.K. But in those two months I enjoyed some of the most pleasant parachuting ever. We jumped from an Argosy at Changi, early each Saturday morning.

Before it was light I would freewheel the car down the slope from our Thomson Rise bungalow so as not to wake the family. The vegetable stalls would already be awake along the Thomson Road, and at Pongol corner the poultry buyers would be tying bunches of live chickens to their motor scooters and stuffing bundles of protesting ducks into car-boots.

On the airfield we would kit up with the new 'Conquistadors' that Mike

Stamford had obtained for us. We would walk out to the Argosy with the stars fading and palm trees leaning against the dawn. Run in over Changi Jail for the streamer drop, then watch the island spread itself as we climbed in early sunlight to 12,000 feet. The fishing traps pointed like arrows out to sea, and Kallang would make a good DZ, and the Padang down there – now that would be a drop ... and there was that little island that we shared with a sea-eagle for one whole idyllic day, and the Thomson Reservoir where we walked on Sundays, and the estate, and the white dot of the bungalow where Ed and the kids would be waking up ...

"Running in ... " someone would say, and we would go through the final checks, and pull our goggles down.

We might go over the tailgate as a grouped four, charging straight off at a run and letting the tumble take us where it would, enjoying the drunken dream of it before we split and scattered. Or we might pile out after Jake and try to get in close to smile at his hand-held camera. Or go off solo and track out over the end of the runway to the sailing club, and back in a wide sweeping turn over the white buildings of the headquarters and above the sports field. Or throw back loops one after the other for the sheer intoxicating joy of it.

The air was like free, sparkling wine.

11 / A Means of Transport

We fitted our parachutes and prepared our loads in a bare hangar, in blue-green light. Those who were ready, and had been checked, went outside for a smoke, or ate chocolate, or squatted around their patrol commanders to pore again over the maps spread on the cold concrete floor.

"All right then lads ... fit up! Let's 'ave you ... "

Sergeant Tommy Atkinson chivvied us along, lining us up in stick order. Two dozen of us.

"Now listen carefully lads ... "

Silence.

"'as everyone got 'is killing knife?"

Some people had been known to take Tommy seriously. Like the course of young Sandhurst cadets at P.T.S. several years before. Early in their training Tommy had taken them to one side and with grim expression had announced that news was just coming through of a serious international crisis. Hostilities were imminent, and a small parachute force was urgently needed for a special mission in Albania. As 16 Para Brigade and the S.A.S. were not available, volunteers were being sought from the trainees then at P.T.S. ... the beguiled cadets stepped forward to a man.

When Tommy had checked us, we filed out of the hangar, wearing our parachutes and carrying our bergens, and crossed the tarmac to the Argosy which squatted humming to itself in the orange lights of the dispersal pans.

We squeezed ourselves into the banks of seats, holding the bergens between our legs for take-off, then composed ourselves as best we could for the flight of nearly three hours. Some still studied their maps. Others munched bisuits. Most dozed, rousing periodically to curse the men who trod on their legs as they made their way through the packed fuselage to the toilet funnel. Two hours gone, and we were looking at our watches. The tins of blacking were passed round, to darken faces and hands, then the lights were dimmed to prepare our eyes for the night outside.

Would it be on? The long-range forecast had not been good. The weather was expected to worsen during the night. We might just get there before the wind and cloud. We wouldn't know until we reached the DZ. The engines maintained their steady chorus as we swung down over the North German Plain. Ten minutes to P hour. We stood up, hooked our static lines to the overhead cable, checked our equipment. Tommy Atkinson came down the stick, tightening and checking.

"You've been compromised," he said with a serious face. "The DZ's surrounded. You'll all be in the bag by midnight, standing there in your shreddies ... "

"Sod off ... "

We shuffled aft to action stations, one hand on the strop, the other grasping the front of the bergen suspended below the reserve parachute. The weight was beginning to drag on the shoulders. The doors were opened, and the coolness of the night eddied up the fuggy fuselage. The first man in the stick was suddenly bathed in red light, then in green, and was gone, the rest of us following, as fast as we could, trying to keep tight to the man in front so that we would be close in the air and close on the ground. My canopy open, I steered away from the dark blobs around me, dropped the bergen to the end of its suspension rope, and looked into the darkness below. There was cloud-filtered moonlight, just enough to show the ground, but not its distance. The bergen hit it, then me. It was made of heather, soft and cold.

I remained lying on the ground, listening to the Argosy droning off into the night sky, checking its direction, for that would be the line of the stick. I stood up, surrounded by silence, and stuffed my parachute, container straps, reserve and helmet into the carrying bag, which I then shouldered with my bergen, and set off cautiously along the line of flight. Humpy figures were converging in the gloom, with the occasional chink of a weapon and the swish of boots in the heather. We lay quietly, the warmth of excitement wearing off and the cold of the night beginning to bite through the combat clothing. The stick commander checked us off. We were all there, nobody injured. We filed towards the zigzag skyline of conifers that bordered the DZ, and in their shelter thankfully dumped and hid the parachute bags.

The group was splitting into its four-man patrols. Some loped straight off into the night, in single file. Others huddled whispering together for a moment. I located my other three. The Corporal confirmed our position on the map, shielding his pencil torch, and reminded us once more of our intended route. There was half a Battalion out there in the darkness, looking for us, and somewhere the interrogation team was rubbing its hands in anticipation. Evasion is a game of bluff. You look at your map and try to select a route that is good, but not good enough to be obvious. You think what you would do if you were on the other side, knowing that they are

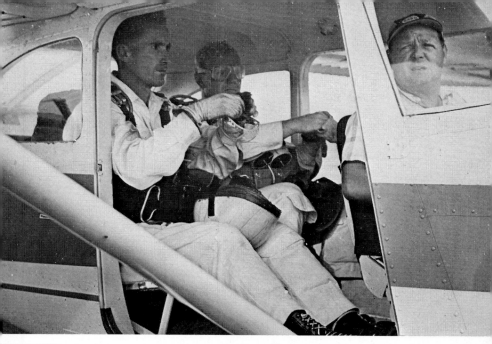

"There was a long wait at the end of the runway. We thought they had forgotton us." Myself, Snowy and Rudi, impatient before take-off at Paya Lebar (*page 121*)

Snowy coming in on reserve and his torn main canopy at Paya Lebar. "It was Dai Hurford's parachute, so he wasn't terribly worried" (*page 122*)

R.A.F. Detachment Special Forces, 1966. About the only time we wore our best blue. Left to right standing: Tommy Atkinson, Bert King, Eric Harrington, Brian Jones, Frank Weatherly. Left to right sitting: Peter Burgess, Bill Last, Myself, Ben Cass

S.A.S. free faller in flight, with the bergen behind the thighs *(Crown Copyright)*

" . . . my presence was essential . . . " With the 1971 Falcons in Hong Kong. Left to right standing: Myself, Gwynne Morgan, Doug Dewar, Harry Parkinson, Doug Peacock, Sid Garrad, Alan Jones. Left to right kneeling: Henry McDonald, Snowy, Bob Souter. On the injured list at this time were Ray Willis, Alan Rhind and Dave Ross (*page 160*)

Tracking across Hong Kong harbour at 8,000 feet (*Crown Copyright*)

Touch down, still smoking, in Hong Kong (*Crown Copyright*)

Falcons at play (*Crown Copyright*)

The 1973 Falcons bale out from the ramp of the Hercules at 12,000 feet (*Crown Copyright*)

Flight Sergeant Ken Kidd fits up a VIP (Very Important Parachutist) who came to P.T.S. in 1971 to make a water jump into Studland Bay. "You ought to get your hair cut," said Ken Kidd to Prince Charles. "We've got royalty around, you know . . . " (*Crown Copyright*)

"Hi ho, hi ho, it's off to work we go . . . " John Mace and myself lead
the staff of No. 1 P.T.S. out of the hangar for the 59-man mass free fall (*page 175*)

" . . . fifty-nine of us, straight over the tailgate at a run . . . " (*Crown
Copyright*) (*page 175*)

As Officer Commanding No. 1 P.T.S., I congratulate Flight Sergeant Andy Sweeney on his thousandth descent (*Crown Copyright*)

The end product of P.T.S. Men of No. 16 Parachute Brigade drop into Turkey on a major NATO exercise (*Crown Copyright*)

thinking what they would do if they were you.

We followed the Corporal, heading south. The first mile through heather and along tracks of soft sand was bad. Twenty to go? The moorland gave way to fields that were nobbly with turnips, and the fields led to a broad valley, its slopes stained black with beech woods in the moonlight. We sat for five minutes, looking and listening, for it was a likely place to be caught. But it seemed as peaceful as countryside should be at midnight, so we followed the Corporal − not too closely − into the vale, over fences that creaked too loudly and through a stream that was too cold and up a far side that was too steep, then across three miles of open upland country with a rhythm of hard breathing and a scuff of boots. The wind was rising, and clouds now hid the moon. We skirted the angular shape of a haystack, and heard men blowing on their hands on the sheltered side of it. They weren't very good. I had a childish urge to shout something rude and run away. We lay in a wet ditch at the side of a main road while three landrovers swept by, then ducked across it, and ran for the shelter of the woods on the far side. Five fast miles along straight paths through beech and pine forest, taking it in turns to carry the heavy bergen with the radio in it. There was a short stop to brew coffee and a curry-block over a fire of solid fuel, then we moved on, stiff and chill from sitting, across open country again, with the wind pressed to one cheek like a slab of ice. Only two miles to go. We waded another stream, skirted a farmyard, and climbed the slope beyond. Snow came with the dawn. The Corporal strung his aerials to a tree. We made a wind-break for him out of our ponchos, and froze slowly while he crouched over the radio, gently coaxing the dials. "Come on darlin' ... come ON ... " he pleaded, then he was holding the earphone tight with one hand, scribbling on his pad with the other. We brought the aerial in while he decoded the target message.

"What are we doing, then?" I asked.

"You're going home," he grinned.

I usually did at that stage. I tried to pretend that I was sorry, gave them the rest of my rations, and went back down the hill. The valley was beginning to look like a Christmas card. I begged a breakfast at the farm while I waited for transport to take me out of the exercise ...

For nearly four years I operated out of an office in King's Road, Chelsea, with a team of well-selected P.J.I.s and with terms of reference and chains of command that were adequately vague to allow me the flexibility of action that was essential in supporting some of our more unconventional airborne units. "R.A.F. Detachment to Special Forces" said the little notice over our door. It was a title impressive enough to persuade many an administrator and official that our work was of the utmost importance and that the validity of our sometimes unusual requests was not a matter for discussion.

"Special Forces" was a collective term for a number of units who were under no single command, but who all had in common a generally covert method of operating. Our principle customers were the Special Air Service, the Special Boat Sections of the Royal Marine Commandos, and several smaller units of signallers.

It was a job that brought us closer to the airborne soldier than one can ever hope to get in a pure training environment. I never fully belonged to them, but I jumped when I could into their exercises, shared their water canteens and their curry blocks, bounced across deserts in their landrovers and over choppy waters in their assault craft, lurked at their cocktail parties, sat in the back row at their conferences, and was able to advise them occasionally on that one small part of their task about which I knew something – parachuting.

My concern was not primarily with what these men did, but with getting them there to do it. To men who had learnt the basic techniques at P.T.S. we taught the fundamentals of clandestine parachuting – how to jump with the bergen rucksack instead of the usual weapons container; how to parachute at night in small sticks on to small DZs; how to rendezvous quickly and silently in the darkness after a drop, to cache their parachutes and leave a 'clean' DZ; how to select and mark areas for furtive resupply drops. And having converted them to their operational parachuting role, we helped them to practise it. Planning the airborne aspects of their exercises was never an easy matter, for air support is by its nature less flexible than most of the units who require it, and I spent much time explaining Army requirements to puzzled R.A.F. staff officers, and R.A.F. operating procedures to equally puzzled 'specials'. Then there was the matter of finding places to jump: I surveyed whole countries for small, inconspicuous DZs, and found many a good pub. When all the planning came to fruition, it was the job of my N.C.O.s to prepare the men and despatch them from the aircraft, whilst my officers and I waited on those small, inconspicuous DZs to receive them. Manning DZs, in fact, was my main active role during this period, during which I spent more time watching parachuting than practising it.

Marking a DZ for a static-line drop appears a very simple matter. There are two basic systems. One is to mark – with coloured panels or flares – an 'impact point', which is that spot on the ground where the first man of the stick should land. It is then up to the navigator in the aircraft to calculate and arrive at his 'air release point', which is the position in the air where he should switch on the green light, so that the first man to jump is thrown forward and drifted on to the impact point. This system of 'bombing' parachutists on to an indicated target is the method favoured for mass drops on to big DZs, as practised by the larger airborne formations. However, the impact point and associated markers require more illumination than is compatible with clandestine dropping, the essence of which is to identify the DZ for the aircraft without advertising its presence to a possibly alert enemy. For Special Forces work, therefore, the man on the ground calculates and marks − with a simple system of torches − the 'release point', over which the first man should jump.

In practice, there were always complications. For instance, in Denmark ... Denmark was a favoured venue for Special Forces exercises, by virtue of the realistic opposition provided by the Danish Army, Home Guard, police, population, and dogs. Even the early reconnaissance to select suitable DZs had to be circumspect, carried out in plain clothes and civilian car, a month before the exercise. I became an accomplished skulker.

One developed an eye for a good DZ: almost a DZ syndrome. On holiday we would admire a stretch of French countryside.

"What a glorious view," Ed would say.

"Glorious," I would agree, automatically selecting a good spot for a stick of four from 800 feet.

Anyway, on this occasion, in a rather populated part of Jutland, I found a perfect DZ for the stick of simultaneous six that was to drop. It was a finely ploughed field, hidden from the nearest track by a belt of trees; bordered on one side by a beech wood that could provide a good RV point and immediate cover for the troops; distant from farmyards with sensitive dogs; and quite free of telephone wires and electricity cables and other things unfair to parachutists. It also had an ideal approach line for the aircraft. Perfect.

In the interests of safety we always had another covert look at our DZ before the night of the drop. On this occasion when I took my brisk and inconspicuous walk I discovered that my perfect DZ had been divided neatly down the centre by a newly constructed and very solid Danish fence. I still had all the length I needed for the drop, but instead of 400 yards of width, I now had a choice of two fields each 200 yards across − not much for a night-time static-line drop. That evening I advised the stick commander by telephone of the fence, and told him that, dependent upon wind conditions, I would put the stick into one or other of the two fields that now existed. With radio, compass, and torches I left for the DZ an hour before drop time, with one Dane for company. We parked the car off the road, behind a haystack, and walked the last mile. It was drizzling. The darkness was like a wet blanket. I hoped that the cloud base was high enough. We came off the track and on to the DZ. It had not only been fenced: it had also been recently manured.

Ideally, I would have aimed my stick right down the centre of the DZ, where the fence now stood. Now I had to choose one of the two smaller fields. There was no surface wind. The drizzle was coming straight down. Nor could I see any cloud movement to give some indication of upper drift. However, the met man had said that there might be a little wind from the south-west at 800 feet. That was all I had to go on, so I set up my release point just to the west of the fence, allowing 150 yards throw forward and 200 yards of drift to take the sticks across the obstruction and spread them down the middle of the eastern field. I sent the Dane to stand with his torch thirty paces in front of me, to give the pattern of two lights aligned on the run-in track. Mine would flash a code letter. I turned on the radio, and squatted in the dark drizzle to wait. Right on time, four minutes to P hour ...

"This is four three calling DZ bravo ... do you read?"

"DZ bravo reading four three loud and clear ... you are clear to drop ... "

"Four three ... understand clear drop ... "

I saw the navigation lights winking over the horizon, disappearing for a moment in low cloud, but coming out again, well on track. We flashed our torches at him. He veered a little as he picked us up. They would be at action stations up there now, anxiously watching the jump lights. I could hear the familiar Argosy whine, and no doubt all the Home Guard in Jutland could too. The dark shape came right over us, on a good run, and spawned black blobs into the sky. They were barely distinguishable. I put my torch out, and watched for the met man's south-westerly breeze to take the blobs across the fence and into the eastern field. Instead, they were gliding silently in the opposite direction. I swore, grabbed the bergen with the radio in it, and set off after them with persistent clods of manure clinging to my boots. All twelve landed safely, in the middle of the western field. I joined them at the rendezvous on the edge of the wood.

"Bloody marvellous," whispered the stick commander, who hadn't known which of the two narrow fields I had aimed for. "Dunno how you do it ... "

"It takes practice," I said.

The met men were more often right, and usually there was a surface wind to measure. That too could cause problems. There is a book of rules that defines the wind limits and the gust ranges acceptable for day and for night descents. But a DZ safety officer requires to exercise judgement as well as the rule book. Is the DZ surface dangerously hard? Or forgivingly soft? How well prepared are the troops? Are they likely to be tired from a long and bumpy low-level flight? How important to the overall exercise is the drop? Is that borderline wind dying, or increasing? Give them a green, or a red? Jock Fox had the answer ...

Jock, at one time School Warrant Officer at P.T.S. and subsequently commissioned, manned many a DZ for 44 Para Brigade. He rarely bothered with a radio.

"The crews can never understand me anyway. Always switch me off ... " he said in his broad Scots accent. He would take a pocket full of Verey cartridges instead, and a small 'Dwyer' anemometer. He had such a device with him on a daylight exercise in Germany where he was to drop his favourites – the 15th (Scottish) Battalion ...

The wind was ... pretty high. The Jocks were coming in from Scotland. The Regulars had already cancelled, and the Americans too, they had cancelled on the weather forecast and were coming in by road. Then Brigadier Pat O'Kane turns up, twenty minutes before P hour, and with him was this American General. And they stood there watching me and Dick Watson getting everything ready, and it was blowing a bit. Then Brigadier Pat shouts across to me, "What's the wind, Jock?" So I held up my Dwyer and I said, "Oh ... marginal sir ... thirteen, fourteen knots ... I think we might just be lucky." Well, we waited. And it was blowing a bit. Then the American General said, "Pat, I don't think you're gonna get your Jocks down." So Pat O'Kane looked at me, and I never said a word. Five minutes before P hour I told Dick Watson to light the flares, and the General and the Brigadier were holding on to their hats and looking a bit old fashioned. Then the aircraft appeared. So I gave him a green. And out the Jocks came, and they piddled across the sky ... psheeeewwww ... Anyway, they landed. UP, and away! Marvellous. It was soft, you see. And Pat O'Kane called me across and said, "Not bad, Jock. By the way, what IS the wind?" So I took out my Dwyer again and said, "Oh, thirteen knots, sir – just on the borderline", and the American General says "Let me have a look at that instrument. How does the goddam thing work?" So I says, "Well, you just hold it up to the wind and the wind blows through this little hole and pushes a little white ball up and down this tube so that you can read off the wind strength." "Does it?" he says. "Oh yes," I says. "Let's have a look," he says, and he and Pat O'Kane stood there holding this thing up and staring at it for about a minute. Then Pat O'Kane says to me, "Where's the little white ball?" "Oh, I forgot to tell you," I says. "I lost the little white ball out of it three months ago ... "

Our DZs were not always on land. The Special Boat Sections of the Royal Marines had a requirement to parachute into water. After they had gained their basic qualification at P.T.S. we put them through a 'water descent course' – six jumps, progressing from 'clean fatigue'* by day to jumps in wet-suits with heavy equipment at night. Water, of course, provides a reasonably soft landing medium. The main hazard lies in being dragged through the water by a parachute that would act as a sail in a wind of more than five knots. So the technique was based on undoing the harness before entering the water, at the same time ensuring that it still gave adequate support. The equipment eventually carried by the four-man teams included an inflatable craft, its associated engine, and fuel. After landing in the water the team would regroup, assemble and inflate their boat, climb aboard, and set about their true business. They were heavy loads with which to parachute, and were later to be superseded by a dropping technique that allowed the boat – already inflated – to be dropped off the back of a Hercules on a platform, with the crew following it out and using steerable static-line parachutes to land alongside it.

Having learnt water-descent techniques in the relatively sheltered waters of Poole Harbour and Studland Bay, the Marines then practised them on more realistic exercises. Kilbrannan Sound, between Kintyre and the Isle of Arran, was a favoured DZ. From the swaying deck of a motor fishing vessel (MFV) I would try to keep the aldis lamp steady on the nav. lights of the aircraft as they came winking up the channel between the black shapes of the hills, then wait anxiously for the parachutists to swim in from the darkness. When they were all on board there would be mugs of hot soup in a fo'c'sle strewn with rubber suits and weapons and wet Marines, while the MFV throbbed and lurched up the coast for an hour or two. The Marines would help each other into their frog-suits again, and I would watch them slip quietly into the black water, hunched into their canoes or trailing phosphorescence as they swam in a close group towards an invisible shore, to blow up the Crinan Canal or Garelochead. Then for me a few hours in the sleeping bag with a lifejacket for a pillow, and wake to early morning stillness and the smell of frying bacon alongside the quay at Largs or Crinan.

Then we progressed from coastal waters to deep-sea dropping, using a submarine as 'reception'. This required more planning than usual. I would arrive at Gosport for the conferences, conspicuous in R.A.F. uniform, to be shown aboard one of several submarines lying at H.M.S. *Dolphin*. I climbed down and up ladders, squeezed and ducked, begged sailors' pardons, cracked my shins and hit my head, and admired men brave enough to be submariners. When I next met the submarine it would be in mid-Channel,

* Without equipment containers or other encumbrances.

lurking silently on moonlit water. We monitored the drops from a 'gemini', scudding over the smooth swell as the Argosy flew overhead and the dark shapes drifted down into the sea. We dragged the 'chutes heavy with water into the boat as the men swam slowly with their loads to regroup, then to board the submarine. We waited until the monster broke wind with a rumbling belch and slid beneath the surface, then scudded back to our lurking MFV.

Finally we put it all to the test with a drop to a submarine in the Mediterranean, rendezvousing with it by direct flight from England. In a Hastings, out of Colerne, we flew across France, down the Rhone Valley at 10,000 feet, and out over the Mediterranean, where we came down low for the final approach over the sea. We called Malta for a weather check. It wasn't good: gusting twenty knots. But the sea-state didn't look too alarming. Just a few flecks of white on waves that looked quite well behaved. We struggled into the rubber suits, fitted our parachutes over them, and sweated greatly. I went forward to the crew compartment to look over the pilot's shoulder for the smoke float that the sub would put up for us at P hour, and right on time, there it was, just a bit to port. The smoke was travelling fast, but the sweat was trickling down into the feet of the rubber suit and the water looked so cool, and the Marines would probably have thrown me out anyway if I scrubbed it, so I declared the drop to be on. We flew into wind, over the smoke float and the dirty grey shape of the submarine lying just below the surface, and dropped the stick 600 yards beyond it. I watched them splash down, then fitted my own equipment container – which held nothing more lethal than my razor and dry clothing – and waited until the R.A.F. rescue launch came creaming through the water from the south, and then I jumped. Usual drills – check the canopy, then get hold of the seat strap and pull it right under the backside to make a sling to sit in — unclip the reserve and lower it on its short cord to one side ... unhook the container and let it drop to the end of the suspension rope attached to a line round the waist ... turn and bang the quick release box on the chest and feed out the leg straps, clearing them with one hand and keeping a tight grip on the harness with the other, then look below. The sea that had looked quite reasonable from higher up appeared far more rumbustious as I came closer to it. I eased out of the seat strap, straightened my body, let go, and disappeared into salty green. The wind whisked my parachute away. I bobbed quickly to the surface. The waves were huge, from sea level. I pulled my load towards me by its suspension rope, and swam on my back with it, enjoying the coolness through the rubber. The launch came see-sawing towards me. I was helped up the scrambling net and handed a civilized tot of rum. For me, the exercise was over, bar the fifty-mile run to Malta. For the Marines, now peeling off their rubber suits and checking their gear in the confines of a submarine somewhere below the surface, it was just the beginning. Somewhere, close to shore, they would slip quietly and unseen into the water again. We were merely a link in their transport system.

Snow was another medium I had to come to terms with. We planned a winter exercise in Norway. I went across in the autumn to find DZs. The ground was frozen and the air delightfully crisp, and the DZs I plotted in the pine woods around Trandum looked ideal. When I went back in January they were under four feet of snow. We had anticipated snow, of course, but not in such good measure. It was also, I was told, unusually soft snow, and the Norwegians were most sceptical of the value of the snow shoes which the troops would be carrying with them when they jumped. Certainly, to reach the DZs I should have to ski.

Had I brought my skis with me?

"Well, no ... I hadn't brought my skis ... in fact ... "

"Not to worry, they would lend me some."

"But ... "

"Absolutely no trouble ... "

The skis were provided. When all were in the bar or their beds, I crept outside, donned the cumbersone planks for the first time in my life, and for an hour slithered and crashed my way round the icy roads of the camp, until I thought that I had them just about mastered. The following night we drove as close to the DZ as we could, leaving two miles to ski through scrub pine. What little balance I had achieved the night before was now destroyed by the added complication of a 40-pound rucksack on my back. I fell at every ditch and sometimes when there wasn't a ditch. My escort of Norwegians picked me up and brushed me down with great care and regularity and believed me, I am sure, to be quite drunk.

For them, of course, snow was no problem. The Norwegian airborne force was a small unit of elite men, impressively led by Major Lasse Laudal. Lasse was crew-cut, squat, broad as a barn. He chewed evil black tobacco, and walked with a swagger that no one begrudged him. In his office, with his pistol and knife hung from the pine wall behind his chair, he explained their parachuting philosophy. Their potential area of operations was northern Norway, where they would provide a reconnaissance and a sabotage capability in the rear of an enemy advancing from the east. They would go in by free fall, with skis and sleds if the time of year warranted their use ...

"We throws out the bundle of skis, with an automatic opener to operate the 'chute at 700 metres. We jumps out after it and follows it down. When it opens, we open. Where it goes, we goes. Where our skis land, we land. Then we gets on with our job."

The skill of his troops matched his matter-of-fact attitude. There was no false glamour attached to their free fall. I jumped with them on to one of their small, snow-covered DZs. We emplaned at dawn, slapping our arms across our bodies and stamping our feet while the C119 was warmed into reluctant life. We kitted up and climbed aboard. Lasse had a last-minute thought as we sat there. He scribbled on the back of a used envelope, and handed it to me.

"Sign here," he said.

"What is it?" I asked.

"Your authority to jump."

I followed a stick of twelve out into the cold slap of the slipstream. I turned on the air to see them all spreadeagled blackly against the white landscape, like a flock of swooping birds. I slipped off to one side for a clear pull, and followed them in towards the target cross. It was pleasant to land in deep snow, going in at an angle like a tent peg. It was a job getting out, though.

Although I spent more time on the DZ than in the air on the Special Forces job, the jumping that I did do was meaningful and full of rich experience — jumps into Danish fields, German heathland, Mediterranean waters, jungle clearings, desert wadis, deep snow ... I achieved a degree of parachuting competence and confidence that I felt could take me anywhere. Above all, I was reminded constantly of the true place of the parachute in the military system ...

In soft evening light I looked down from the open door of the little U 10 monoplane of the U.S.A.F. 'Air Commandos' as it flew above the forested hills of southern Germany. It was one of my last jumps with Special Forces. Toy caravans in lakeside sites reminded me of holidays past and holidays to come. Villages were putting on their yellow lights. Daylight lingered in the sky, but the fields and forests below melted rapidly into a uniform blackness. "Five minutes," called the American pilot. I knelt, looking over his shoulder. We saw Peter Burgess's torch winking at us on the horizon, coming slowly closer. I sat on the door sill, dangling my legs in the air blast. The pilot turned his head.

"Good night," he said.

I pushed off from the sill. A minute later I settled into the stubble field under the big American steerable canopy. Peter pointed me towards a dark clump of bushes on the ridge where I was to rendezvous with my escort. I climbed the slope. There was the click of a safety catch. I gave the password.

"Good evening," said the S.A.S. Lieutenant from the darkness.

That just about summed it up. "Good night," and "Good evening". What happened in between had been immaterial: just a means of transport.

12 / Lady Be Good

We took off from El Adem at first light.

"Straight down the pipeline and turn left," said Major 'Cal' to his co-pilot, and closed his eyes behind his sunglasses. The Dakota lifted sweetly into the air and turned inland, heading south from the Libyan coastline. The aircraft bore discreet U.S.A.F. markings. It was crewed by Air Commandos, whose full-time role was the airborne support of special operations. Cal was Texan and tall, with a ready grin and a boyish enthusiasm for flying aeroplanes that was fortunately matched by great professionalism. One felt safe with Cal, even when he was dozing behind his sunglasses.

We settled down to sleep away the three-hour flight to the south. Nobody chose to sit next to me, because I stank ...

Two days previously we had been jumping at Timimi, along the coast to the west of Tobruk. I had already spent several days out there, manning the DZ for a series of static-line drops for the S.A.S. squadron at that time exercising itself in the desert. The DZ was a vast half-circle of sand, backed by a crescent of low but rocky hills and fringed on its open side by the surf of the Mediterranean. The flat surface was interrupted only by bleached camel-bones. We had worked early in the mornings, before the wind and the heat came to spoil the day. Tired of curry blocks, and frustrated by watching others jumping in such perfect conditions, I had briefed the S.A.S. sergeant who was with me on the rudiments of marking the DZ, and went back to El Adem for a steak, and to join the next morning's drop. I intended to jump as 'drifter', before the troops, so that I could check the conditions and the DZ markings before they followed.

The breeze was barely awake as we emplaned at dawn, and half an hour later all looked well as the Dakota run in towards the big half-moon of yellow sand tucked into the coastline. The orange markers were there, about half-way up the DZ, and there was nothing on the barren surface to indicate that it was anything but calm, just as it had been on previous mornings.

The green light came on and I launched myself from the door. I checked my canopy in no great haste, then looked down. The earth, 800 feet below, was rushing past like a brown conveyor belt. I couldn't believe it. I had never travelled so fast in a parachute before. I felt like a leaf in a gale, and the gale was blowing me straight towards the jagged ridge at the eastern end of the DZ. I grabbed a liftweb, tore it down and began to haul on the rigging lines in a frenzy of fear ... I had to lose height rapidly, or be hurled into the rocks. I almost had the periphery in my hands before the canopy shuddered and rippled and began to slip down through the air. I held it as long as I dared, watching the ground coming up alarmingly fast, then let everything go and grabbed the liftwebs again as the canopy reinflated with a jerk ... I tucked my head down, saw a blurred, greeny-black surface rushing sideways beneath my feet, had one second to wonder why it was greeny-black, then hit it, bounced, somersaulted, caught a foot in the rigging lines as I went over, and with the parachute billowing like a sail, took off after it on my backside with something that was slimy and smelly flowing over me like a bow wave. I was dragged by the ankle some fifty yards to the edge of the rocks, where the canopy at last draped itself over a boulder, exhausted.

I stood up, scraped the slime from my eyes, and looked shakily around. I had landed at the foot of the ridge, in the over-spill of a well where camels and donkeys had been drinking and defaecating for centuries; I was covered from head to foot in generations of liquid dung.

The El Adem showers, a bottle of cologne, a scrubbing brush and two packets of Daz had failed to sweeten my clothes and I.

So I dozed alone as we flew south. The Dakota followed the pipeline that carried the oil from the heart of the Libyan deserts. Wheel tracks followed it too, but not so well disciplined as the metal pipe, they wandered and weaved on either side of it as it ran across the lifeless plain of rock and gravel and through the dune country. The visibility was poor; immediately below, the ground was bright yellow and threw the sun back at us, but the horizons faded quickly into a glowing haze.

"Holy cow, that's rough country out there!" decided Cal from behind his sunglasses.

We flew down the line for nearly two hours, then the aircraft banked on to a south-easterly heading, over high dunes flowing across the land in giant crescents, then into a featureless plain that stretched like a dirty yellow carpet between walls of purple haze. The navigator said that we should be getting close. As the Dakota began a square search of the unbroken flatness, we all pressed our faces to the windows, screwing our eyes against the reflected glare of the overhead sun. Nothing. Swing round on a parallel track, further east. Again, nothing. Back once more. "Got it!" someone was shouting "Two o'clock ... " The Dakota swung right, banking sharply, everyone crossing to the starboard windows, and there she was, spreadeagled on the gravel plain, with a broken back – the 'Lady Be Good'.

She was a B24 bomber – a Liberator of the Second World War. Hers was a sad story. On 4 April 1943, the 'Lady Be Good' was returning to her base near Benghazi from a bombing raid against Naples harbour. It was night time. Short of fuel, Lieutenant William Hatton and his co-pilot Robert Toner looked hopefully ahead for the Libyan coastline. For a friendly light. They could see nothing. Fuel and hope ran slowly out as they peered into the darkness. One by one the engines coughed and spluttered and with the aircraft losing height on its one remaining motor, Hatton closed the throttles, ordered the crew to bale out, and followed them into the night. As they swung under their parachutes, they had been able to hear the 'Lady' still flying south, dipping and fading slowly. They landed – perhaps to their surprise – on dry ground. By dawn, with the aid of signal flares and revolver shots, eight of the nine-man crew had managed to rendezvous. Of John Worovka, the bomb aimer, there was no sign.

Where were they? Some fifty miles inland, they estimated. At the very most, a hundred. Somewhere near the coastal strip, within range of search aircraft from the Libyan bases. They had only to walk north until they were picked up, or if necessary until they reached the coast. And the 'Lady' was no doubt a smouldering wreck somewhere to the south, with nothing remaining in it that would be of use to them. So taking the canopies of their parachutes to leave as markers and to give them warmth at night, and with a few rations and one flask of water between them, they turned their faces to the north: towards those fifty miles.

Fifty? How wrong they were. Between them and the nearest point of the coast lay 300 miles of some of the worst country in the world – an incinerator by day, a refrigerator at night. Hastened on their flight across the Mediterranean by an unforecast following wind, they had overflown the Libyan coast well before schedule. Whilst they had been searching ahead for the safety of the coastline, it had been receding steadily behind them. Unwittingly they had plunged on into the heart of the Libyan wilderness, and had parachuted on to the biggest DZ in the world – 200 square miles of flat gravel in the centre of the great Libyan sand sea. To add to the dreadful irony, twenty miles to the south the 'Lady' had made a passable landing on her belly. Her survival equipment and water urns were intact.

So the eight men walked north, confidently at first, and periodically screwing their eyes against the sun to scan the skies for search aircraft. They walked all day, and shivered all night. A second day, and a third. They would walk for fifteen minutes, then rest for five, closing their eyes gratefully against the unremitting glare that was gradually blinding them. They drank one mouthful of water each day. Their strength ebbed in the cauldron.

"Everyone getting weak. Can't get very far; prayers all the time," wrote Lieutenant Toner in his diary, on the fourth day.

They came to the dunes. Perhaps their hopes rose when they saw them through the heat haze, thinking that this was the coast at last. But when they had staggered up the soft, shifting slope to stand on the crest of the first dune, 200 feet high, all they could see stretching before them was wave upon wave of silent sand.

"Everyone very weak," scrawled Toner. "La Motte's eyes are gone."

By the sixth day, five of them could go no further, and laid down on the slope of a dune to wait. The others struggled on, with no water, hopefully for help ...

Sixteen years later, oil prospectors in a chartered Dakota spotted and marked on their maps the position of a crashed Liberator bomber lying in the middle of the Caashino 'serir'. It was another year before prospectors, travelling overland, reached the wreck and identified it as the 'Lady Be Good'. The name was still easily legible where it had been painted on the nose of the aircraft. The fuselage was polished and rustless in the dry desert air. Flying jackets hung limply in the crew compartments. There was water in the urns, and drinkable coffee in the flask. What of the crew? There was no sign, neither in the wreck, nor close to it.

In February 1960, a British oil team came across five bodies in the sand sea, and the diary of Lieutenant Toner, with his last entry, barely legible, dated 12 April 1943 – eight days after they had baled out. Later, twenty miles to the north, was found the body of Ripslinger the engineer, then Guy Shelley, who had struggled a further seven miles before dying on an upward slope as though striving to see over the crest of one more dune. Moore, the third man of that party, was never found. And what of John Worovka, the man who had failed to rendezvous with the rest of the crew? His death had been the swiftest and perhaps the kindest of all, for he was finally discovered embedded in the sandy gravel where he had fallen from the 'Lady Be Good' with his parachute unopened.

Now, we circled the dead 'Lady', looking down on her in silence. She wasn't alone. There were five landrovers and their shadows drawn up around her. This landmark in the desert wilderness now provided a goal for exercises in desert navigation and travel for the S.A.S., and we had flown south to rendezvous with the landrover troop and to resupply it with fuel and water. The Dakotas were to land alongside the wreck, but before they could do so the most suitable stretch of gravel had to be located and marked. Captain Lo Walker, one of the Commando pilots, was parachute-trained for this type of mission. Lo came from the southern States, and was for ever complaining of the lack of Louisiana hot sauce in the El Adem mess.

We fitted and checked our 'chutes. The troops threw a smoke grenade on to the gravel to show what little wind drift there was. The spotting was complicated by the glare and by the lack of reference points on the featureless surface, but it didn't really matter: the DZ was a hundred miles wide. Mindful of the last occasion on which men had parachuted on to the gravel plain — twenty-five years earlier — I swung out through the door. You could feel the heat, even in free fall. A spreadeagled speck above that vast gravel pit, I felt a great humility. We opened, and spiralled down to gentle landings alongside the 'Lady' and the pink-painted landrovers. The bronzed troops were not impressed, for they had arrived the hard way — overland. The sun hit me on the back of the head when I took my helmet off. The stillness and the silence were tangible things. It was the most impressive cemetery I had been in.

Lo found his strip, and marked it with two smoke canisters. The Dakotas settled gingerly on to the gravel, which billowed up behind them in khaki clouds, then the aircraft turned and taxied back with their noses in the air like big birds curious to examine their broken sister. The 'Lady' was still rustless, and didn't look her age, although occasional visitors like ourselves had torn much that was easily transportable from the fuselage. The crews from the Dakotas went to work on her with screwdrivers and cameras, while we stripped to the waist to offload the drums of fuel and the cans of water. The troops were loudly hoping that the aircraft might not be able to get off again, for they envied us the cold showers and cool beer that awaited the airborne party at El Adem. But trailing plumes of blown sand we lifted off the level plain, to circle the 'Lady' and her transient company once more before setting our course to the north — the way those eight men had headed hopefully a quarter of a century ago. As I lay on my belly looking out of the open door, I found myself searching for them.

13 / Problem Parachuting – Desert and Jungle

Usually the delivery of a Special Forces unit to its operating area requires to be unobtrusive, and the selection of the best available means of transport is often crucial to the success of its mission. To meet the varying demands of surprise and secrecy, of terrain and weather, of distance and time, the commander needs as many options as possible – legs, vehicles, canoes, helicopters, skis, submarines, camels, parachutes ...

Always keen to widen these options, the S.A.S. had long been interested in free-fall parachuting, as a possible alternative to conventional static-line parachuting from low altitude. There could be situations where greater security and surprise might be achieved from altitudes where the dropping aircraft was neither visible nor audible. Also, the greater accuracy potential of free-fall parachuting in visual conditions commended it for use in areas where dropping zones were either too small or otherwise too hazardous for conventional parachuting. So it was that I became involved in testing and adapting the techniques of military free fall in some of the traditional S.A.S. hunting grounds – the desert and the jungle.

Like all S.A.S. systems, tactical free fall had to be adaptable. There could be no one standard operating procedure: we had to develop techniques that could be adjusted to meet a wide variety of circumstances. In the desert, the possibilities ranged from a visual drop into a confined wadi or on to a rocky plateau of limited size, to a 'blind' drop at night into a more extensive area, free of major hazards.

To achieve this flexibility of operation, the basic skills of free fall and canopy control that the S.A.S. troops had learnt at Abingdon were in themselves not going to be enough. Our parachutists would have to learn how to apply those skills to a wide variety of parachuting situations. They would have to be capable of planning the drop themselves with the minimum of information on DZ and wind conditions; they would have to be able to orientate themselves rapidly in free fall, and read the ground like a map; under the canopy they would have to assess wind strengths and drift angles without the help of an accurate met forecast and signal-smokes; on a 'blind' drop they would have to be able to follow their leader in free fall and under the canopy, to land as close to him as they could. In short, they were going to have to *think* their way on to the ground, from the moment the drop was conceived. I therefore worked on the principle that every training descent should give them something to think about. It should have a definite aim, and it should present a definite problem. If there wasn't a problem inherent in the situation, I would create one.

For our desert training we operated with Andover aircraft, out of Sharjah in the Persian Gulf. Our DZ was Manama airstrip, at the foot of the rugged Jebel, thirty miles inland across a plain like brown parachment pimpled with thorn trees. At Manama the aircraft would land after each drop to take us straight up for another, giving that concentration of jumping that is so important when basic skills are being grooved. The thorn trees ensured that everyone rapidly learnt the techniques of obstacle avoidance. We piled on other problems. We began by giving the stick commanders the minimum of dropping information necessary for safety. Then we gave them none at all. Then we fed them wrong information. We would follow the sticks out to hover above them in free fall and under the canopy, and watch them sort it out: watch them *thinking*. When we ran out of problems at Manama, we moved into rougher terrain, where drops were less frequent, but more realistic and more demanding.

On the edge of the Jebel were large bays of sand between headlands of sun-shattered rock: ideal tactical DZs. With no markings on the ground, it was up to the stick leader to pick his spot, and for the others in his team to fly with him in free fall, open their 'chutes higher than his, and follow him down to land in as tight a group as possible. It bore some resemblance to a team accuracy jump in sport parachuting, except that there was no pin-point target, and no drift indication. Another difference was the fifty-pound rucksack that we carried.

Several years earlier, as free-fall loads became heavier and more bulky, we had discovered that a smoother fall was obtained by carrying the rucksack behind the thighs instead of in front of them, where it tended to disrupt the airflow unduly and create buffeting. Strapped tightly to the back of the thighs, it was a hindrance when standing, and one had to approach the door at a fast waddle, but in free fall it was no impediment to stability provided that it was correctly balanced and well secured. Should it slip, it would introduce a built-in asymmetry and a consequent tendency to spiral. On one occasion, hurrying to prepare my kit and to brief the aircrew before a drop, I asked one of the troopers to load and service my bergen for me. "Yes, *sir*," he said. When I rejoined them later in the aircraft, the rucksack was waiting for me, sitting on the floor. When I tried to pick it up, I thought at first that it was tied down. It weighed all of a hundred pounds. It gurgled. There was a jerrycan of water in there, amongst other things. "You bastards," I said, but I had to jump with it. They watched with interest as I fitted it, grinned as I stood sagging and sweating on the run-in, and laughed as I staggered to the door and fell out. As I fought to get on to my belly in the airflow, the load shifted, and started spinning me to the right. I had to screw my upper body into a tight left-turn position and hold it all the way down to 2,000 feet, where I pulled high because I wasn't sure what the extra weight might do to the canopy. It served me right. With the S.A.S., sir looks after himself and his own kit.

But it was good jumping. Hard, but purposeful. On the instructional side, we were able to retire more and more into the background, leaving the planning and conduct of each drop to the troops themselves. Each stick commander would make his calculations on the little information available to him, and relate them to the aerial photograph of the region we were aiming for. On the run-in, as he crouched in the open door to guide the aircraft over his selected release point, I would watch over his shoulder, ready to stop him if I thought he was too far out, or too close to the high rocks. But they never were. He would call for the green light, then lead his stick out. I would follow the last man, watching from above as they turned on their leader and flew down towards him, following if he needed to track for his opening point. I would open high to see how they were using their canopies to group in on the stick commander. If they were scattered, he would need to come back and meet them, staying low by stalling his 'chute if necessary, and when he had shepherded them together, they would turn into wind for landing, and pick their spot amongst any minor obstacles there might be. I would watch my own shadow come galloping over the dunes to meet me, then pick a smooth slope and plough ankle deep into the soft red sand. I would take off my helmet and listen to the silence of the desert and the great rocks as I bundled my parachute.

If operational drops into the desert were to be truly clandestine, the cover of darkness would be essential. Free falling at night required a certain amount of faith, and an adaption of the 'follow-the-leader' techniques we had used for the grouped descents in daylight, with red 'tail lights' for identification. As soon as the team was ready for the night training phase, we began with familiarization jumps in the darkness on to a marked DZ, at

Juweiza, an area of the plain east of Sharjah that was relatively free of obstacles. Operationally, however, DZs were unlikely to be marked, and might not be visible nor indeed identifiable. In such cases the drop would have to be made on a timed run from a 'target approach point' (TAP) – an identifiable feature such as a coastline or the lights of a village, at a known distance from the desired landing area. Obviously, the further the TAP from the DZ, the greater was likely to be the dropping error, and this would be taken into account in any planning. In fact, it was exactly the same system that we had used on our first tactical free-fall demonstration on to Fox Covert on that night many years earlier. Now, at Juweiza, we marked the TAP with an aldis lamp 2,000 yards to the north-west of the DZ. The release point was calculated in the normal way, and the navigator translated the distance between these two points into a time, based on his calculated speed of flight over the ground.

The green flashing aldis signal, the only light in the desert, was visible from many miles out. As we passed above it, the stick leader pressed his stopwatch, then stood back to watch the hand trot round the dial, while we all watched him. It seemed an awful long time. He finally nodded to the rest of us, and was gone. Launching out over complete blackness, unrelieved by any surface lights, and with only an altimeter to believe in, is disconcerting. I turned, and picked up the red rear light of the man below, and followed it, in free fall and under the canopy. We all landed close together, with only one man swearing in a thorn bush, and there wasn't too far to walk through the sand to where the three-tonner began flashing its lights.

For subsequent jumps, we moved the TAP progressively further from the landing area, until we were taking our timings from overhead Sharjah runway and still not having to exercise our legs unduly to reach the rendezvous point after the drop.

It wasn't all tactical work with heavy loads. On one such training programme we were asked to display our skills before Sheikh Zaid of Abu Dhabi. Sheikh Zaid was noted for his generosity with gold watches. It was Race Day, and we were to jump into his presence on the course. There was one minor problem. Major 'J' was insistent that this was to be an S.A.S. display, and I was equally insistent that there would be a Royal Air Force representative in the line-up for gold watches – me. We compromised. I borrowed a blue belt and a fawn beret and became Trooper Hearn for the day. We flew down the coast to the modern airport of Abu Dhabi, and were driven over to look at the race course and to pick our landing spot. The course itself was of sand, and in front of the small grandstand was only fifty feet wide. We thought that it would be more spectacular and certainly more worthy of gold watches to land on the course rather than on the vast area that it enclosed, so asked for the target cross to be placed on the sand, right in front of the Sheikh. Then we went back to the airport and took off in the Andover, full of confidence. We could hear those gold watches ticking. There was little wind. It was, however, very hazy. At least, that was the stick commander's excuse when we all landed on the far side of the race course, a thousand yards from the grandstand, the Sheikh, and the gold watches that had suddenly stopped ticking.

Perhaps the Abu Dhabi drop had been too easy. Perhaps the absence of 'problems' caused us to relax our concentration. Certainly, in far more demanding situations there were no such failures.

Towards the end of a desert training programme we would put the techniques to the test in some realistic exercise situations. We parachuted on to hard-baked clay on the firing ranges at Jebajib, where the troops set up the radios we had carried in and directed Hunter rocket strikes against the hulks of old tanks. In a twenty-knot wind we jumped on to Yas – a stark, sunbaked island in the Persian Gulf – to mark a DZ for a static-line assault. At night we dropped into a sandy re-entrant in the high Jebel. With a touch of moon, it was a prominent enough feature, tucked into the side of the black rock. We came out of the aircraft slightly off track, right above the mountain that sprawled under our bellies like a hump-backed monster sleeping in the moonlight. As I watched all the little red tail lights below me go streaking off towards the paler bowl of sand, I knew with some satisfaction that we had indeed trained some 'thinking' parachutists, and I tucked my belly in and set off after them through the night sky.

We turned our attentions to the jungle.

Although the helicopter had proved itself the most valuable means of tactical transport in jungle warfare, we were again looking for options. There might be occasions when a less noisy and more inconspicuous method of arrival was required.

In the desert the emphasis had been on accuracy as a group on unmarked and extensive DZs. In the jungle we were more concerned with inserting patrols into the very restricted open spaces that the terrain occasionally offered – jungle clearings, villages, or river sandbanks. There was no need to jump at night to achieve surprise, for from the jungle floor the sky was barely visible through the tangled canopy of vegetation, and a descent from altitude was likely to go quite unperceived except by anyone in the immediate landing area. Although desirable, it was not essential to have a clear space; parachuting into the tree-tops was not new to the S.A.S., and part of our training would be to adapt free-fall techniques to the already tried methods of tree jumping. But our immediate concern was accurate dropping on to small DZs, again with the minimum support and information. Once more, we had to train men to think for themselves, and to think fast. Although the environments were totally different, the qualities required for parachuting into the desert and the jungle were the same; the same, indeed, as those needed to live in them — adaptability and awareness.

The first troop I had for jungle training included a number of beginners who were barely at the stage of free-fall stability. Their free-fall skill was perhaps of less concern than their ability to handle a steerable canopy, for where we were going one bad error would have them dangling from a tree. Our training ground was to be the hilly jungle country of north-west Malaya, inland from Penang. Fortunately I had the stalwart backing of Flight Sergeant Stan Phipps, and the troop also included some old hands like Pete Sherman, to whom I had nothing to teach.

Before moving inland, we managed to obtain some preliminary training on a more extensive DZ — the sports ground of the Gurkha training base at Sungai Patani. These early jumps enabled us to iron out a few individual problems over basic techniques, but otherwise did little to create confidence. We designated one whole soccer pitch as the DZ. Some managed to miss it consistently, and seemed little worried by the fact.

What chance Grick, I thought. Grick was to be our training base. It was an airstrip with plenty of length, but only 25 yards of width. Along one edge were high trees, not particularly dense, although uncleared jungle lurked only 50 yards further back. The other side of the strip was bordered by low scrub, not particularly hazardous, but unpleasant, and potentially injurious to nylon canopies. The carcase of a Scout helicopter had been dragged to one side of the landing area, and an unserviceable Belvedere was a permanent feature at the southern end. It would not have been too bad if the prevailing wind had been down the length of the strip, but the drift was almost always across it, allowing no room for undershoot or overshoot errors. We weren't going to have to build in any problems at Grick.

We were using the relatively new Tactical Assault Parachute, designed by GQ specifically for tactical free fall, based on the vented configuration of the

American 'Paracommander' but with far less drive and holding power: the emphasis was on a slow and steady rate of descent, with enough 'push' for grouping purposes, but not for pin-point accuracy.

With some misgivings, I briefed the troops for their first drop at Grick, emphasizing the basic principles. There was no great strength in the wind, but what there was tended to be variable. They should make sure of their opening point, and pull high if they were too deep. Under the canopy they should work in close, to hold a position just outside the strip, always keeping it within a distance that the 'chute could drive on its own should the wind die on them altogether, then at 300 feet they should strike for the grass and start their turn into wind again as they crossed over the near edge of the landing area. They didn't look as worried as I felt.

I jumped with the first stick of more experienced men. The strip looked awfully thin from 7,000 feet, but we all made it without any trouble. I then stood by the target to monitor the rest of the jumping. I needn't have worried; every one of them touched down on the grass as though they had been jumping into jungle strips for months, then went straight up and did it again. The flippancy of Sungai Patani had gone. Faced with a realistic situation, they responded with some realistic parachuting.

The jumping at Grick followed a set pattern. We began as early as we could in the mornings. After rain in the night, the valley would be dripping with mist. We would carry our gear down to the strip from the 'bashas' where we slept, and wait by the fuel drums for the sun and Flight Lieutenant Rusty Ironsides to find their way through to us. Sometimes Rusty would win, the Twin Pin appearing almost miraculously through the mist at the end of the strip.

"Thought it was somewhere here," he would say.

I would jump on the first sortie, then stay reluctantly on the ground to watch the others and make notes on the canopy handling for subsequent debriefs. We tried to get three jumps for each trainee before midday, for by then the heat would be shimmering over the hard ground and the wind and the turbulence would start to play tricks on us. An unexpected gust would change a good approach on one side of the strip to a tangle of curses on the other. On one jump our smallest man found himself hovering in the air that rose from the hot surface of the landing area. Making no progress earthwards, he turned back over the scrub, where he began to lose height. Once more he tried to get in, but hung again in the updraft. "Come down, Jimmy — all is forgiven," mocked the rest of his stick, already bundling their parachutes. He turned, and swearing loudly disappeared into the tall ferns and bushes by the side of the runway. The turbulence and the gusts would finally call a halt to the training, and we would climb up the path to the camp to brew tea and curry while the Twin Pin headed back over the jungled hills to Butterworth. We would repack for the next day's jumping while the storm clouds built up amongst the hills.

Progress was fast. Certainly nobody ever made the same mistakes twice. A target cross in the middle of a large DZ might be a fair incentive to good spotting and sensible canopy handling, but a jungle clearing is a better one. Furthermore, take away the drift indicator and the DZ guidance, and the clarity of thought and sense of awareness induced are remarkable. Not that I would advocate small and hazardous DZs for all parachute training. I was preparing operational jumpers, and they were men who by the very nature of their selection, training and task were well able to cope with an element of risk: indeed, they thrived on it. Men who less than two weeks earlier had barely mastered stability were now jumping with full equipment, could track to opening points, and were handling their canopies with assurance. So we looked for variety, and more problems. Further inland, in a broad valley among the hills, lay Fort Kemar, an aborigine settlement with a fortified police post and its attendant airstrip. The landing area was again 400 yards long, but even narrower than Grick and flanked on both sides by tall, primary jungle. The northern end dropped almost sheer to a curving river. It was an impressive setting. I wondered what we had let ourselves in for as the Twin Pin hopped over the rim of the bluff and bounded down the narrow corridor between the green banks of vegetation which rose to almost 200 feet on either side. Certainly, I thought, parachuting into it would be far preferable to flying in. I never do like landing in aeroplanes at the best of times.

I waited on the strip, chatting with the Captain of Police who commanded the fort, while the Twin Pin flew back to Grick for its first load, who would fly straight in for the drop. It was one of those jumps that I would much rather have been doing than watching, but again I need not have fretted, for the little black dots left the high-flying aircraft in just the right place, and it was gratifying to watch the troops come in over the high timber under their big khaki canopies, and swing gently down into the centre of the clearing one after the other, politely applauded by the dapper Malay policemen and the aborigine children who had swarmed from the school-house to watch.

Pete Sherman and I went up to 9,000 feet armed with Captain Zabri's police baton, which we passed ceremoniously from one to the other as we dropped back to the rolling green waves of primary jungle and the thin ribbon of the airstrip. In return the Captain presented us each with a native blow-pipe and quiver of darts, then took us all to the fort for a cold beer. A small cluster of buildings was positioned on the bluff, overlooking the river where children splashed in play and women bent at their washing. Good views are rare in the jungle, but from there we could see a panorama of green hills and ridges rolling into purple distance. A breeze coming up from the river brought coolness, and sounds of water and laughter, and a velvet butterfly as big as a blackbird.

We turned, reluctantly, to the next phase of our training – parachuting into the jungle trees that we had been so carefully avoiding for many weeks. An aircraft flying and dropping by static line at 1,000 feet, even though not easily visible through the layered vegetation, might well advise an alert enemy that he was being visited. Not so from 12,000 feet: free-fall parachuting would give an even greater possibility of security and surprise. Furthermore, the closer grouping of a stick using steerable parachutes would hasten the subsequent rendezvous on the ground, and steerability would also increase the safety factor by enabling parachutists to avoid the less promising parts of the jungle canopy.

We adapted for free fall the 'bikini' abseil gear which I had previously used with the Jungle Rescue Team. On a rickety water-tower at Grick we practised tying ourselves to the superstructure, releasing ourselves from the harness, and abseiling gingerly to the ground.

An aura of exceptional hazard had grown up around tree jumping. Certainly the injury and fatality rates did not commend it. But I could think of no other reason for not doing it myself. We kitted up in the hot sun at Grick. I stuffed a small towel down inside my trousers for extra protection where it might be most needed ... then the canvas 'bikini' and tape, main and reserve parachutes, weapon, rucksack, knife where it was handy, emergency signal flare, radio beacon, helmet, goggles, gloves ... "Are you enjoying yourself, sir?" inquired Rusty. He was advised to get stuffed, and I waddled into the aircraft, sweating profusely.

We took off and circled out over the jungle to the south-east of Grick. It wasn't the best jungle to jump into. Ideally one looks for a thick, well-matted canopy that will ensure a hang-up rather than induce only a partial collapse of the parachute. The area below us had been worked on by loggers and was not as dense as we would have liked. We thought, however, that the steerability of the parachutes we were using would compensate for that by allowing us to avoid the gaps and to steer for the thickest tree within range. I leant out of the door, examining the green landscape below rather dubiously. Too late now – we were running in. I spotted for the centre of the area we had chosen, and we heaved ourselves and our heavy loads out of the aircraft in a tight stick of four. I just laid on the airflow, watching the jungle come closer, with a sense of relief and excitement now that we were committed. We opened at 2,000 feet, to drift gently down to a vast sea of foliage; a rough sea, of different shades and depths. The jungle lost even more of its apparent solidity as we dropped towards it. It dispersed into individual clumps, with thin gaps between, and here and there the bony limbs of a dead jungle-giant reaching out from the greenery. I lowered my rucksack and pushed it under my feet to absorb the first impact of branches. I picked what looked like a good solid patch, steered for it, missed it, and swung hard into a confusion of crackling branches and leaves, snagged, broke free, fell cursing through a whiplash of twigs, going down much too fast, then snagged again, jerking as it held ... bouncing gently as though suspended by elastic, swinging in dappled green shadow. I looked down. My boots were about four feet from the ground. Above, my parachute was draped – much tattered – from an apologetic sapling. I dropped to earth, gathered my gear, gratefully patted the thin tree, and struggled through the undergrowth towards the sound of muffled cursing. I found one of the troopers sitting on his rucksack, picking thorns from his forearms. He too had slid straight through to the ground, but less comfortably than I. We located the others, and made our way to the rendezvous on an old logging track. The other sticks jumped, with similar results, some hanging up and others breaking right through, but none seriously hurt.

For subsequent jumps we found ourselves a more substantial patch of jungle, but there is little to be learnt from the repeated practice of parachuting into trees, other than that it is largely a game of chance and usually painful. We did no more than was necessary to satisfy ourselves that the procedure and equipment were adequate.

After one jump, nursing our bruises and treating our scratches at the rendezvous, we were approached by a party of aborigines from a nearby encampment. The men were squat and stocky, and their women carried wide-eyed babes in slings on their backs. They gave us to understand that they would retrieve our 'chutes from the high trees where we had abandoned them. This we thought unlikely, for jungle trees of ironwood and teak are not made for scaling, but within the half-hour they were back with four canopies. The parachutes were beyond economic repair, and neither did we wish to carry them out with us, so we signified to the natives that they could keep them. They thanked us gravely. Sitting in a quiet circle, they then dismembered the parachutes with their knives, and carefully and equably shared the treasure between them – lengths of rigging line and webbing, buckles, and stretches of nylon material. We watched them for a while, then shouldered our packs and left them, and their trees.

14 / Falcons and Other Birds

It was the first time that I had strapped on a free-fall 'chute for many months. I had been otherwise occupied in the Defence Intelligence Staff for almost two years. I pretended that it didn't seem that long, and tried to look as nonchalant as the others sitting in the Hercules as it trundled noisily towards the end of the runway. They were well relaxed, self-assured young men, unhurried in their actions, impressive in their uniform black overalls and bright red helmets. I suppose that I had looked like them once. Ten years ago, in fact. For these were the 1971 Falcons. The successors of the display team that had stepped backwards from the Beverley still almost a decade ago to the day.

Now, returned to No.1 P.T.S. as Commanding Officer, I had taken the first opportunity to join them for a routine practice descent on the airfield.

"Okay, sir? Remember all about it?" Doug Peacock had said.

"Yes thank you, Flight," I had lied.

We tightened and checked our equipment as the aircraft roared towards 12,000 feet. The buckles felt unfamiliar. The aerial photograph was passed round, with release and opening points clearly marked, and we lined up in two sticks, watching Alan Jones crouched at the open door, spotting the run and passing final corrections direct to the pilot. He called for the green, stood back, disconnected his radio link, and waved the first men out. I followed the port stick, running straight through the door into the sunlight. Any uncertainty I may have felt was whipped away on the slipstream; any doubts were swamped by the exhilaration of flight. With outstretched arms I welcomed the air like an old friend, and laughed as I watched the Hercules lift away. Without thought I dipped a shoulder and turned. Below me, against the familiar backdrop of the Abingdon runways, black figures were converging, two already linked, others flying down and in, approaching from either side, gripping the sleeves of the base men, tugging them apart and grabbing their wrists to complete the four-man star. It looked so effortless. Others of the twelve-man stick had tracked out in different directions, would have turned at 7,000 feet and would now be swooping back towards the opening points. The star broke and scattered, each man diving off to find his own airspace for that very private function of opening a parachute. I pulled as I saw the first extractor flash from someone's back. I followed them down, watching them land below me in tight clusters around the two small orange crosses on the grass. I joined them. The team had come a long way since that Beverley sill ...

After its debut in 1961 I had been fortunate enough to lead the team for a second year. 1962 was again a season of development: development of ideas, techniques, and scope. As an official R.A.F. display team we were directed to major air displays throughout the country, made our first overseas appearance at the Rouen Air Show, and again jumped at Farnborough.

We wanted something new for the Farnborough show. We had just learnt to 'track', which was an improvement on the delta position for moving across the sky. From the basic delta attitude, the belly was sucked in, the backside lifted slightly, shoulders rolled forwards, legs brought closer together, and the arms straightened along the sides with the palms down, cupping the air. Thus the body became a simple airfoil section, deriving lift and thrust from the airflow. 'Tracking' was all the rage. Everybody wanted to get out and hurl themselves through the sky in all directions. Many finished up several ploughed fields away from Weston until their map reading became as effective as their tracking position. From this new-found skill we evolved a 'follow the leader' display technique, whereby I would work out a feasible track pattern on the information passed by the DZ, and plot an outbound track which we could fly in 20 seconds, and an inbound leg to return us to the opening points. I would then fly that track over the ground in free fall, with the rest of the team following me, our combined smoke trails making a definite zigzag across the sky.

My number 2 on the 1962 team was Flight Lieutenant Peter Williams, who achieved instant fame and almost brought a smile to the face of Ron Ellerbeck on the DZ when he made an immaculate stand-up landing on the very centre of our red target cross at Farnborough. It was the first 'dead centre' we had seen in this country. Peter was also the first to free fall from the balloon, when he led the team himself in 1964. It was an experiment that he considered too costly in hydrogen and adrenalin to be repeated.

Thereafter a new leader each year developed progressively exciting display patterns, and took the team to further successes. Trophies from France, Italy, Germany, Holland, Belgium, Norway, Denmark, Iran and Canada soon decorated the crewroom. Under John Thirtle in 1965 the team expanded to twelve men, and the name of the 'Falcons' was officially adopted. In 1967, led by Flight Lieutenant Stuart Cameron, they achieved the first British six-man link in free fall, and even more indicative of the standards then being achieved in relative work, this feat was captured on air-to-air film. That same year, the 'Paracommander' appeared in Royal Air Force colours. The 'PC' was by then widely accepted as the foremost precision landing machine available to parachutists. The partial inversion of a canopy made of ultra low porosity nylon, and elliptical shaping of the front skirt, ensured maximum diversion of air flow through the drive apertures and steering slots to give a revolutionary forward drive of 13 miles per hour and a descent rate of 13 feet per second, both of them highly controllable. 'Toggling' was brought to a precise art. The toggles served as steering wheel, brake pedal, and accelerator, enabling the competition parachutist to drive his machine on a downwind approach from a pre-calculated set-up point, both toggles at shoulder level on half brakes, holding a reserve of forward speed to be turned loose by gentle letting up should he be dropping short, or further reduced by depressing the toggles should he appear to be overshooting the little white disc ... reach for it with one foot, and bingo! Dead centre! For display jumpers, the great inherent drive of the 'PC' was a comfort in high winds and an obvious aid to overall team accuracy, although the precision of the competition parachutist was not required – nor, indeed, attempted, for the downwind approach needs the compensation of a landing surface of yielding pea gravel. Like most high-performance beasts, the 'PC' proved sensitive. It didn't take kindly to rough handling. If so abused, it would hurl its rider in wide spirals or swing him in violent oscillations, and if exceptionally angry, could drop him out of the sky with little support at all. It was not a parachute for novices.

Although the Falcons, like all parachutists, collect their share of bumps and bruises, more serious injuries are rare. Flight Lieutenant Geoff Greenland, leader of the Falcons in 1968, came the closest to real disaster when jumping early in the season at Biggin Hill ...

"It was a misty, squally sort of day," Geoff recalled. "We could only manage a hop and pop from 3,000. I was first out, and just managed to land on the edge of the DZ. It was really gusty, and before I could get the canopy down, I was off across the pans, being dragged on my backside. The next thing I knew was a sudden battering as the canopy and myself were whiplashed under the fuselage of an aircraft. When I got out, my helmet was fractured, my smokes flattened, and the canopy in shreds, wrapped round the props of a Mustang. Another couple of turns, and I've have been in there too. All I got was a busted finger, a bang on the nose, and a rollicking from Val when she read it in the papers the next day ... "

"Parachutist Cheats Death," said those papers, and gave the pilot of the Mustang great credit for switching off his engine in the nick of time, when of course he shouldn't have had props turning at all.

A new member joined the team that year – a real feathered Falcon, officially named 'Quinquaginta' to mark the fiftieth anniversary of the Royal Air Force, but to become more widely and conveniently known as Fred.

Flight Lieutenants Mervyn Green and David Cobb had each led the Falcons to further successes, and when I returned to P.T.S. in 1971, Alan Jones was team leader. Already the team had completed a rewarding early-season tour of Australia, and was now coming towards the end of its normal U.K. and continental display programme. But one highlight remained on the calendar: Hong Kong. My presence there, I decided, was essential.

A series of displays was to be one of the attractions of the 1971 Festival of Hong Kong – an extensive trade fair and cultural festival. It was a new and challenging experience for the Falcons, for instead of the airfields or otherwise extensive areas over which they were accustomed to launch their high-level display, in Hong Kong they would be using extremely small DZs, most of them within the congested urban area of the city. The Government Stadium, into which the team was to jump at night on six seperate occasions, was particularly awesome. On three sides towered cliffs, themselves topped with tall buildings. A Chinese cemetery clung precariously to one almost vertical slope: It would be like jumping into a funnel, in darkness. We surveyed it with thoughtful expressions. Weather conditions were unlikely to favour accuracy, for we were advised by the local met men that the low-level Hong Kong winds were temperamental, tumbling as they did over the mountains into the city to wander aimlessly around with the tourists amongst the skyscrapers and local geography.

We would be giving displays from helicopters for the first time. Three Whirlwinds would fly in V formation, and from each would jump a stick of four, each group tracking outwards in a dispersal pattern for 20 seconds, then flying back in for the opening points. Jumping out of helicopters is a sensation of its own. With no slipstream there is an acute but not unpleasant sensation of actually falling. There is also – until speed picks up – no airflow to get hold of, no pressure to work on, so that for a few seconds the body feels sluggish and off balance. Furthermore, the door of the Whirlwind is low. It was all right for Snowy – he could walk straight out. But I needed to duck, and usually forgot.

There were press conferences, publicity photographs, and television interviews, in which Fred featured prominently and misbehaved on the carpet of the Hilton. Then we got down to some practice. It was going to be jungle-jumping again, I mused as we studied the aerial photos of the tiny DZs — except that this was a concrete jungle and the penalties for missing the 'clearings' would be painful. But the DZs looked less fearsome from the door of the helicopter at 10,000 feet. They always do. You can stand on the ground in a tiny space hemmed in by vicious obstacles, thinking "How the hell are we going to get in here?" but from altitude with a 'chute hugging you tight it will look quite attainable, surrounded though it might be by blocks of flats looking like upended match boxes, coiled in streams of traffic, and with the harbour waters lurking close.

And so, with the confidence that is absolutely essential to successful display jumping, we set about the twelve shows that were crammed into the eight-day festival.

Kai Tak airfield. Reluctantly, I watched this one from the ground, with Fred, who showed no interest at all as the twelve smoke trails erupted from the high-flying formation of dots and spread outwards like a slow-motion shrapnel burst against the blue sky, then streaked in again to explode into tri-coloured canopies upwind of the airfield. Fred, in fact, was fully occupied in staying on his perch, for it was rather windy.

Victoria Park, on the other side of the water. We tumbled out of the helicopters high above the waterfront, and my track pattern took me out across a narrow neck of the harbour, over the bustling ferries and the motorized junks and the moored freighters with lighters alongside them like litters of puppies, then back again to open in a good stack and drive the 'PC' in over the typhoon harbour and between the skyscrapers to land on the sun-baked soccer pitch in the park.

Aberdeen. We clacked away in the Whirlwinds over the hump of Hong Kong Island to the famed fishing harbour, with its floating restaurants standing aloof from the brown jostle of junks that crammed the bay. Offshore islands drifted on the horizon. We parachuted into a small stadium set in a deep valley of eddying winds and tall buildings. I jumped behind Doug Peacock from the starboard helicopter and tracked out after him, trying unsuccessfully to catch up with his smoking boots, then turning to zoom back to the opening point. Under the canopy I made the mistake of following the man below me instead of keeping my eyes on the DZ and the smoke drift, and was suddenly dismayed to see his parachute collapse on the ground amongst a clutter of tin roofs just short of the stadium. A slight shift of wind had caught us out. Others, who had read the situation better, were dropping in around the crosses in the centre of the stadium. I wasn't going to make it. Cursing loudly, I turned away from the tin roofs and selected a small vegetable patch. I recognized lettuces as I milked the toggles gently for the final approach, and carefully placed a foot on either side of a neatly planted row as I came in for a soft stand-up landing, which was no consolation at all for the embarrassment of having to climb over the stadium fence to rejoin the team.

Yuen Long, in the New Territories. We parachuted into another stadium, flanked with tall buildings on one side, and by paddy fields and a murky grey canal on the others. It was only 4 miles from the Red Chinese border. No mistakes this time; everyone in the penalty area around the crosses.

Happy Valley Race Course, back in Hong Kong. One block of flats can look very like another when you are hurtling down from 10,000 feet looking for your opening point, and Sergeant Henry McDonald tracked off for the wrong block. As we swung and spiralled beneath our canopies in a well-positioned cluster, we could see him hanging lonely in the distance, and as we glided down one side of a sky-scrapered ridge to land in front of the packed grandstand, Henry drifted down the other side. Fortunately, there lay the Government Stadium, in which Henry made a perfect though unannounced arrival. With his parachute bundled in his arms, he hitched a lift through the teeming streets and was supping his cold ale in the Jockey Club almost as soon as the rest of us.

"Where you been Henry?"

"The stadium's tonight, Henry."

The Government Stadium, in fact, was every night, for six nights. It was undoubtedly the highlight of the Hong Kong tour, for parachutists and spectators. A system of dropping was evolved whereby the three Whirlwinds would fly in at 3,300 feet, at one-minute intervals, with individual exit and opening points well spaced so that each of the twelve jumpers would have a clear run in the darkness for the floodlit bowl below. The result was fantastic. Thirty thousand Chinese can't be wrong. They would hum with anticipation as team manager John Parry began his commentary, then rise to their feet peering upwards into the night as the first of the helicopters clattered high across the bowl. The more observant would shout and point as they caught perhaps a flicker of the altimeter torches dropping through the darkness, and then after a long half-minute of anticipation the loud buzz would erupt into a roar as the first canopy ghosted into the glow of the floodlights at 700 feet, tacking, spiralling, orange smoke billowing behind ... and the roar would in turn rise to a screaming crescendo as each man in turn, coming in fast in the airless stadium, swung down on to the target crosses, each one greeted like a World Cup goal.

Most other places have seemed easy after Hong Kong.

The concentrated periods of intensive training that the Falcons need to bring them to the standards they display require a guarantee of better weather than the British Isles normally provides, so twice a year venues with climates more favourable for parachuting and suntans are sought. In 1972, the combination of airstrip and DZ, clear skies and acceptable winds, was found at Ampugnano in northern Italy. Much useful pre-season work was done. On the final day of training, the team gave a formal display for local dignitaries and spectators. It was a perfect jump. After speeches and presentations, the team strapped themselves into the Andover for their return trip to Pisa, thence home. Midway down the runway the aircraft tipped on to one wing, cartwheeled horrifyingly, crashing back on to its belly, and burst into flames. Squadron Leader Bill Last − my second-in-command at P.T.S. − and Sergeant Roy Bullen died in the crash, with two crewmen. It seemed a miracle that anyone escaped, yet within a week the team was re-equipped, and jumping again, with a noticeable tendency to favour the rearmost seats when next flying in an Andover. "It doesn't burn so well back here," they said with a jovial callousness that is the only way to live with that measure of tragedy.

Flight Lieutenant Gwynne Morgan's phlegmatic leadership did much to see the Falcons through that particular season. Probably the only time that Gwynne was in any way ruffled was on his last descent with the team − or rather without them, for when he disconnected his RT lead and swung out through the door of the Hercules 12,000 feet above Teeside for the final show of the season, nobody followed. Gwynne, busy with his own track pattern in free fall, and with the live running commentary he was giving for the B.B.C., didn't realize until he was swinging under the canopy and happened to look round for the others, that he was quite alone in the sky. His team of practical jokers followed him down on the next run, as previously and clandestinely arranged with the display organizers. Flight Lieutenant Alec Jackson, who took over the Falcons from Gwynne, was also the victim of team trickery on his final show in 1973. It was considerably less subtle this time. On the run in for a drop at Episkopi, in Cyprus, he was forcibly overpowered, tied up, and left fuming in the Hercules while his team waved farewell and stepped out.

Flight Lieutenant Johnny Johnson led the 1974 Falcons, and handed the ceremonial baton to Peter Watson in the skies above Canada at the end of his season.

The role of the Falcons is primarily and unashamedly to entertain and impress the public: to portray before as large an audience as possible the spirit of adventure and the mastery of the air that is symbolic of the Royal Air Force. Some might think it an expensive luxury. Not really. In pure financial terms it is a very cost-effective way of bringing the Service to the public, either live or on television. And the Falcons as individuals are certainly no luxury: they are not trained or maintained specifically for the role of aerial stuntmen, but as parachute jumping instructors, who when not launching themselves into the skies above Brisbane or Birmingham are yelling "getcher-feet-an-knees-together" to a trainee airborne soldier in the P.T.S. hangar. And the display skills themselves have more military applications. The techniques that we had used in Hong Kong, for instance, were almost exactly those I had taught the S.A.S. in the desert wadis and the Far Eastern jungles. No, not an expensive luxury at all. Great fun, though ...

Parachute displays are not the sole preserve of major air shows and festivals – nor, of course, of the Falcons. There are now some forty civilian and military sponsored teams who at weekends during the summer leap into carnivals, fetes, social functions, and sports meetings throughout the country. Usually, those jumping are sport parachutists, augmenting their club or personal parachuting funds, as well as enjoying themselves. Back at P.T.S., I came again into contact with civilian sport parachuting, which I found greatly matured since Moussatchevo. From the handful of sport jumpers then struggling for recognition, the British Parachute Association (B.P.A.) was formed in 1962, and has now risen to a membership of over 5,000, with over thirty affiliated clubs, and recognized by the Civil Aviation Authority as the governing body of the sport in this country. Advance has been achieved through the dedication of a hard core of committee members, early sponsorship by the *Daily Telegraph*, the work of secretary Bill Paul, and above all the growing sense of responsibility and the enthusiasm of the sport jumpers themselves.

The absolute commitment of the modern competition jumper to his chosen sport is exemplified in John Meacock, three times overall national champion, and our most consistent and frequent performer in international events. Slight in stature, bespectacled, and with a quietly unassuming manner, John is perhaps not the popular image of our most successful sport parachutist to date, with over 3,000 jumps in his log book. John trained as a T.A. soldier at P.T.S. in 1961, and began sport jumping at Thruxton two years later. Like many other enthusiasts at that time he furthered his skills in France and the U.S.A. Although embarked on a career in printing, John eventually decided to make his sport his life, and opened the Peterborough Parachuting Centre as a business enterprise, through sheer love of the game and his determination to get to the top of it. His dedication is typical of many.

The present standards of competition, like the people achieving them, are impressive. Britain is no longer the poor relation in international competition. In the 1968 world championships, Doug Peacock, Brian David, Ken Mapplebeck and Geordie Charlton took the bronze medals for third place in the team accuracy event, and the British team in 1972 was unlucky not to get amongst the medals again. Indicative of the accuracy standards being achieved were the nine consecutive dead-centres scored by Kumbar of Czechoslovakia in the 1972 individual accuracy event. In the tenth and final round, he missed the disc by over a metre, and dropped to tenth place! In the 1974 championships, held in Hungary, Sidov of Poland won the individual accuracy with a total 'miss' of one electronically measured centimetre for six jumps. Style performances have reached a similarly high level. In 1974 the style event was won for the second time by the Frenchman Armaing, with an average time of 6.662 seconds for his four sequences of turns and loops.

The Paracommander and its imitators provided the accuracy competitors with a vastly improved vehicle in the 1960s. Now in the skies is the most revolutionary advance in parachuting technology – the ram-air parachute. In flight, the Para Plane and its successors look like fast flying mattresses. Two rectangular sheets of ripstop nylon are linked by airfoil shaped ribs, making a layer of open-ended cells which fill with air when the device is opened, to create a stiffened surface with true aerodynamic features. It is hardly a parachute in the conventional sense, but a flying machine which planes through the air like a glider in descending flight, with a forward drive of more than 25 m.p.h. And the man who jumps with it is no longer a conventional parachutist: he is a pilot, and it is essential that he thinks of himself as such once the machine is open and roaring windily above his head. Although – as with the 'PC' – control is exercised by a system of brakes applied through the toggles, the precise application of that control is greatly different from that used for the 'round' parachute, a fact that has been demonstrated effectively and sometimes fatally by those who in moments of stress or forgetfulness have applied ingrained 'PC' reflexes to a Para Plane. But it is a joy to watch an expert fly it on its downwind and base legs, turn smoothly into wind for the final approach, then stop it almost dead in the air just above the disc and step down as though from a low box. Such an expert is Bob Hiatt, who has combined his skilled use of the Para Plane with the natural 'eye' and aggressive instinct of the accuracy man to become British champion for the past two years. Although the 'squares' have not ousted the 'rounds' for accuracy competition, they have heralded a new dimension in parachuting sensations, and surely have yet further potential.

And now, on the competitive scene, we have a new type of event altogether – relative work. This was the inevitable outcome of the 'star building' craze that swept American sport parachuting in the late 1960s, and subsequently spread further afield. Great circular links of twelve, twenty, and eventually over thirty free-fallers have been put together, but true relative skill was seen to be not in the size of star – which is a product of organization, altitude, and adequate aircraft – but in the speed with which it can be constructed. Parachuting administrators viewed with some concern a tendency for parachutists to rush into star-building before they were capable of flying in potentially dangerous proximity to others, but the popularity of the game was undeniable, and when discipline was added to infectious enthusiasm, relative work became an event in its own right. The first world relative championships were held in the U.S.A. in 1973, and now take place bi-annually. The ten-man star is the main event, the aim being for ten jumpers to leave the aircraft individually, and faster than peas from a pod, then fly their bodies to link up in a ten-man circle as quickly as they can – which is somewhere under 25 seconds in international competition. Smaller stars and more intricate patterns such as 'snowflakes' and 'caterpillars' can be formed. Nor need it end there. One pattern of linked bodies can be formed, then broken, and a different formation immediately put together, to give us 'sequential relative work', with almost unlimited scope for imagination and flying skill. It requires great individual ability, team work, and safety consciousness – for fast-flying humans in close proximity are potentially lethal.

Although our climate does not favour high-altitude relative work, teams led by Dave Waterman and Jim Crocker have been active in international competition. They seem to typify the more joyous and extroverted aspects of sport parachuting. "This is the scene, man!" they grin as they waddle out to their aircraft in the floppy, flared jumpsuits they wear to give them extra flying surface. Indeed, relative work has become more than a sport. With some, it is a way of life. "A brotherhood of free fall", the Americans call relative work – the natural outcome of the fellowship of parachutists. They see significance in the human relationships involved, with harmony in the air relating to harmony on the ground. I can believe it. Even in my humble relative experience, I have derived a great sense of concord from linking up in a mediocre six-man circle. On the other hand, when I have busted a star into flailing bodies by zooming in too hard or by flying below it and stealing its air, people haven't spoken to me for days ...

Keeping pace with the growth of the sport, the Royal Air Force formed in 1966 its own Sport Parachute Association – R.A.F.S.P.A. As well as offering low-cost parachuting facilities to Service and civilian sportsmen, R.A.F.S.P.A. also presents its own display team – the 'Robins'.

"They pick up the crumbs which the Falcons leave", is the inevitable but unjust comment.

For me, display jumping with the Robins is now the most enjoyable parachuting of all. So pleasant, to don anonymous red overalls and huddle up as one of seven on the floor of the Rapide, with Jerry Schellong in his cloth cap at the controls, and Doug Peacock or Ken Mapplebeck or Peter Smout doing all the work in the back.

"You go number one on the first pass, sir, all right?"

"Whatever you say."

Nice, to be told what to do. To just sit back and enjoy the slow spiralling climb to altitude through puffs and wisps of cloud, and when the spotter steps back and the engines cut, to duck through the low door, rip the smoke flare on the right ankle, and dive headfirst off the lower wing, facing aft, with the arms flung forward to keep from somersaulting. A lovely sensation ... and then the thrill of free flight and the challenge of a small DZ at some country fete or suburban carnival. Quite therapeutic after a hard week's parachuting.

They aren't all fetes and carnivals. In 1973 we were invited to make a water descent as part of the ceremonies to mark the opening by the Prime Minister of the Holme Pierrepont National Water Sports Centre, outside Nottingham. We were to land in the water in front of the impressive grandstand at the finishing point of the 2,000 metre course. It was blowing a bit, as Jock Fox would have said. Fortunately, it was blowing almost straight down the length of the course, so as long as we were on the wind-line, a wet arrival was almost assured. It is greatly embarrassing to land on dry ground when you are prepared for a splash. We had been promised that the various races and aquatic events that were the main features of the entertainment would be suspended during our slot in the programme, and that the water would be clear for our arrival. It was thus with some surprise that – after a pleasant fall from 7,000 feet and a smooth opening at 2,000 almost immediately above the course, with the Trent curving alongside it and

Nottingham smoking quietly beyond – I saw far below my boots a quartet of coxless fours leap suddenly from the starting point and begin to lever their way energetically down the channel, leaving regular rows of little dimples on the water. We were all travelling at the same speed, in the same direction, for the same destination – the finishing line. It was a very good race, with all the inevitability of a silent comedy film. We did have the advantage of being able to see the oarsmen, whereas they, heads down and labouring hard, were quite unaware of our approach and took the screams of the crowd as encouragement to even greater effort rather than a warning of impending catastrophe. I flew down-wind, directly above one of the boats, hooked hard into wind so that the swing would take me to one side of them, and let go. We all arrived at the finishing line in a confusion of oars, splashing bodies, and billowing nylon. I lost by a canvas.

Another unusual venue was Berlin, where we took part in an air display at Royal Air Force Gatow in 1974. The political sensitivity of airspace above and around the divided city does not normally allow for the vagaries of parachuting, but special dispensation was given on this occasion. On the ground, of course, there was the Wall to consider, for at Gatow it practically borders the western edge of the airfield. A bad miss would cause some embarrassment. " ... like a bullet up the backside," said Ken Mapplebeck. Just before we were about to take off, a black cloud came from East Germany to squat right over the airfield and empty itself. In swirling winds and sheets of rain, the crowds streamed for the car parks. It looked as though we had come a long way for nothing. We fumed on the ground, but the skies lightened, the rain eased, and with a great show of flexibility, the organizers rearranged our jump times. We flew over the airfield perimeter, and across the Wall – a stark boundary of grey concrete, with the open space and coils of wire beyond, and observation posts and machine-gun towers at intervals. It stretched away around Berlin, a wide swathe cut through the countryside and the built-up areas, like an unfinished ring road. It was an enjoyable drop, from 6,000 feet, in lightening winds that needed watching all the way down. We drove in over the heads of the remaining spectators, to hook back and plop down just in front of them. We rather hoped that the East Germans in the tall observation post that looms like a nosey neighbour above the Gatow skyline to keep a constant telescopic watch on the airfield and its happenings had enjoyed the show, for theirs must normally have been a tedious occupation, and there weren't many spectators left on our side of the Wall.

Display jumping, as well as being fun, is a welcome source of income for parachute clubs. R.A.F.S.P.A. funds have also benefitted periodically from film contracts. One of our more unusual filming ventures was to advise on and portray the parachuting sequence used in the major production *Juggernaut*, which loosely drew its story from the occasion in 1972 when a team of Royal Marines and Bomb Disposal personnel parachuted to a bomb-threatened QE2 in mid-Atlantic. The main difference in the delivery system was that Richard Harris and his team were, for greater effect, to be portrayed as going in from high altitude by free fall, through complete cloud cover, and into stormy seas ... in full frogman gear.

"Thank you very much," we said.

However, it is remarkable what the camera can do. By breaking down the descent into component parts, the hazards were isolated and dealt with one at a time and quite safely. Free falling in wet suits, though, was a new sensation. The smoothness of surface made the body feel slippery in the airflow, and the flippers acted as outsize ailerons. Without the drag effect of normal clothing, rate of fall was considerably faster, and landing on dry ground in flippers required a certain finesse. The drops had to be made through cloud, so some of the free-fall exit shots were taken above the safe expanse of Salisbury Plain, where the sight of seven fully equipped frogmen appearing through the clouds 50 miles from the nearest sea may have caused some concern to casual observers.

A film of a different sort was the BBC production "The Long Fall", in which John Noakes of "Blue Peter" fame added a high altitude jump with the Falcons to his impressive list of achievements. John had made seventeen previous descents with R.A.F.S.P.A. and with the Army's "Red Devils", so was not a complete novice. However, he was an outstanding pupil, for after oxygen familiarisation and drills, some intensive ground training, and five preparatory jumps from 12,000 feet, he made a perfect descent from 25,000 feet – two minutes of free fall, some of it through cloud, captured on cine and still film by Bob Souter and Ray Willis, who both linked with John in free flight. John impressed himself on PTS as a most modest and pleasant pupil, as well as an able one. "Quite a guy," summed up Ray Willis.

Although the more unusual jumps may be the more memorable ones, the real satisfaction for me of jumping with the Robins comes from the relaxed pleasure of the normal run of weekend displays for local schools and charity occasions, and for fetes, carnivals and sporting events further afield. There is that feeling of individuality and comforting unconformity as you fly over countryside and suburbs, looking down from the open door of the Rapide on white dots sprinkled on cricket fields, on toy cars queueing at roudabouts, on Saturday afternoon normalcy. Then the challenge of a new and usually tiny

DZ, watching the streamer as Jerry Schellong or Keith Field banks the aircraft in a wide circuit, working out the drift and the approach and the opening point as you spiral slowly upwards ... goggles down for the run in, then that joyful dive into sunlight, looking for the opening point and beyond it for the flicker of the flare on the pocket handkerchief DZ. Pull at 2,000 feet above Eynsham market square; or over the edge of a Wantage housing estate; or a bend in the Thames speckled with swans; or a field and a half away from Barnet rugby ground; or above the traffic on the Gloucester ring road ... Set another smoke flare going when the canopy is open and pointed in the right direction, then tack to and fro upwind of the slowly approaching DZ, assessing the drift with eyes and experience, then turn and drive in, over the back gardens, over the marquees and the flags and the colourful flicker of the kiddies' roundabout still turning, above the upturned faces and the yells of the children, over the boundary rope, easing the toggles down, knowing it's a good one, and hook into wind to try for a stand-up, close to the cross. Applause as each one lands, and a self-conscious line-up when all are down. Take off the smouldering flares, bundle the 'chute into its sleeve, and sign autographs on sticky programmes, with leaking biros.

"Isn't it scary, mister?"

"Don't your feet ever catch fire?"

"Can I 'ave a go?"

A pint of shandy in the beer tent; a smell of hot dogs and trampled grass; the local band sprawling with their instruments in the shade, their tunics unbuttoned; donkey rides and swing-boats in the background; and the bells of the Morris dancers now jingling in the roped-off arena that was our DZ. Marvellous. We are all barnstormers at heart.

15 / P.T.S.

Wing Commander Norman Johnstone made no attempt to disguise his unhappiness at handing over to me the Command of No.1 P.T.S. in the summer of 1971. I made no attempt to disguise my pleasure. I did, however, try to hide a certain unease.

Since leaving Special Forces I had spent a year at Staff College and almost two more on the Defence Intelligence Staff – worlds far removed from parachute training. I was also newly promoted. In fact, I felt distinctly uncomfortable sitting behind the big desk across which Jimmy Blythe had viewed me with some misgivings fourteen years earlier.

There were a number of familiar faces in the hangar and the crewroom to smile a welcome: Norman Hoffman, Ron Ellerbeck, Stan Phipps, Jim Hurford, Wilf Jones, Doug Peacock, Ken Kidd, Keith Teesdale, Andy Sweeney – they were still there, the parachutists with whom I had learnt my trade. Ben Cass was my Warrant Officer, as he had been at Special Forces; Major Peter Baynham was again commanding the Army element of P.T.S.; eighty-year-old Bert Poynter was still making the Headquarters coffee; and Snowy Robertson grinned and said, "Fancy a game of cards, sir?"

But there were also many new faces, to view me with a certain suspicion. In particular, the younger officers disconcerted me, for in them I could see myself fourteen years ago. I didn't feel that much older than them, that far removed from them. I had to consciously hold in check the familiarity that I felt.

As for parachuting, I was undoubtedly very much out of practice, which worried me – not the worry of injury or malfunction, but concern that I should make a fool of myself. I was aware that I had a reputation, and equally aware that those first few descents were not going to live up to it. So I sidled off to Weston one morning to join a continuation training course that was jumping from the balloon. I hid myself amongst them, and jumped last of a cage of four.

It was all vaguely and pleasantly familiar – the step into space; the drop; the rustle of nylon activity above. I smiled up at the big khaki canopy, then looked below at the green grass coming closer.

"Getcher legs back Number four ... " a voice was yelling, " ... Getcher bloody long legs back!" Number four ... ? That was me ... I landed, not very elegantly. "Hello, sir," said Sergeant Butch Casey, "I didn't know it was you."

But it soon returned – the perception of distance and direction, the timing, and the confidence. And once I was parachuting well again, and stepping out of the sky for smooth stand-up landings when the wind was right, I also found that I was sitting more comfortably behind that big desk.

Nothing at P.T.S. seemed greatly changed from the day I had arrived as a trainee. The hangar was still the same noisy hive of activity, although a little more spruce, with the dusty coir-mats of the landing area now replaced by rubber ones, and the 'swings' replaced by static flight-trainers for more economical use of space.

All parachuting was now from the Hercules and the Andover, and the old 'X' type parachute had long since been replaced by the more stable and slower-descending 'PX', which now wore around its periphery a 14-inch band of nylon mesh, known as a net skirt. Thus attired it was rapidly earning the reputation of being an exceptionally reliable parachute, with the incidence of 'blown peripheries' apparently eradicated.

Although the character, the organization, and the training philosophy of the school were little changed when I returned, parachuting itself is a constantly evolving technique. Moreover, its military application and the methods of its teaching must reflect the airborne operational requirement of the time. This in turn is influenced by national defence policies. I found that I was no longer involved solely in the enjoyable practicalities of parachuting: I had now to concern myself with the politics of the matter as well.

The major policy requirement during my tour of command at P.T.S. was to bring the dropping heights for airborne assault down to as low a level as possible. If the Hercules fleet was to deliver a complete, self-supporting battalion group on to the NATO flanks direct from bases in the U.K., it would need to fly in at low level, keeping below enemy radar surveillance until the final approach, when they would 'pop up' to drop their troops and heavy loads on to the DZs. The lower the height to which they had to 'pop up', the better. Drop heights of 650 feet by day and 750 feet at night were eventually considered acceptable. No other airborne force in the West jumps from such low altitudes, yet the penalties have been negligible. The 'PX', with its net skirt, is probably the most reliable statichute in the world, not given to major malfunctions. A normal descent from 650 feet under a 'PX' canopy gives a fully loaded man approximately 30 seconds to check his canopy after deployment, look around him and steer away from other parachutists, lower his equipment container, look down at the ground to assess his drift, pull down on the correct pair of liftwebs to reduce that drift, then run through a quick mental check on his body-position for landing. All this he can do in the time available, provided that these basic drills are not complicated by having to kick out of too many twists, or by excessive steering away from others, or by having to sort out an entanglement. Then 30 seconds becomes a little tight.

So in preparing men for lower drop heights one of the aims must be to keep the incidence of 'complications' to a minimum by encouraging good aircraft drills and smooth exits. Although entanglement and the consequent partial or even complete collapse of canopies remains one of the hazards of parachuting, its occurrence is rare. An alert parachutist will usually avoid it, and a cool-headed one will usually cope with it if it does occur. We endeavoured to encourage this alertness by introducing a more visual approach to flight training, in which there has always been a tendency to talk too much. "Parachutist rear ... steer away!" yells the instructor, and the pupil does so. In reality − which is under the canopy just below 600 feet, in the middle of simultaneous sticks of thirty-one − he will need to use his eyes rather than his ears to keep clear of others, although the occasional request to "Sod off!" has been known to have effect.

This basic instruction of the airborne soldier in static-line parachuting techniques remains the primary function of P.T.S., and the responsibility of Basic Training Squadron, commanded during my tour by Squadron Leader Fred Marshall, and subsequently by Ron Smith. Ron had been a N.C.O. at Ringway and at Chaklala during the war, and had been engaged in P.J.I. duties almost continuously ever since. Low-level dropping held no worries for him. He had been one of the 1943 Chaklala team who jumped in soccer kit from 400 feet into Rawalpindi stadium to play in a charity march. Right up to his retirement at the age of fifty-three Ron was still parachuting regularly, albeit heavily, scorning the use of the new-style 'Para-boots' and not seeing the ground, I am sure, until it hit him. As the officer directly responsible for our bread-and-butter work, he had the right attitude of slightly amused tolerance for his junior partner − Advanced Training Squadron, under Squadron Leaders Arthur Johnson and John Mace during my time.

It was in Advanced Training Squadron, with its responsibilities for trials, for P.J.I. training, and for free-fall parachuting, that major changes and advances were being made.

Although it accounted for only a small proportion of our output, the training of military free fallers had by 1971 become a well-established task. It was gratifying to find many of our early proposals come to fruition, and others long overtaken by even better ideas. In particular the 'short cut' to high altitude jumping has at last been achieved by a combination of the HALO and 'buddy' systems that we had evaluated in the U.S.A. in 1962. Gone are the banana positions; the semi-cross; the rigid breath-holding five seconds of disorientation; the tedious progressions towards altitude. Now, after learning basic free-fall skills and emergency procedures in a suspended harness, our military free-fall trainee climbs aboard a Hercules for his first free drop – from 12,000 feet ...

The rear of the Hercules yawns open. The spotter moves aft, and crouches on the tailgate. The trainee has his equipment checked for the final time, slips his goggles down, tosses an apprehensive look at all that space out there and the earth two miles away, then the spotter jabs his thumb up, and the pupil, with the instructor on his heels, pivots off the sill. He goes straight into a tight delta position, as the easiest way to achieve immediate symmetry and to pick up the speed that makes stability that much easier, then slowly he relaxes into the frog position that he has been taught in the 'stabiliser'. If he sees the distant earth beginning to slowly rotate beneath him he has been taught to lean back into the turn and so correct it: if that fails, or if the earth isn't there, or if it is chasing the sky round and round, he will sweep his arms back into a tight delta to speed out of his instability. Eyes are never far from the altimeters on that first jump, and at 3,000 feet the pull that has been practised so often in the hangar is now tried for real. And should, for any reason, the pupil himself fail to operate the parachute before 2,500 feet, the pack will automatically fly open and the life-supporting canopy will bang open above him, with the compliments of the Irvin 'Hitefinder' – an automatic opening device, working on a barometric principle, that gives the assurance of an opening and with it the confidence that makes the high altitude training scheme possible and acceptable.

After a full debrief from the instructor who has hovered alongside to watch his every action during the long fall, the pupil is up there again for another 50 second's worth. It is this length of time in the air that is the key to progress: time to relax, to think, to remember the theory and to put it into practice, to sort things out if they go wrong. Most pupils are stable ones from the start. There are a few exceptions. "You ought to have a bloody rev counter, not an altimeter," said John Mace to one habitual spinner. But even these problems are solved by time in the air, and within ten jumps the basic skills of aerial manoeuvre have been mastered. Then a bergen rucksack, oxygen kit, and a weapon are progressively strapped on to the pupil, until after some twenty descents in all we have an operational free faller, capable of jumping at night as one of a group, through cloud if necessary, with full military equipment, from 25,000 feet.

Jumping from heights above 12,000 feet requires the use of oxygen. We are in a potentially hazardous area here, for oxygen deficiency causes a blurring of the senses and, ultimately, unconsciousness. Thus the use of oxygen equipment in the aircraft and the transfer just before drop-time to the parachutist's individual 'bottle' are carefully monitored and carried out in accordance with a strict drill. In addition, every high altitude trainee is lectured on the physiological aspects of high altitude exposure, and in a decompression chamber he is subjected to oxygen deprivation in order to appreciate its effects and to help him to recognize its symptoms.

The break-through in training techniques has at last killed the mystery of free fall. It is no longer for the chosen few: for all instructors it is now a natural progression from the static line, and I introduced free fall into the basic training syllabus for P.J.I.s so that all would sample it.

Before the end of my tour we were able to fill a Hercules with free fallers. Fifty-nine of us (number sixty failed to turn up) boarded the aircraft at Abingdon ...

"Hi ho, hi ho, it's off to work we go, we work all day for sod all pay, hi ho, hi ho ... " sang the fifty-nine as we circled high over Oxford, climbing to drop height. We lined up in two sticks stretching the length of the fuselage. I was last man on the port side. We watched the lights. Dummy run. We relaxed.

"Why are we waiting, why are we waiting, why are we waiting, why, why, why ... " we sang on the long circuit. Another dummy run. There was an obstinate lump of low cumulus sitting over Weston. Nobody sang the next time round. It looked as though we wouldn't jump. We prepared ourselves again, not very hopefully, then suddenly the green light was on and the lines' were moving, slowly at first, then picking up momentum — fifty-nine of us, running straight over the sill at 12,000 feet. It was some sort of record. But it was so easy. So natural. That was the most important thing. That, and the happy singing when we thought we were going to jump and the silence when everyone feared that we weren't. That was important.

In addition to the two main squadrons — basic and advanced — the school had a small administrative cell under the second-in-command, Squadron

Leader Ernie Helsby, responsible for daily programming and forward planning. Not that there was much scope for forward planning during my tour. The years since 1971 were not the best ones for a virile unit, always eager to progress and to improve itself still further. They were years of economic stringencies and defence cuts, and we had our share of attendant problems. My view that parachuting is a damned sight easier to do than to organize was well confirmed. But whenever the paper and the problems piled too high in the IN tray, I would lock them in the drawer and call for a parachute ...

If there was a free-fall training lift, I would jump as an observer, following a pupil from the tailgate of the Hercules, to fly alongside the orange-overalled figure and watch him trying to come to terms with his strange new world. Or perhaps a couple of training jumps in quick succession on the airfield at Abingdon with the Falcons. If there was a high altitude sortie, I would go for that, to savour that delicious sensation of launching out into four miles of cold, clear space, perhaps above a rolling blanket of white cloud with no sign of the earth beneath it ... lying on the airflow, watching the whiteness come closer, slowly at first, then with a sudden uprush as you dive into it, swaddled, watching the altimeters, wiping ice from the goggles, falling flat stable to avoid any relative movement and possible collision with others hurtling through the cloud, then bursting out into clear sky just before the automatic opener fires, and there is Salisbury Plain rolling away beneath your feet as you swing down under the canopy. "Marvellous!" you say, as you lift your goggles, "Bloody marvellous ... "

Or I might join the current basic course making its first descent from the balloon. I would listen to the nervous jokes and the forced laughter of those sitting on the grass in rows of four, kitted up and awaiting their turn. Silent ones filed into the balloon cage. "Up eight hundred feet ... four men jumping!" I felt for each of them. These are the brave ones, these lads making their first jump, not us with our hundreds behind us, leaping from 25,000. I would watch them make their mistakes under the canopy, watch the ground take them by surprise, watch them carry their bundled parachutes jauntily off the DZ. "Nothin' to it, mate ... " they would say to those still anxiously waiting.

If there was a course in the aircraft phase of jumping, I would go along as drifter.

"Do you know your reserve is on the lower D rings, sir?" the despatcher would ask politely.

"Yes, thank you," I would say. I preferred it there, and it was my prerogative. I would jump on the green light, kick out of the twists I normally got, then fiddle for a stand-up landing if the wind was right. I would stay out on the DZ to watch the troops jump: the fruits of our labour, dropping from the sky. I would fill my helmet with mushrooms, have a cup of tea with Peter Burgess in the control tower, and then drive back to the office to find all the problems reduced to their correct size.

I went on occasions to Boscombe Down to jump with the team of P.J.I.s who operate as trialists for the Procurement Executive, responsible for the live testing of airborne equipments before they are released for Service use. I jumped there for the first time with the Para-Wing, a device shaped like a paper dart, with uncertain opening characteristics but a very positive forward speed. I jumped it into dense cloud, on a radar-controlled drop, with no sight of the DZ. Although I had both toggles down to reduce the forward speed, and a compass needle on top of the reserve pack to keep me flying straight, I had the impression as I flew it through the grey cloud of driving a fast car down a foggy road, waiting for the crash. It was pleasant to come out of the murk 500 feet above Fox Covert, and to see the flare not 200 yards away.

With the Boscombe Down team I was also able to sample 'stabilized fall'. When military free fall was a concept and not a fact, one of the foreseen problems was the length of time it would take to train an operational free faller by the then conventional means. It was therefore suggested that instead of teaching him the skills of body control in free fall, the high altitude jumper should be provided with some means of automatic stabilization. Various systems of reefed parachutes and drogues were tried out. It was a lengthy and hazardous trials process, which claimed one life at Boscombe Down – that of Sergeant Les Hicks – and by the time that a viable piece of kit was produced, our free-fall training system had overtaken the need for it.

It was certainly a fascinating and well-engineered device, but to me – a great believer in simplicity of parachuting equipment – it was disturbingly complex. I was well briefed on the stages and manner of its deployment, and on the various emergency procedures to undertake should any of those stages of deployment fail to occur. I emplaned in the Boscombe Down Argosy burdened by the excessive weight and intricacy of the device. At 9,000 feet I hooked up. Green light, and away I went, with a normal 'statichute' exit. I rolled down the slipstream. There were long seconds of disorientation as the man-alignment-drogue presumably aligned me, then there was a jolt on the shoulders as the small stabilizer parachute took over, and I was hurtling downwards at about 100 m.p.h. in an upright position. It was a most helpless sensation: I felt trussed, like a bundle of stores, with nothing to do but watch the altimeter unwind and the earth come closer, and to try to recall what should happen next and what I would have to do if it didn't ... at 3,000 feet there was a sudden lurch, a moment of free drop, and then the big TAP canopy took over, and we were back to normal. No, not for me! It is no alternative to the freedom of body-flight, and the flexibility of operation that goes with it.

My responsibilities as O.C. P.T.S. extended beyond the Abingdon-based elements of the school, to the detachments – the teams of P.J.I. officers and N.C.O.s attached permanently to Airborne units to provide them with continuation training and exercise support. I was fortunately blessed with good detachment commanders who needed little advice and guidance from me, and I was able to let them conduct their business as they and their army commanders saw fit. But I visited them at frequent intervals, for a breath of fresh air and a draught of airborne realism. When I could, I joined their exercise drops, which were rarely comfortable occasions.

With 16 Parachute Brigade I was miserably airsick on one low-level flight in a packed Hercules, and have never been so happy to get out of that door. I didn't mind all those twists at all. More pleasant were balloon-jumping programmes on Hankley Common, with Lieutenant Colonel Peter Walter of the Depot of the Parachute Regiment, and the Regimental Colonel, Joe Starling. 'Yo Yo Joe' the troops called him, so keen was he to get his jumps in.

With the Territorials of 44 Parachute Brigade, I jumped on to Ginkel Heath – the DZ in Holland on to which men of the 1st Airborne Division had parachuted in 1944 in their glorious but vain attempt to capture and hold the bridge across the lower Rhine, at Arnhem.

Lieutenant Colonel Ronny Jenkins, who commanded the 10th Battalion and was a friend from school days (we used to high-jump together for the school athletics team) invited me to join the drop on to Ginkel Heath that was to mark the thirteenth anniversary of the battle. As I stood in the open door of the Hercules, watching the orderly fields and the broad Rhine slide underneath us as we flew in for the DZ, I was mindful of Danny Sutton, and of those who had done this for real. " ... they went out all right. No bother. A good stick ... "

The green light flicked on, and I launched myself into the slipstream. Twists, as usual. I hoped that the Brigade Commander – Brigadier Ken Came – who had jumped number one from the other door, wouldn't notice. He did. Just time to kick out the twists, grab the front liftwebs down, tuck my head in, and take a fast backwards landing in the gusty wind. I got up, to watch the others of our simultaneous sticks of tens swinging down into the heather.

The Dutch had come in their thousands to watch, ringing the vast brown DZ with colour. The event seemed more symbolic to them than perhaps it did to us. There was a brief, impressive ceremony at the simple memorial that stands by the edge of the heath, and on the following day – a Sunday – the drop itself faded into its proper insignificance as we viewed the relics of battle in the Arnhem Museum, visited the now peaceful places where the fighting had been bloodiest, and finally paid our tributes amongst the white headstones on permanent parade in the Oosterbeek Cemetery.

With Special Forces I jumped into Denmark on a night exercise, as one of simultaneous tens, on to a large enough DZ whose only small obstacle was an invisible and odious pond. I found it.

There were occasions when the laugh was on others, as on another exercise with S.A.S., free-falling this time. Flight Lieutenant Graham Hand, newly posted to Mervyn Green's Special Forces Detachment, was making a descent from the Scout helicopter, in which there is little room for fully equipped parachutists, for the first time. He was on the right-hand side of the bench seat, Mervyn was in the spotting position on the left, and I was in the middle, out of the draught as a Wing Commander should be.

"I'll give you a thumb when it's time to go," Mervyn told Graham, who was viewing with some misgivings the yawning door beside him and the helicopter skid rail just outside it.

"How do I get out?" he asked.

"Imagine it's on fire ... "

We climbed towards 7,000 feet in a wide circuit. As the helicopter swung on to the approach run for the DZ, still some three miles distant, Mervyn leant out, got his bearings, and to let the pilot know that he was well on track, he gave him a nod and a thumb-up. The seat on my right was suddenly vacant. Graham had mistaken the gesture to the pilot as his own signal to jump. He had found no trouble at all in getting out, but it was a long walk back to the DZ.

The detachments are a vital part of P.T.S. We have inevitably lost something of the closeness of association that was developed between the P.J.I. and the paratrooper in the formative and operational years of military parachuting. Not only is the bond lessened by circumstances, but our Service structure is now such that we no longer have the same continuity in the job –

particularly at officer level – that was once enjoyed. It is through the detachments that we maintain a link with airborne forces, and it is they who constantly remind us that we are training fighting men, not gymnasts.

Our links with our own predecessors are also valuable. When one serves most of a Service career with one unit, there naturally develops an individual sense of attachment, coupled with a strong corporate spirit. In the case of P.T.S., this identity and spirit is perpetuated in the 'Canopy Club'. At one stage, the club seemed in danger of becoming purely a gathering of the dwindling Ringway vintage, and it was in an endeavour to inject new blood that we organized a summer reunion at Abingdon in 1973.

All current and former P.J.I.s were invited, with their families. Into our hangar storeroom, suitably renovated by Sergeant Ted Marwood, we crammed a mixture of nostalgia and current parachuting information, and presented it as the P.T.S. Museum. With undiminished wit, Group Captain Maurice Newnham formally declared it open at that summer reunion. J.C.K. was there too, and Jimmy Blythe, and Eric Brice, and a whole wealth of P.T.S. tradition and folklore.

There was 'Big Robbie', who had retired as a Warrant Officer five years previously. Robbie's speciality had been to ride a bicycle out of the balloon cage at 800 feet in the days when a 'comic cage' was part of every P.T.S. demonstration. When regulations caught up with such antics, Robbie had taken to free fall – when nearly fifty years of age. A former heavyweight wrestler of repute and a man of dogmatic opinion, there were few prepared to argue with Robbie when he wagged a ponderous finger and declared that "Ye canna dae it!", as he was wont to do.

Taff Harriss, who had been P.T.S. Warrant Officer in Upper Heyford days, had once received two broken ribs from a friendly hug administered by Robbie. He was there.

So too was Monty Zeff, a tailor by trade and looking as spruce as his Ringway reputation, in contrast to his great friend Taf Watkins who arrived at the reunion looking as happily untidy as apparently he always had. Taf had been one of the Chaklala P.J.I.s who had flown on operations over Burma, Indo-China and Malaya to despatch the special operators of clandestine Force 136 from their Hudson and Liberator aircraft. Another had been Jimmy Walsh, who now came to meet old friends as a Group Captain in the Education Branch.

Jack Roy – heavyweight boxer and coach to the 1960 Olympic Team – was there. Bill Jevons, Bert Price, John Saville, Red Summers, Stan Kellaway, Danny Sutton ... many, many others, who had made P.T.S.

In the crewroom, in the hangar for the ground training display, in the bar, on the DZ to watch the demonstration drops with critical eyes – these, our predecessors, mingled with the young instructors of today. All were talking a common language, with a common enthusiasm. The youngsters found that their admiration for the Ringway pioneers was matched by the deep respect which the older ones had for modern techniques and standards. Past and present – talking, laughing, gesticulating, exaggerating – were brought together by a bond that transcends age, rank, and background. It is a bond that is not peculiar to P.T.S. Wherever jumpers – sport or military, professional or amateur, current or long past it – foregather, it is there.

Since 1797, when Andre Jacques Garnerin oscillated wildly to the ground in his wicker basket suspended beneath the forerunner of the modern parachute, people have been asking us why we do it. Some of us, like myself, are parachutists by profession; for others it is a means of military transport; for some it is a pleasurable sport. But all, at some stage, have made a very personal decision to hurl themselves into space, and then to go on doing it. Why?

Psychologists who have never donned a parachute often have ideas about us. Some see parachuting as a manifestation of a death wish. At the other extreme, some see it as the essence of death defiance – giving the body to the destructive power of gravity, then snatching it away again with a symbolic tug of the ripcord. Rubbish! Then why?

We can babble on about the sheer, sensuous enjoyment of it. About challenge, exhilaration, satisfaction. We might even get carried away and talk about the sense of personal freedom, of individuality, of the clarity of thought and action that comes from leaping out of aeroplanes which – as Doctor Johnson said of hanging – "concentrates the mind wonderfully". But these are intangibles that we toss about, so difficult for others to grasp. Indeed, sometimes we ask ourselves why we do it. We ask it when our kit is weighing us down and the shoulder buckles biting as we stand waiting for the call to action stations in a swaying, dimly lit Hercules roaring through the night. We ask it when we rise from a warm bed into a shivering dawn to get the jumps in before that damned wind wakes up. We ask it as we kneel with stiffening knees and nothing to wipe our noses on in the open door of an over-crowded Cessna, trying to find a gap in the clouds and a glimpse of the target. But when we have launched ourselves through that door; when we have fallen, flown, and floated to earth; when we are carrying our bundled 'chutes from the DZ – then we never think to ask ourselves why we do it.

Nor did I need to ask it that day of our summer reunion. It was there all around me, one of those elusive reasons for doing it. It was the spirit of people who chose to leap from the sky: the exclusive fellowship of the parachutist.

I made no attempt to disguise my unhappiness at handing over to Wing Commander Brian White the command of P.T.S. in September of 1974 ...

Bibliography

My story has but touched on various aspects of parachuting. For those whose interest has perhaps been whetted and who wish to read further, I would recommend the following. The list is selective, not exhaustive.

MAINLY AUTOBIOGRAPHICAL

Birdman by Leo Valentin (Hutchinson)
The Man in the Hot Seat by Doddy Hay (Collins)
Alone in the Sky by Mike Reilly (Robert Hale)
Panic Takes Time by Dumbo Willans (Max Parrish)
Free Fall by Cathie Williamson (Robert Hale)

MAINLY HISTORICAL

Parachuting and Skydiving by Dumbo Willans (Faber & Faber)
Bailout by Dwiggins (Collier Press)

SPORT PARACHUTING

Skydiving by Bud Sellick (Prentice Hall)
Sport Parachuting by Charles Shea Simmonds (Adam & Charles Black)

MILITARY PARACHUTING

Prelude to Glory by Maurice Newnham (Sampson Low)
Airborne to Battle by Maurice Tugwell (William Kimber)
The Special Air Service by Phillip Warner (William Kimber)

PICTORIAL AND POETICAL (AND QUITE MARVELLOUS)

Skies Call by Andy Keech (Dept 436, The Old Pines, Epsom, Surry)

Those whose appetite has been stimulated beyond the reading stage might wish to know the address of the British Parachute Association, who will put them in touch with their nearest club: The British Parachute Association Ltd, Kimberley House, 47 Vaughan Way, Leicester, LE1 4SG.

Index

A

Abingdon, Royal Air Force, 17, 34, 157, 180
Abu Dhabi, 148
Aerodynamics, of free fall, 58-59
Air Commandos, USAF, 137, 139
Aircraft, parachute descents from:
    Andover, 146, 163
    Antonov A.N.2, 68-69
    Argosy, 124, 127, 132, 177
    Beaver, 80
    Beverley, 20, 35, 36, 53, 62, 81
    C119, 88, 137
    C130, 103
    Caribou, 92, 93
    Cessna 172, 96, 120
    Dakota, 33, 139-140, 143
    Hastings, 34, 135
    Hercules, 157, 172, 175, 178
    Huey helicopter, 92
    Pioneer, Single, 123
    Pioneer, Twin, 77, 151-152
    Rapide, 66, 167, 169
    Scout helicopter, 179
    U10, 137
    Valetta, 34, 109, 111
    Vimy, 26
    Wessex helicopter, 116
    Whirlwind helicopter, 109, 160
    Whitley, 26-28
Anikiev, 74
Arender, Jim, 72
Arnhem, 33, 178
Arter, Harry, 71
Atkinson, Tommy, 127, 128
Auriole, Lieutenant, 43, 47
Australia, parachute display 1958, 52-53

Australian Parachute School, 52
Automatic Opening Device, 92, 174

B

Baldwin, Thomas, 78
Balloon, descents from, 28-29, 38, 176
Bario, Sarawak, 111
Baton Pass, first all-British, 79
Baynham, Peter, 171
Berlin, 168
Berry, Albert, 78
Biscarosse, France, 49
Blackman, Victor, 83
Blank Gore Parachute, 51, 68
"Blue Peter" BBC Programme, 169
Blythe, Jimmy, 24, 180
Brice, Eric, 43, 180
British Parachute Association, 164
British Skydivers Club, 61
Broadwick, Charles, 78
Brown, Douggie, 100, 103
Browning, General "Boy", 33
Bruneval, France, 33
Buddy System, 94-96
Bullen, Roy, 163
Burgess, Peter, 137, 177
Burgess, Sue, 66
Burt, Dave, 94, 95

C

Came, Brigadier Ken, 178

Cameron, Air Chief Marshal Sir Neil, 11, 13
Cameron, Stuart, 159
Canadian Airborne School, 88
Canarozzo, 54
Canopy Club, 180
Card, Alf, 43, 55, 63, 66
Casey, Butch, 172
Cass, Ben, 171
Changi, Singapore, 107
Charlton, Geordie, 61, 66, 72, 74, 165
Chasak, Sam, 76
Cobb, David, 160
Crane, Joe, 65, 67
Crocker, Jim, 166

D

Dare Wilson, Lieutenant Colonel, 87
Davies, Jim, 53, 113
Denley, Pete, 52
Dropping Zones marking systems, 23, 130-133

E

El Adem, Libya, 139
Ellerbeck, Ron, 86, 158, 171
Elsinore, California, 96

F

Falcons, RAF Parachute Display Team, 157-164
Far East Air Force Jungle Rescue Team, 107-118
Far East Air Force Parachute and Survival School, 107-118
Farnborough Air Display
    1961, 83-86
    1962, 158

Field, Keith, 169
Fort Bragg, USA, 90-93
Fort Kemar, Malaya, 152
Fortenberry, Dick, 73-74, 92
Fox, Jock, 133
Francombe, Dave, 87
French Military Parachute School, 43-50

G

Gale, General "Windy", 33
Gallimard, Monique, 73
Galloway, Bev, 90
Garnerin, André Jacques, 181
Gavin, Frank, 111
Gebolys, Julian, 30
Gilpin, Kip, 115
Golden Knights, US Army Display Team, 92
Green, Mervyn, 160, 179
Greenland, Geoff, 159
Gurkhas, Parachute Training, 107

H

HALO Parachuting Techniques, 91, 174
Hall, Jim, 94-96
Hand, Graham, 179
Hanson, Mike, 111
Harrison, Arthur, 65
Harriss, Taff, 180
Hatton, William, 141
Helsby, Ernie, 176
Henry, Daryl, 89-90
Hewitt, Paul, 87, 93
Hiatt, Bob, 166
Hicks, Les, 177
High Altitude Parachuting, 91-92, 175-176
Hoffman, Norman, 61, 66, 171
Hong Kong, 160-163
Humphries, Lofty, 29
Huntingdon, Jack, 113
Hurford, Dai, 100, 104, 112, 171

I

Ironsides, "Rusty", 151
Irvin, Leslie, 41, 78
Istel, Jacques, 89

J

Jackson, Alec, 163
Jenkins, Ronny, 178
Jenkins, Group Captain Roy, 13
Jevons, Bill, 180
Johnson, Arthur, 173
Johnson, Johnny, 164
Johnstone, Norman, 171
Jolly, Bill, 89
Jones, Alan, 157, 160
Jones, Wilf, 171

K

Kaplan, 74
Keane, Paddy, 111
Kellaway, Stan, 107-108, 180
Kidd, Ken, 53, 108, 171
Kiesow, Bud, 96
Kilkenny, John C., 30, 180
Kluang, Malaya, 116, 122
Kuala Lumpur, 122

L

"Lady Be Good", 141-143
Lambirth, Bluey, 53
Lang, Peter, 66
Lard, Pierre, 49
Last, Bill, 163
Laudal, Colonel Lasse, 136
Leary, John, 82
Lee, Denis, 61, 66, 72

M

Mace, John, 173

Malaysian Skydiving Championships, 1964, 122
Maloney, Tommy, 43, 80
Mapplebeck, Ken, 165, 167
Marshal, Fred, 173
Marwood, Ted, 180
Masterson, Glenn, 76
McCardle, Mike, 61
McDonald, Henry, 162
McLoughlin, Jake, 61, 66, 80, 115, 122
Meacock, John, 164
Military Free Fall Parachuting, 61-63, 146-157
Minter, Errol, 30
Morgan, Gwynne, 163
Moussatchevo, Bulgaria, 65, 67, 70
Mullins, Dick, 87, 90, 109, 111

N

Newnham, Maurice, 11, 29, 180
Nicolan, Adjutant Chef, 43, 48, 50
Night Descents, 22, 61-63, 148
Noakes, John, 169
Norman, Mike, 123
Norwegian Parachute School, 136

O

Olsen, Tom, 91, 93
O'Kane, Brigadier Pat, 133
Orange, Massachusetts, 89

P

Parachutes:
    Conquistador, 69, 83, 124
    Double L, 80
    Para Commander, 159
    Para Plane, 165
    Para Wing, 177
    PX Type, 172
    Tactical Assault Parachute, 150
    T.10, 88, 94
    X Type, 19, 31

Parachutes Incorporated, 89
Parachuting Techniques, free fall:
    Aerodynamics, 58-59
    Back Loop, 59
    Banana position, 44, 54
    Delta position, 44, 54
    Equipment carriage, 61, 146
    Frog position, 55-56
    Full Cross position, 55
    Half Spreadeagle position, 55
    Relative Work, 79-80, 166
    Semi Cross position, 46
    Tracking, 158
    Turning, 59, 72
Parachuting Techniques, static line:
    Aircraft Drills, 18
    Exit technique, 18
    Flight technique, 18, 31
    Ground Training, 18, 31
    Landing Technique, 18, 30, 91
Para Ventures Incorporated, 95
Parry, John, 162
Pau, France, 43
Paul, Bill, 164
Paya Lebar Airport, Singapore, 120
Peacock, Doug, 80, 157, 161, 165, 167,
    171
Perry, Neil, 42
Peterborough Parachute Centre, 165
Phipps, Stan, 150, 171
Poynter, Bert, 171

Q

Quilter, Sir Geoffrey, 65
Quinney, Pete, 53

R

"Red Devils" display team, 169
Reilly, Mike, 57, 66, 70
Reserve Parachute, 35
Richardson, Jack, 62
Robertson, "Robbie", 180
Robertson, "Snowy", 80, 100, 104, 120-
    123, 160, 171

Robins display team, 167-170
Rock, John, 25
Roy, Jack, 180
Royal Air Force Sports Parachute
    Association, 167
Royal Singapore Flying Club, 119, 120

S

Sanborn, Lew, 89
Saville, John, 180
Schellong, Jerry, 167
Seal, John, 111
Seegar, "Ram", 122
Sharjah, 146
Sherman, Pete, 150, 152
Sinclair, Bob, 95-98
Sleeve deployment of parachute, 51-52
Smith, Ron, 29, 108, 173
Smout, Peter, 167
Sohn, Clem, 42
Souter, Bob, 169
Special Air Service, 28, 87, 108, 119, 130,
    139, 145-155
Special Boat Sections, Royal Marines,
    130, 133-135
Special Forces, Royal Air Force
    Detachment, 129
Sport Parachuting history, 65-66
Spotting techniques, 60
Stabilised free fall, mechanised system,
    177
Stamford, Mike, 122
Starling, Joe, 178
Stevens, Leo, 78
Summers, Red, 180
Sutton, Danny, 18, 41, 33, 180
Strange, Louis, 25
Sweeney, Andy, 122, 124, 171

T

Taylor, John, 82, 84
Teesdale, Keith, 52, 119, 171.
Tengah, Singapore, 124

Thailand Airborne School, 102
Thirtle, John, 11, 43, 79, 80, 84, 158
Thompson, Chuck, 65
Thomson, Glen, 111
Toner, Robert, 141
Traquino Viaduct, Italy, 28
Tree Descents, 110, 113, 153

U

United States Airborne Forces, 91
Upper Heyford, 34

V

Valentin, Leo, 42
"Varsity", Airborne Operation, 34

W

Walter, Peter, 178

Walsh, Jimmy, 180
Ward, Harry, 27, 29
Water Descents, 133-136, 168
Waterman, Dave, 166
Watkins, Taff, 180
Watson, Peter, 164
Weston On The Green, 20, 53, 83, 171, 175
Wheeling, George, 65
White, Brian, 182
Willians, Dumbo, 65
Williams, Peter, 158
Willis, Ray, 169
Wiltshire, Bob, 16, 24, 36
World Parachute Championships
    1951, 65
    1954, 65
    1960, 67-77
    1968, 165

Z

Zeff, Monty, 180